WORLD
THE DEFINITIVE VISUAL GUIDE
WAR I

D1338711

WORLD
THE DEFINITIVE VISUAL GUIDE
WAR I

FROM SARAJEVO TO VERSAILLES

R.G. GRANT

LONDON, NEW YORK, MELBOURNE, MUNICH, AND DELHI

Senior Editor
Janet Mohun

Senior Art Editor
Ina Stradins

Editor
Laura Wheadon

Project Art Editor
Anna Hall

Pre-Production Producers
Rebekah Parsons-King, Rachel Ng

Producer
Alice Sykes

Jacket Editor
Manisha Majithia

Jacket Designers
Mark Cavanagh, Paul Drislane

Managing Editor
Angeles Gavira Guerrero

Managing Art Editor
Michelle Baxter

Cartographers
Simon Mumford
Encompass Graphics Ltd,
Brighton, UK

Art Director
Philip Ormerod

Publisher
Sarah Larter

Associate Publishing Director
Liz Wheeler

Publishing Director
Jonathan Metcalf

DK INDIA

Editorial Manager
Rohan Sinha

Deputy Design Manager
Sudakshina Basu

Senior Editor
Vineetha Mokkil

Senior Art Editor
Mahua Mandal

Editors
Sudeshna Dasgupta, Dharini Ganesh

Art Editors
Sanjay Chauhan, Suhita Dharamjit,
Arijit Ganguly, Amit Malhotra,
Kanika Mittal, Shreya Anand Virmani

Production Manager
Pankaj Sharma

DTP Manager
Balwant Singh

DTP Designers
Neeraj Bhatia, Syed Md Farhan,
Shanker Prasad, Sachin Singh,
Tanveer Abbas Zaidi

TOUCAN BOOKS LTD

Managing Editor
Ellen Dupont

Senior Art Editor
Thomas Keenes

Senior Editor
Dorothy Stannard

Picture Research
Roland Smithies (Luped)

Assistant Editor
David Hatt

Indexer
Marie Lorimer

Proofreader
Caroline Hunt

Editorial Consultants
Barton C. Hacker, Senior Curator of Armed Forces History, National Museum of American History, Kenneth E. Behring Center, Smithsonian Institution; Richard Overy, Professor of History, University of Exeter

First published in Great Britain in 2014 by Dorling Kindersley Limited
80 Strand, London WC2R 0RL
A Penguin Company

Copyright © 2014 Dorling Kindersley Limited

2 4 6 8 10 9 7 5 3
004 – 184796 – June/2014

All rights reserved. No part of this publication may be reproduced, stored in a retrieval system, or transmitted in any form or by any means, electronic, mechanical, photocopying, recording, or otherwise, without prior written permission of the copyright owner.

A CIP catalogue record for this book is available from the British Library.

ISBN: 978-1-4093-4761-3

Printed and bound in Hong Kong

See our complete catalogue at
www.dk.com

CONTENTS

3

STALEMATE
1915

4

YEAR OF BATTLES
1916

5

REVOLUTION AND
DISILLUSION
1917

6

VICTORY AND DEFEAT
1918 262

7

AFTERMATH
1919–1923 326

Foreword

When Winston Churchill reflected on World War I in the 1920s he claimed that "all the horrors of all the ages" were brought together in a terrible conflict that sucked in "not only armies, but whole populations". The war of 1914–1918, or the "Great War" as it came to be known, was indeed a war of exceptional intensity, scale, and ruthlessness. It destroyed the fabric of European political life and set in motion movements worldwide that did not come to rest until much later in the 20th century. The effects of the war were deadly and devastating for every country dragged into its orbit.

A war that was supposed to be over in weeks soon became a long, drawn-out war of attrition. Military and naval belief in the decisive battle between rival navies and armies shifted inexorably towards a new concept of "total war" in which whole populations found themselves unexpected participants. This book describes and illustrates the war in all its many guises, from the brief colonial skirmishes in the Far East, when Japan seized Germany's Pacific colonies, to the slaughterhouses of the Western Front, which consumed millions of young men in four years of unabated combat.

Almost a century later, historians still debate why the Allies won and why the Central Powers – Germany, Austria-Hungary, and Turkey – were forced late in 1918 to sue for an armistice. The answer has a lot to do with resources: the Allies controlled the seas and denied trade to the enemy; the British and French empires, and the United States, could supply food and raw materials to keep populations fed and factories supplied. Germany was forced to improvise and invent in order to keep the war effort going, and shortages slowly undermined the domestic war effort of all the Central Powers.

The war changed the map of the world. In 1919, four of the great pre-war empires – German, Russian, Austro-Hungarian, and Ottoman – disappeared, while Britain and France faced an uncertain future in their surviving empires, where nationalist sentiment had been woken by the world crisis. Peace was welcomed, but its survival was uncertain. On 11 November 1918, Armistice Day, Churchill, then Minister of Munitions, looked out of his office in Whitehall as people streamed out on to the street in scenes of "triumphant pandemonium". But in his history of the war, Churchill concluded on a more sombre note: "Is this the end? Is it merely to be a chapter in a cruel and senseless story?" Sadly for humanity, it proved to be the prologue to the devastations to come a generation later.

Richard Overy,
Richard Overy,
University of Exeter

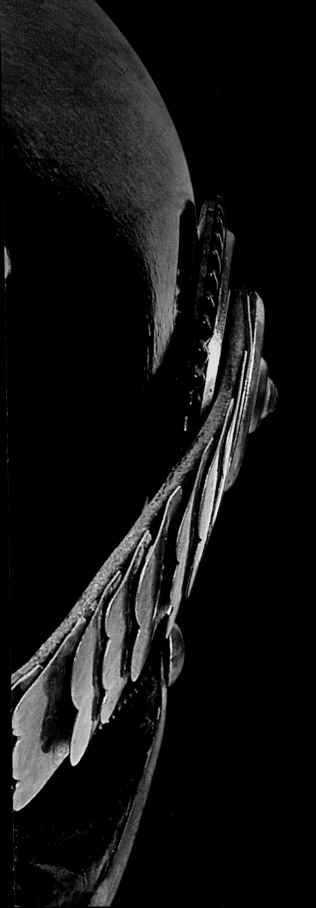

1

THE TROUBLED CONTINENT
1870 – 1914

In the early 20th century, Europe was
dominated by ambitious imperial states.
This produced an unstable international
system and fuelled an arms race. War broke
out in Europe with the assassination of
Austrian Archduke Franz Ferdinand
in the summer of 1914.

THE TROUBLED CONTINENT

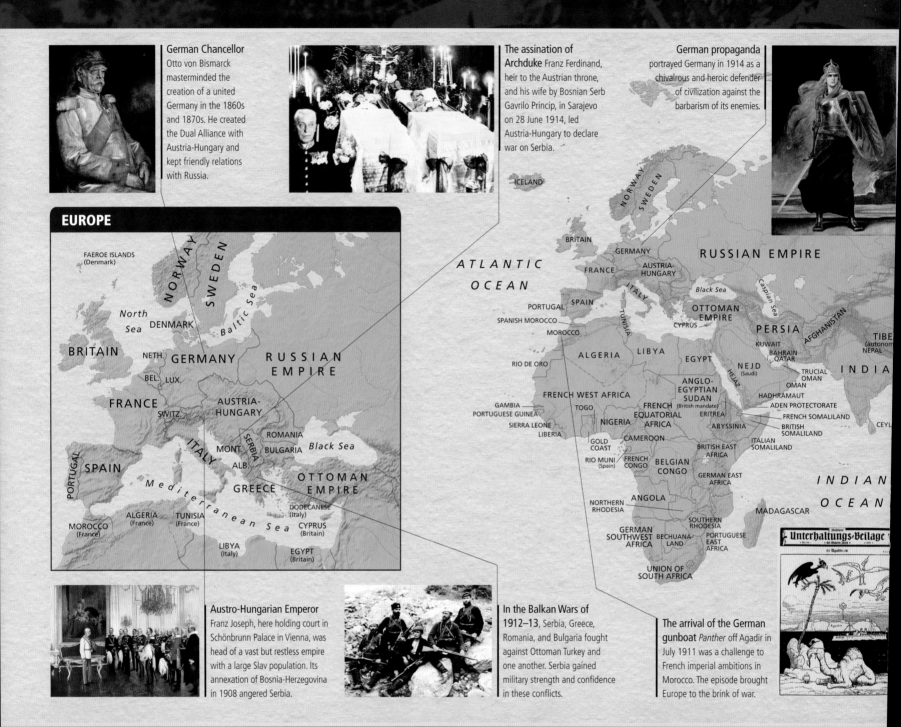

German Chancellor Otto von Bismarck masterminded the creation of a united Germany in the 1860s and 1870s. He created the Dual Alliance with Austria-Hungary and kept friendly relations with Russia.

The assination of Archduke Franz Ferdinand, heir to the Austrian throne, and his wife by Bosnian Serb Gavrilo Princip, in Sarajevo on 28 June 1914, led Austria-Hungary to declare war on Serbia.

German propaganda portrayed Germany in 1914 as a chivalrous and heroic defender of civilization against the barbarism of its enemies.

EUROPE

Austro-Hungarian Emperor Franz Joseph, here holding court in Schönbrunn Palace in Vienna, was head of a vast but restless empire with a large Slav population. Its annexation of Bosnia-Herzegovina in 1908 angered Serbia.

In the Balkan Wars of 1912–13, Serbia, Greece, Romania, and Bulgaria fought against Ottoman Turkey and one another. Serbia gained military strength and confidence in these conflicts.

The arrival of the German gunboat *Panther* off Agadir in July 1911 was a challenge to French imperial ambitions in Morocco. The episode brought Europe to the brink of war.

A series of wars in the 1860s and 1870s established Germany as Europe's dominant military power. In the 1890s, France and Russia formed an alliance to counter the might of Germany and its close ally, Austria-Hungary. In the first decade of the 20th century, Britain, feeling threatened by the growth of the German navy, abandoned its traditional isolationism and a formed an entente – a loose unofficial alliance – with France and Russia. In the years leading up to World War I, peace was maintained by a balance of power between the two hostile alliance systems. The European states expanded their armed forces and equipped them with the latest technology. They developed plans for the rapid mobilization of mass conscript armies that threatened to turn any confrontation into full-scale war. Every country felt that the side that struck first would have a decisive advantage.

1870–1914

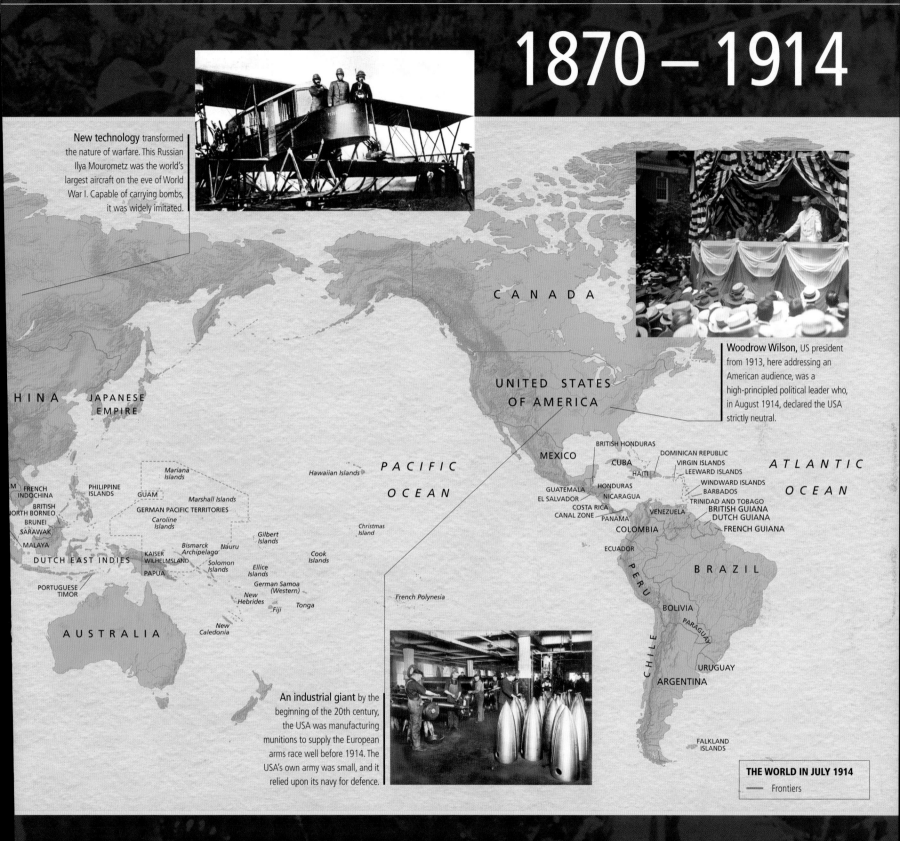

New technology transformed the nature of warfare. This Russian Ilya Mourometz was the world's largest aircraft on the eve of World War I. Capable of carrying bombs, it was widely imitated.

Woodrow Wilson, US president from 1913, here addressing an American audience, was a high-principled political leader who, in August 1914, declared the USA strictly neutral.

An industrial giant by the beginning of the 20th century, the USA was manufacturing munitions to supply the European arms race well before 1914. The USA's own army was small, and it relied upon its navy for defence.

THE WORLD IN JULY 1914
— Frontiers

The behaviour of Germany's leader, Kaiser Wilhelm II, was aggressive and erratic, particularly during the Moroccan crisis of 1911. But the spark that ignited war came in the Balkans, where states such as Serbia had become independent of Ottoman Turkish rule in the 19th century. Russia had ambitions to spread its influence in the Balkans as the champion of the Slav peoples. This led to hostile relations with Austria-Hungary, which was at odds with restless Slav

minorities, including Serbs, within its own borders. In June 1914, a Serb terrorist assassinated the heir to the Austro-Hungarian throne. Austria-Hungary was determined to use this as a pretext for a war with Serbia.

When Russia mobilized in defence of Serbia, Germany declared war on Russia and France. The German invasion of neutral Belgium then ensured that a hesitant Britain would enter the conflict.

TIMELINE 1870 – 1914

Franco-Prussian War ▪ Rival military alliances ▪ **Wilhelm II is Kaiser** ▪
Boer War ▪ **Anglo-German naval race** ▪ Moroccan crises ▪ **Wars in the**
Balkans ▪ Assassination in Sarajevo ▪ **Declarations of war**

1870 – 1880	1881 – 1890	1891 – 1900	1901 – 1902	1903 – 1904	1905 – 1906
JULY 1870 Outbreak of the Franco-Prussian War. **JANUARY 1871** France is defeated. The King of Prussia is declared Emperor of Germany.	**1881** Russia joins Germany and Austria-Hungary in the League of the Three Emperors. **1882** The Triple Alliance is formed between Germany, Austria-Hungary, and Italy.	**1891** Architect of Germany's pre-war planning Alfred von Schlieffen becomes German Chief of the General Staff. **JANUARY 1894** Franco-Russian Alliance is concluded. ⌄ Alfred von Schlieffen	**1901** Discussions about a possible alliance between Britain and Germany come to nothing. **JANUARY 1901** Death of Queen Victoria.		
⌃ French Legion of Honour medal	**1884** The Maxim gun, the first true machine-gun, is invented. The Berlin Conference formalizes the division of Africa between European colonial powers.		**MARCH 1901** In the Boer War, the British adopt the policy of moving Boer civilians into concentration camps. **SEPTEMBER 1901** China signs a humiliating treaty with foreign powers after suppression of the Boxer Rebellion.	**MARCH 1903** Germans make plans with Ottoman Turkey to build a railway between Berlin and Baghdad. **DECEMBER 1903** The Wright brothers make the first powered heavier-than-air flight.	⌃ King Edward VII visits Paris for the Entente Cordiale **1905** German army adopts the Schlieffen Plan for fighting a war on two fronts.
	JUNE 1888 Wilhelm II becomes Emperor (Kaiser) of Germany. **1889** Russia begins a rapprochement with France.	**1898** Germany begins naval expansion, starting an Anglo-German naval race. **OCTOBER 1899** The Boer War in South Africa reveals deficiencies in the British Army.	**JANUARY 1902** Britain agrees a military alliance with Japan.	**FEBRUARY 1904** Russo-Japanese War begins. **APRIL 1904** Britain forms the Entente Cordiale with France.	**MARCH 1905** Japanese army defeats the Russians at the Battle of Mukden. Germany provokes the First Moroccan Crisis to test the Anglo-French Entente, which holds firm.
MARCH 1878 Defeated in war with Russia, Ottoman Turkey is forced to recognize the independence of Serbia and Romania. **1879** Germany and Austria-Hungary form the Dual Alliance.	**1890** European armies begin to adopt bolt-action repeater rifles, increasing infantry rate of fire.	**1900** First effective submarines come into service. First flight of Zeppelin airship.	**MAY 1902** Boer War ends in British victory. **JUNE 1902** Triple Alliance between Germany, Austria-Hungary, and Italy is renewed.		**MAY 1905** The Imperial Japanese Navy destroys a Russian fleet at the Battle of Tsushima. **SEPTEMBER 1905** Russo-Japanese War ends in humiliating defeat for Russia. **FEBRUARY 1906** HMS *Dreadnought* is launched, rendering all earlier battleships obsolete.

≫ Belgian machine-gun

≪ Kaiser Wilhelm II

"The accelerating **arms race is… a crushing burden** that weighs on all nations and, if prolonged, **will lead to the very cataclysm** it seeks to avert."

TSAR NICHOLAS II, ADDRESSING THE HAGUE CONFERENCE, 1899

1907 – 1908	1909 – 1910	1911	1912	1913	1914

MARCH 1909
Germany backs Austria-Hungary over the annexation of Bosnia-Herzegovina, forcing Russia to withdraw its opposition by threatening war.

« Political postcard of European balancing act

JULY
General Joseph Joffre is appointed commander-in-chief of the French army.

1 JULY
Arrival of German gunboat in Tangier provokes the Second Moroccan Crisis, taking Europe to the brink of war.

12 FEBRUARY
China becomes a republic as the last emperor abdicates.

23 MARCH–30 MAY
Bulgarians capture Adrianople, Turkey, in First Balkan War. Treaty of London redraws boundaries.

29 JUNE
Second Balkan War begins. Bulgaria fights Serbia, Greece, and Romania.

AUGUST 1907
Russia and Britain sign a convention settling outstanding disputes in Central Asia.

1908
German army adopts the MG 08 machine-gun.

APRIL 1909
Young Turks depose Ottoman Sultan Abdul Hamid II and replace him with Mehmed V.

⌃ The German High Seas Fleet in the North Sea

≫ German holidaymakers, summer 1914

28 JUNE
Archduke Franz Ferdinand is assassinated by a Bosnian Serb in Sarajevo.

6 JULY
Germany agrees to support Austro-Hungarian action against Serbia.

≫ German Uhlan helmet

NOVEMBER 1909
Britain creates an Imperial General Staff to coordinate military planning in Britain and its dominions.

29 SEPTEMBER
Italy declares war on Turkey in pursuit of territorial claims in Libya.

28 MARCH
British House of Commons rejects votes for women, provoking suffragettes into adoption of militant tactics.

7 AUGUST
France enacts the Three-Year Law, extending conscription.

10 AUGUST
Second Balkan War ends with defeat of Bulgaria.

23 JULY
Austria-Hungary issues the Serbians with an ultimatum.

28 JULY
Austria-Hungary declares war on Serbia.

1910
Armies and navies of the major powers begin to acquire planes and train military pilots.

UNITED SUFFRAGISTS

USQUE AD FINEM

8 OCTOBER
First Balkan War begins, pitting Turkey against the Balkan League: Serbia, Montenegro, Greece, and Bulgaria.

18 OCTOBER
Italo-Turkish War ends. Italy takes possession of Libya.

JULY 1908
Young Turk revolution begins drive to modernize Ottoman Turkey.

≫ Suffragette banner

OCTOBER 1908
Austria-Hungary announces the annexation of Bosnia-Herzegovina.

MAY 1910
In Britain, George V becomes king on the death of Edward VII.

1 NOVEMBER
First combat use of aircraft by Italians in North Africa.

4 NOVEMBER
Treaty of Fez resolves the Moroccan crisis.

NOVEMBER
Britain and France agree to share naval responsibilities, the French concentrating on the Mediterranean.

5 NOVEMBER
Woodrow Wilson is elected president of the USA.

⌃ Announcement of war in Berlin

30 JULY
Russia begins general mobilization.

Royal visit
A state visit by the British King Edward VII to Paris in 1903 was the prelude to a diplomatic agreement between Britain and France, the Entente Cordiale, signed on 8 April 1904.

« BEFORE

A series of localized wars in the 1860s and 1870s redrew the borders of major European states.

GERMAN UNIFICATION

In 1860, Germany was a collection of separate states. **Prussia** was acknowledged as its **leading power** and, in 1870–71, defeated France in the **Franco-Prussian War**. This victory led directly to the founding of the German Empire under the king of Prussia, who later became the German Kaiser.

AUSTRIA-HUNGARY

The Austrian Habsburgs survived in power by forming **Austria-Hungary**, the Dual Monarchy, held together by allegiance to the emperor of Austria, who was also the king of Hungary.

GERMAN ARMY HELMET

Europe's High Noon

Convinced of the superiority of their civilization, Europeans had achieved a dominant position in the world, rooted in the spectacular growth of their industries and populations, and in the strength of their military forces.

At the dawn of the 20th century, Europe was at the height of its military and economic power. States such as Britain and France controlled huge empires, encompassing nearly all of Africa and large parts of Asia. European capital and commerce created enormous influence and wealth. Worldwide transport and communication networks tied the global economy to its European hub. The US was the only major non-European economic power, although Japan had emerged as an industrializing military force in the 1890s. The leading European powers were Britain, France, Germany, Russia, and Austria-Hungary. Italy and Ottoman Turkey aspired to join them. Of these states, Germany was the most dynamic force.

Since the unification of Germany in 1871 the country had undergone rapid industrialization. The population had grown a massive 43 per cent between 1880 and 1910. France, in contrast, had an almost static population growth and less developed industries, despite ruling an extensive empire. Russia lagged even further behind industrially, but was by far the most populous European state. Britain had lost its industrial lead but still exercised unchallenged dominance over international finance, maritime trade, and its vast overseas empire.

1.63 BILLION The estimated global population in 1900. Around one-quarter of this number resided in Europe.

Precarious balance
A 1910 postcard shows various heads of state embarked upon an uncertain journey, precariously mounted aboard a motor vehicle. In the early 20th century, the political balance was always threatening to tip over into war.

Oppressed nationalities' demands for self-rule were a threat to the multinational Austro-Hungarian Empire. Governments feared a breakdown of order and responded by asserting the military and diplomatic prestige of the state. They hoped this would serve as an antidote to internal forces of disintegration and subversion.

All the major powers spent large amounts on their armed forces. Mass education and a popular press united in spreading a message of patriotism that easily slipped into jingoism. As no formal institution existed for regulating international affairs, states sought security in alliances. Germany allied itself with Austria-Hungary and Italy, and France with Russia. Britain was

Imperial splendour
Emperor Franz Joseph of Austria receives guests at Schönbrunn Palace in Vienna. A member of the Habsburg dynasty, he was Europe's longest-ruling monarch in 1914, having come to the throne in 1848.

traditionally isolationist, but its fear of Germany led to agreements with France, and later Russia. These divisive alliance systems existed among nations bound by cultural similarities, economic interdependence, and the ties that linked the various royal families. The inability of the countries to stop the slide to war was to be a catastrophe for Europe, from which it would never recover its global power.

Political systems
Most European states were ruled by hereditary monarchs. In Germany, Austria-Hungary, and Russia, these monarchs retained a large measure of political power, despite the existence of elected parliaments. Britain had retained its monarchy, but kings and queens scrupulously respected the authority of the Houses of Parliament. France, conversely, was a republic. Both Britain and France had restricted electoral franchises – women could not vote, and in Britain the poor were also excluded.

Threats and alliances
Although often seen in retrospect as a golden age of tranquil prosperity, the years before World War I were racked by political conflict. Mass Socialist movements preached the overthrow of the capitalist system. Anarchists practised "propaganda of the deed", assassinating monarchs, such as the Italian King Umberto I in July 1900, and bombing symbols of power. Suffragettes turned to violence in their quest for women's voting rights.

AFTER

Tensions between the European powers mounted over disputes outside Europe and in the Balkans.

THE MOROCCAN CRISES
Germany challenged French **imperial ambitions in Morocco**, leading to diplomatic crises in 1905 and 1911 **18–19 ≫**.

CENTRAL POWERS Name given to Germany, Austria-Hungary, and their allies in World War I.
ENTENTE POWERS Name given to Britain, France, and Russia, which are also referred to as the Allies.

OTTOMAN DECLINE
The long-term decline of the **Turkish Ottoman Empire** was a serious source of instability, triggering an **Italian invasion of Libya**, an Ottoman-ruled area of North Africa, in 1911, and two **Balkan Wars in 1912–13 18–19 ≫**. Ottoman weakness and Balkan conflicts were a temptation for both Russia and Austria-Hungary to intervene in an area on their southern borders where they had competing interests. This was where World War I would start, after the assassination of **Austrian Archduke Franz Ferdinand** in June 1914 **28–29 ≫**.

European alliances, 1878–1918
By 1900, shifting military alliances had resolved into a fixed confrontation between Russia and France on one side and Germany and Austria-Hungary on the other.

KEY
- Austro–German alliance 1878–1918
- Three Emperors' alliance 1881–87
- Austro–Serbian alliance 1881–95
- Triple alliance 1882–1915
- Austro–German–Romanian alliance 1883–1916
- Franco–Russian alliance 1894–1917
- Russo–Bulgarian military convention 1902–13
- Anglo–French Entente 1904–1918
- Anglo–Russian Entente 1907–1917

ALLIANCES DURING FIRST WORLD WAR 1914–18
- The Allies (and allied states)
- Central Powers (and allied states)
- Neutral states

Crises and Conflicts

In the years before the outbreak of World War I, the European powers engaged in brinkmanship and an accelerating arms race. A series of diplomatic crises and conflicts in the Balkans accustomed Europeans to the possibility of a major war.

Germany was indisputably a major military and economic power by the end of the 19th century. However, it lacked two of the attributes then regarded as indicative of great power status: a substantial overseas empire and an ocean-going navy.

Under the unstable Kaiser Wilhelm II, Germany set out to flex its muscles on the world stage. A plan to build a world-class fleet, proposed by Admiral Alfred von Tirpitz, was adopted in 1897. To Britain, this appeared a hostile act. The German naval programme presented a direct challenge to the Royal Navy's dominance of its home waters, the cornerstone of Britain's national security. The British responded with a massive warship-building programme of their own, setting a new standard for battleships with HMS *Dreadnought* in 1906. As the naval race gathered pace, the British buried old rivalries to form an entente with France in 1904 and with France's ally, Russia, in 1907.

Moroccan crises

While making an enemy of Britain, Germany also manufactured a confrontation with France. In 1905, Kaiser Wilhelm made a provocative visit to Morocco, a nominally independent country that France was absorbing into its sphere of influence. He called for all the powers to be given equal access to Morocco, a claim rejected by a subsequent international conference. The Germans took up the issue again in 1911, sending the gunboat SMS *Panther* to the Moroccan port of Agadir. This move provoked a diplomatic crisis, briefly raising fears of a general European war. By the end of 1911, a settlement had been negotiated, involving a small concession of territory to Germany from French Equatorial Africa. This sabre-rattling, along with some anti-British remarks dropped by the Kaiser, drove Britain to strengthen its links with France.

When the crisis of 1911 blew over, the prospect of a general war appeared to recede. Yet at a private meeting in December 1912, the Kaiser and his senior military commanders discussed launching a preventive war against France and Russia. They argued that with the strength of the Russian

Crisis in Morocco
The dispatch of the German gunboat *Panther* to Agadir, caricatured in this contemporary German illustration, took Europe to the brink of war in 1911. Diplomacy solved the crisis but strengthened Anglo-French resolve.

army increasing, it was in Germany's best interest to make the conflict happen sooner rather than later.

Slav nationalism
In southeastern Europe, tensions were rising. The Balkans was a traditional area of rivalry between Austria-Hungary and Russia. The Russians had adopted the role of protectors and leaders of the area's Slav states,

« BEFORE

The accession of German Kaiser Wilhelm II in 1888 was followed by a fatal shift in great power relations.

LEAGUE OF THE THREE EMPERORS
In 1873, German Chancellor Otto von Bismarck tried to stabilize Europe through an **alliance of three empires**: Germany, Russia, and Austria-Hungary. In the 1880s, **rivalry between Russia and Austria-Hungary** undermined this system. Germany formed the **Dual Alliance** with Austria-Hungary, but maintained friendly relations with Russia. This policy was abandoned by Wilhelm II. By 1894, **Russia had allied itself with France** against Germany.

OTTO VON BISMARCK

German fleet, pre-1914
Dreadnought battleships of the German High Seas Fleet steam into the North Sea before World War I. The navy was a source of pride to the German people, its expansion supported by a patriotic Navy League with more than a million members.

German troops on manoeuvres
A crowd watches soldiers cross a pontoon bridge during Germany's 1912 military manoeuvres. These annual occasions were a testing ground for new tactics and technology and a display of military strength.

Austria-Hungary faced a problem of split objectives. The Austro-Hungarian chief of staff, Conrad von Hötzendorf, favoured an offensive war against Serbia, and was inclined to stand on the defensive against Russia. But Austria-Hungary's German allies needed Austro-Hungarian forces to attack the Russians in Poland, to relieve pressure on Germany's Eastern Front. Despite Austro-Hungarian plans for a "swing force" to be mobilized against Serbia or Russia as required, the issue was still unresolved in 1914.

British commitments

Britain's front line of defence was its Royal Navy, which had long enabled British governments to adopt a detached pose in relation to European

affairs. But its entente with France in 1904, designed to deter German aggression, led to the development of war plans that would commit the British to a European war.

From 1911, informal talks between British and French army commanders resulted in an understanding that, were France attacked by Germany, Britain would send an expeditionary force across the English Channel to take up position on the left of the French line, facing the border with Belgium. However, the British were careful to avoid making any formal promise to carry out this commitment to their French allies.

The pre-1914 war plans were worked out in great detail by staff officers, with timetables that had to be adhered to if the military machine was to function smoothly. Collectively they created a situation in which the mobilization of armies could only with great difficulty be prevented from leading to large-scale battles. The planners had written the script for a Europe-wide war that could be precipitated at any moment by a single incident.

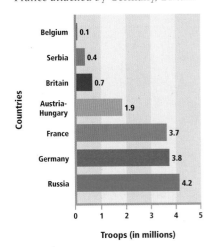

Countries	Troops (in millions)
Belgium	0.1
Serbia	0.4
Britain	0.7
Austria-Hungary	1.9
France	3.7
Germany	3.8
Russia	4.2

Army sizes at the outbreak of war
Russia's army was substantially larger than those of other European nations, but it was poorly equipped and badly organized. Britain had a relatively small army, and depended on the Royal Navy for defence.

AFTER ≫

The mobilization of European armies in 1914 mostly proceeded with an efficiency that was a credit to the professionalism of army staff officers. Once the fighting had started, however, little went as planned.

THWARTED EXPECTATIONS
None of the plans of the initial protagonists worked out as they had expected. Attacking on their eastern frontier, the French army quickly discovered their troops' **vulnerability to defensive firepower**. At the same time, instead of achieving the rapid defeat of France they had envisaged, German forces were driven back at the **Battle of the Marne** in September 1914 **54–55 ≫**. On Germany's eastern front, **advancing Russian armies** suffered heavy defeats. There was to be no quick victory for anyone.

Evolving Military Technology

"Everybody will be **entrenched...** The **spade** will be **indispensable.**"

JAN BLOCH, POLISH FINANCIER AND INDUSTRIALIST, IN "THE FUTURE OF WAR", 1897

The European armies and navies of 1914 were the beneficiaries of a century of progress in industry, science, and technology. Change was often not specifically driven by military requirements. Railways transformed the speed at which armies could be deployed to frontiers. New means of communication, from the electric telegraph to the telephone and radio, were adapted to military uses. Progress in precision engineering made it much easier to mass-produce weapons with complex mechanisms. Chemists experimented with new explosives that would provide a more powerful replacement for gunpowder.

Arming the infantry

In 1815, at the end of the Napoleonic Wars, armies fought with smoothbore flintlock muskets, loaded by ramming a ball and powder down the barrel, and cannon firing solid shot. Navies went to sea in wooden sailing ships. The pace of change was slow at first, but by the 1870s a firepower revolution was under way.

In the Franco-Prussian War of 1870–71, both sides armed their infantry (foot soldiers) with breech-loading single-shot rifles. By the 1880s, these already effective infantry weapons were being replaced by bolt-action rifles with ammunition fed from a magazine. A well-trained soldier using the Lee-Enfield, the British Army's standard rifle from 1895, could fire more than 20 rounds a minute. This rate of fire was far exceeded by machine-guns. The Maxim gun, the first true machine-gun, brought into active service in the 1890s, fired 600 rounds a minute. The German army took to machine-guns enthusiastically, while other countries struggled to find a good tactical use for the weapon.

Rapid-fire artillery

Artillery guns (long-range weaponry used for bombardment) also adopted rifled barrels and breech-loading. The range of guns greatly increased, and gunners began practising the bombardment of targets beyond their field of view.

The invention in the 1870s of a hydraulic mechanism that returned the gun's barrel to its original position after recoil cleared the way for rapid-fire artillery. Most important of all, scientifically designed shells packed with nitrate-based high-explosives ensured that artillery fire

Potential bomber
Just before the outbreak of World War I, Russian aviation pioneer Igor Sikorski (right) built the first multi-engine aircraft. These flying machines could carry a substantial load and were turned into bombers during the war.

High-explosive shells

Mass-produced in factories and fired from breech-loading rifled guns, these shells marked a revolutionary advance in destructive power over the gunpowder and smoothbore cannon of the mid-19th century.

The rapid developments in military technology from the 1870s occurred during a long period of peace between the great powers. The Russo-Japanese War of 1904–05, the first conflict to use modern armaments, provided a preview of what was to come in World War I. At sea, torpedoes and mines proved capable of sinking the largest warships. On land, troops were entrenched behind barbed wire. Invented to control cattle in the American West, barbed wire inflicted massive casualties on infantry attempting frontal assaults.

The old ways die hard

In Europe, naval commanders continued to focus on bigger and better battleships, while army commanders preached the triumph of offensive spirit over defensive firepower. Openness to technological innovation coexisted with an attachment to venerated traditions, such as the cavalry charge with sabre and lance, and the infantry assault with fixed bayonets. World War I would be characterized by the contrast between the efficient exploitation of weaponry supplied by science and industry and the persistence of many attitudes to war belonging to an earlier era.

TIMELINE

- **1840s** Prussia is the first European state to equip its infantry with a breech-loading rifle, the Dreyse needle gun.

- **1859** In France, the army makes the first mass movement of troops by railway, transporting an army to fight the Austrians in northern Italy.

BELGIAN MACHINE-GUN, 1869

- **1860s** The first hand-cranked rapid-fire weapons are introduced, including the Belgian Montigny Mitrailleuse and the American Gatling gun.

- **1866** British engineer Robert Whitehead invents the first self-propelled naval torpedo.

- **1870–71** In the Franco-Prussian War, Krupp's rifled artillery guns prove their effectiveness.

- **1880s** High explosives such as picric acid (Lyddite) and TNT come into widespread use as fillings for artillery and naval shells, greatly increasing their destructive effect.

- **1884** The first recoil-operated machine-gun is invented by Sir Hiram Maxim. The Maxim gun, as it is known, is used by the British Army in colonial wars in the 1890s. Its derivatives include the German MG 08 (1908) and the British Vickers gun (1912) used in World War I.

- **1886** Replacing gunpowder with a smokeless propellent makes rifle fire more effective.

- **1890s** European armies are equipped with the bolt-action repeater rifles they will use in World War I, such as the German Mauser Gewehr 98, French Lebel, and Russian Mosin-Nagant.

- **1897** The US Navy adopts the first successful powered submarine.

- **1898** France introduces the 75 mm field gun that can fire up to 30 rounds a minute to a range of 8.5 km (5 miles).

- **1904–05** In the Russo-Japanese War, the combination of trenches and barbed wire, artillery firing high-explosive shells beyond line of sight, and the use of field telephones and radio anticipate the warfare of World War I.

- **1906** The British battleship HMS *Dreadnought* enters service, making all previous leading warships obsolescent.

- **1911** The military use of aircraft begins as Italy drops grenades on Ottoman Turks in Libya.

"Aviation is fine as a **sport**. But as an **instrument of war,** it is **worthless.**"

FERDINAND FOCH, FRENCH GENERAL, 1911

was more destructive. Rifled guns and high-explosive shells were also used at sea, mounted in rotating turrets aboard steam-driven steel warships.

New technology

By the early 20th century, armies and navies were keen to explore other new inventions that might give them an advantage over the enemy. Wireless telegraphy (radio), first demonstrated experimentally in the 1890s, was in use by navies by 1904. However, early radio equipment proved cumbersome on land, and armies preferred to use field telephones.

Inventors Wilbur and Orville Wright developed a heavier-than-air flying machine between 1903 and 1905. European armies showed interest but adoption of the invention was delayed by the brothers' refusal to demonstrate their aircraft in public.

Meanwhile, airships were developed by, among others, German Count Ferdinand von Zeppelin. From 1909, the year in which French pilot Louis Blériot flew a monoplane across the Channel, an air craze gripped Europe. Air enthusiasts and fantasy fiction writers envisaged future aerial wars with mass bombing of cities. More

12,000 The number of machine-guns in service with the German army in August 1914. In contrast, the British and French armies had only a few hundred machine-guns each.

soberly, armies and navies explored the potential of aeroplanes and airships for reconnaissance, integrating both into manoeuvres from 1911.

By that date, motor transport was having a major impact on civilian life, but armies remained overwhelmingly reliant upon horse-drawn vehicles. Armoured cars began to come into service, and were used by Italy in its war with Turkey in 1911.

Clément-Bayard II airship

Built in 1910 for the French army, this airship never entered service. It was the first airship to fly over the English Channel, and its wireless transmitter achieved the first air-ground radio communication.

1 MAUSER GEWEHR 98 (GERMAN)

2 7.92MM X57 MAUSER CARTRIDGE (GERMAN)

5 PATTERN 1907 SWORD BAYONET (BRITISH)

7 KNIFE BAYONET (GERMAN)

8 .303 MKVII CARTRIDGE (BRITISH)

9 SHORT MAGAZINE LEE-ENFIELD (BRITISH)

11 HALES NO. 3 RIFLE GRENADE (BRITISH)

Rifles

The infantry was armed with bolt-action rapid-fire rifles, with ammunition fed from a box magazine. These were reliable, efficient weapons, and armies saw no need for substantial innovations during the war.

1 **Mauser Gewehr 98 (German)** entered service in 1898. This model has been fitted with a telescopic sight for use by a sniper. 2 **7.92mm X57 Mauser cartridge (German)** was adopted in 1905. Its use with the Gewehr 98 rifle led to the name "Mauser" being added. 3 **Ross .303IN MK III (Canadian)** Produced until 1916, the Ross was favoured by many snipers due to its long-range accuracy. However, it often jammed in the muddy conditions of the trenches. 4 **M91 Moschetto de Cavalleria (Italian)** This was a shorter variant of the Carcano M91 rifle, the standard Italian infantry weapon. 5 **Pattern 1907 sword bayonet (British)** Designed for the Lee-Enfield rifle, this was based on the Japanese Arisaka bayonet, but its long blade was unwieldy in the trenches. 6 **Steyr-Mannlicher M1895 (Austro-Hungarian)** was used by Austro-Hungarian troops, who called it the "Ruck-Zuck" (very quick) due to its high firing rate. 7 **Knife bayonet (German)** Short and double-edged, this fitted to the Gewehr 98 rifle and doubled as a trench knife. 8 **.303 MKVII cartridge (British)** This version of the Lee-Enfield cartridge had a heavy lead base, which caused

the cartridge to twist and deform, inflicting more severe wounds on the enemy. 9 **Short Magazine Lee-Enfield (British)** was the standard British infantry weapon. The rifle shown is the Mark III Star, introduced in late 1915. 10 **Berthier MLE 1916 (French)** A modified version of the earlier MLE 1907/15, this increased the magazine size from three rounds to five. 11 **Hales No. 3 rifle grenade (British)** Rifle grenades, which clipped to the muzzle, provided greater range for explosives. 12 **Cartridge belt (American)** Standard issue for infantrymen, these belts enabled them to carry extra ammunition. 13 **Mosin Nagant M1891 (Russian)** was the main weapon of the Russian infantry. Due to shortages, Russia issued contracts to American firms for over three million of these rifles. 14 **M1903 Springfield (American)** After encountering Mauser rifles in the Spanish-American War of 1898, the US negotiated a licence to manufacture a Mauser-style rifle of its own. 15 **Cartridge belt (Turkish)** This belt with its cartridge pouches was made in Germany, as was most of the equipment used by the Turkish troops.

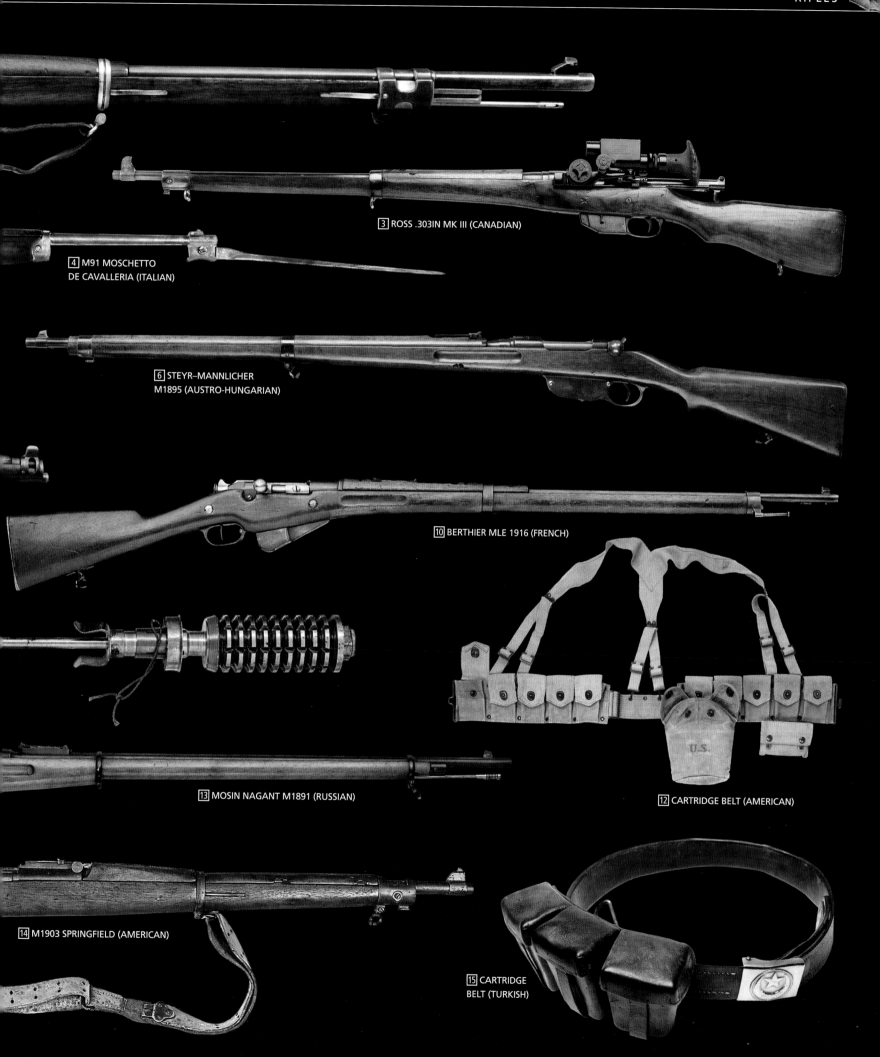

3 ROSS .303IN MK III (CANADIAN)

4 M91 MOSCHETTO
DE CAVALLERIA (ITALIAN)

6 STEYR–MANNLICHER
M1895 (AUSTRO-HUNGARIAN)

10 BERTHIER MLE 1916 (FRENCH)

13 MOSIN NAGANT M1891 (RUSSIAN)

12 CARTRIDGE BELT (AMERICAN)

14 M1903 SPRINGFIELD (AMERICAN)

15 CARTRIDGE
BELT (TURKISH)

◀◀ BEFORE

Austria-Hungary was a multi-ethnic state in crisis. Its stability was under threat from growing discontent among its Slav subject peoples.

AUSTRO-HUNGARIAN WEAKNESS
The country's ruler, **Emperor Franz Joseph**, had come to the throne in 1849. His regime was splendid in its public ceremonies but shaky in its political foundations. In 1908, Austria-Hungary **annexed Bosnia-Herzegovina ≪ 18–19**, a province with a mixed Serb, Croat, and Bosnian Muslim population. This annexation **angered Serbia**, an aggressive Balkan state with ambitions to unite the region's Slav population under its rule. The Austro-Hungarian government felt the **rising power of Serbia** was a threat to its authority over its restive Slav subjects in the Balkans.

EMPEROR FRANZ JOSEPH

Assassination at Sarajevo

On 28 June 1914, the heir to the Austro-Hungarian throne, Archduke Franz Ferdinand, and his wife, Sophie, were shot dead by a Bosnian Serb in Sarajevo. This act triggered a chain of events that would lead to the outbreak of war.

Archduke Franz Ferdinand's visit to Sarajevo, the capital of Bosnia-Herzegovina, was a blunt assertion of imperial authority in a recently annexed province. Even its timing was provocative – 28 June was a day sacred to Serb nationalists as the anniversary of the 1389 Battle of Kosovo, in which a defeat by the Turks had cost Serbia its independence.

Bosnian Serb separatists, who were armed, trained, and organized by shadowy nationalist groups and military intelligence officers in Serbia, had been carrying out attacks against the Austro-Hungarian authorities in Bosnia-Herzegovina. The Austrian government had received specific warning of a planned assassination attempt against the Archduke, but the

> **The Habsburgs of Austria-Hungary were one of Europe's oldest royal families. They took their name from a castle in Switzerland.**

visit went ahead regardless. To cancel it, or even to mount a heavy-handed security operation, would have been an admission that the Habsburgs did not fully control one of the provinces in their empire. The archduke's planned route and schedule were publicized in advance of the visit.

Imperial visitor
Franz Ferdinand arrived in Sarajevo by train at 9:50am. He was delighted to be accompanied by his wife, who was usually excluded from all public ceremonies under the terms of their marriage. The archduke first inspected troops drawn up on the Filipovic parade ground and then set off for the town hall in a procession of cars.

Assassin apprehended
Gavrilo Princip is arrested after shooting Archduke Franz Ferdinand and his wife on 28 June 1914. Princip declared himself inspired by a mission to free Slavs from Austrian rule "by means of terror".

Waiting among the crowds along the route were seven young conspirators bent on assassination. Six of them were Bosnian Serbs and one a Bosnian Muslim, apparently chosen deliberately to give the operation multicultural credentials. Between them they had six bombs and four Serbian army pistols.

Assassin's gun
The assassination was carried out with a Belgian-manufactured Fabrique Nationale Model 1910 semi-automatic pistol, supplied by the Serbian army.

The assassination

As the motorcade drove along the quay by the Miljacka river, one of the conspirators, Nedjelko Cabrinovic, threw a bomb that bounced off the back of the archduke's car and exploded. This injured a number of bystanders, including a police officer. The would-be assassin then swallowed a cyanide pill and jumped into the shallow river, where he was arrested, the cyanide dose proving non-lethal. Angry and shocked by the incident, Franz Ferdinand continued making his way to the town hall. The conspirators dispersed into the crowds, their assassination bid having seemingly ended in failure.

Nineteen-year-old Gavrilo Princip went into a delicatessen to buy a sandwich. Coming out of the shop, he found the archduke's car stopped directly in front of him. Franz Ferdinand had decided to visit the injured police officer in hospital, but his driver had taken a wrong turn and was trying to reverse. Seizing his opportunity, Princip pulled out his pistol and fired twice, hitting the archduke in the neck and his wife in the abdomen. The couple died within minutes, while still in the car. Princip tried to kill himself but was overpowered by onlookers and arrested.

Austria-Hungary reacts

The news of the couple's death was a shock to the Habsburg court. There was no state funeral. Franz Ferdinand and Sophie were interred side by side in a private crypt at Artstetten Castle in the Danube valley. Emperor Franz Joseph was privately relieved that he would never be succeeded by a nephew he neither liked nor trusted. "A higher power," the emperor said, "has restored that order which I could unfortunately not maintain." But the public affront to the Austro-Hungarian state was gross. Although there was no clear evidence that the Serbian government had been directly involved, the operation had definitely been planned and organized in Serbia. This was enough.

A band of assassins, with Serbian backing, had killed the heir to the throne. Austria-Hungary's honour, prestige, and credibility required that Serbia be made to pay.

The road to war

Austro-Hungarian ruling circles were split between hawks and doves. Chief of the General Staff Count Franz Conrad von Hötzendorf had long sought a war with Serbia. He saw the assassinations as an ideal pretext for military action. Other important figures, including Count István Tisza, prime minister of Hungary, were more cautious, preferring a diplomatic solution. In the first week of July,

47 PER CENT of the population of Austria-Hungary were Slavs. They included Poles, Czechs, Croats, Slovaks, Slovenes, and Serbs. Only 24 per cent of the population were ethnic Germans.

Austria-Hungary sought the opinion of its ally Germany. Kaiser Wilhelm II had been outraged by the assassinations. His advisers, including Chancellor Theobald von Bethmann-Hollweg, agreed that Austria-Hungary should be encouraged to take decisive, but unspecified, action against Serbia. Whatever the Austro-Hungarian government chose to do, it could be assured of Germany's support.

This loose guarantee of German backing – often referred to as the "blank cheque" – put the hawks firmly in control in Vienna. Austria-Hungary then drew up a series of demands deliberately designed to prove unacceptable. Their rejection by Serbia would provide a pretext for an attack by the Austro-Hungarian army.

No one was planning for a full-scale war. The idea was for a swift punitive invasion followed by a harsh peace settlement to humiliate and permanently weaken Serbia. However, nothing could happen quickly. Much of the army was on leave, helping to bring in the harvest. After some hesitation, the date for delivery of an ultimatum was set for 23 July.

Private burial

Franz Ferdinand knew his Czech wife would be denied burial in the Habsburg imperial crypt below the Capuchin Church in Vienna. He therefore specified in his will that they be buried at Artstetten Castle, Austria.

ARCHDUKE (1863–1914)

FRANZ FERDINAND

Franz Ferdinand was the nephew of Emperor Franz Joseph. He became heir apparent to the Habsburg throne in 1889. His relations with Franz Joseph were soured by his insistence on marrying an impoverished Czech aristocrat, Sophie Chotek, in 1900. He was forced to agree to humiliating terms in order to marry her. She was denied royal status, and any offspring would be barred from inheriting the throne. Franz Ferdinand's political position varied over time, but he was viewed by the Austro-Hungarian establishment as dangerously liberal on the key issue of Slav nationalism.

AFTER »

The interrogation and trial of the conspirators failed to dispel the mystery surrounding the event.

TRIALS AND EXECUTIONS
Twenty-five **Bosnian conspirators** implicated in the archduke's assassination were **tried in Austria-Hungary** in October 1914. Sixteen were found guilty and three hanged. Gavrilo Princip was spared execution because he had been under 20 years old when the crime was committed. He died of tuberculosis in prison in April 1918.

The **planning of the operation** was traced to the head of **Serbian military intelligence**, Colonel Dragutin Dimitrijevic. Using the code name Apis, he also led a Serbian secret society known as the **Black Hand**. In 1917, the Serbian government had Dimitrijevic and three other Black Hand members executed after a rigged trial.

THE OUTBREAK OF WAR
Austria-Hungary **declared war on Serbia** on 28 July 1914 **30–31 »**. Within a week, a wider European war had broken out. World War I led directly to the collapse of Austria-Hungary and the fall of the Habsburg dynasty.

"Sophie, Sophie, **don't die!** Stay alive for our children!"

LAST WORDS OF ARCHDUKE FRANZ FERDINAND, 28 JUNE 1914

The Slide to War

In late July 1914, an Austro-Hungarian confrontation with Serbia plunged Europe into crisis. Such situations had been resolved before by diplomacy, but this time the major powers slid with startling rapidity from peace to a long-anticipated war.

On 23 July, at 6pm, the Austro-Hungarian ambassador delivered an ultimatum to the Serbian government, starting the world on the road to war. The ultimatum demanded that the Serbs suppress anti-Austrian terrorist organizations, stop anti-Austrian propaganda, and

BEFORE

The assassination of Archduke Franz Ferdinand and his wife by a Bosnian Serb in Sarajevo on 28 June 1914 **« 28–29** was followed by an interlude in which, in public at least, little happened.

PLANNING FOR WAR
Dominant figures in Austria-Hungary, notably Chief of Staff Franz Conrad von Hötzendorf, were determined to use the assassination as a pretext for **war against Serbia**. They had received clearance from Germany to take whatever action they wanted. It took time for Austria-Hungary to organize its blow against Serbia, so through the first three weeks of July the crisis appeared to subside.

BUSINESS AS USUAL
Maintaining a facade of normality, Kaiser Wilhelm left for a summer cruise. Meanwhile, French President Raymond Poincaré made a prearranged visit to Russia to confirm the long-established **Franco-Russian alliance**. The issue of Serbia was mentioned, but without the urgency of a matter that might **threaten war**.

TSARIST STATE EMBLEM

allow Austro-Hungarian officials to take part in the investigation of those who were responsible for the Sarajevo assassinations. The Serbians were given 48 hours to accept the demands of the ultimatum or face war. Serbia accepted most of them but, assured of support from Russia, rejected outright the idea of Austrian officials operating on its territory.

A diplomatic solution was still possible. On 26 July, British Foreign Secretary Sir Edward Grey proposed a conference of the major powers. Kaiser Wilhelm, returning from his holiday cruise in the North Sea, enthused over the humiliation of Serbia and suggested that war was no longer necessary.

The Russian reaction

The dominant elements within the Austro-Hungarian military and political establishment did not want a diplomatic triumph. They wanted a military victory to dismember Serbia and bolster Habsburg authority. Thus on 28 July, Austria-Hungary formally declared war on Serbia.

To stand by while Serbia was defeated by Austria-Hungary would have been a severe humiliation for Russia. It would have signalled the end of its long-nourished ambition to expand its influence in the Balkans and towards Constantinople (modern Istanbul). So, on 28 July, Russia declared the mobilization of its armed forces in those regions facing Austria-Hungary, but not along its border with Germany. Suddenly the great European powers

faced the prospect of war spreading to engulf them all. The insecurity and crises of the last decade had strengthened rival alliances and hardened mutual suspicions. France and Russia felt that they must stand or fall together. Neither had the military or industrial capability to stand up to Germany alone. By making no effort to restrain their ally, the French in effect abandoned all influence over the evolving situation.

German mobilization

At this point in the crisis, a general war was still far from inevitable. Yet leading figures in the German political and military ruling circle, including the Chief of the General Staff, Helmuth von Moltke, and Prussian War Minister Erich von Falkenhayn, decided the moment for the long-predicted war with France and Russia had come. Moltke had argued on previous

Life as usual
The gravity of the diplomatic crisis in July 1914 was masked by summer holidays. Relaxation in the sun distracted ordinary German citizens and cloaked the machinations of military and political leaders.

occasions that, for Germany, it was better the war should come sooner rather than later. On 29 July, he urged mobilization to support Austria-Hungary. German war plans dictated that this had to be directed against both Russia and France and involve the invasion of neutral Belgium.

Meanwhile, in St Petersburg, debate raged about the practicality of partial mobilization. The Russian foreign minister Sergei Sazonov, fearful of German intentions, forced through a shift to general mobilization on the evening of 30 July. This played into the hands of the German hawks, who could now present themselves as responding to Russian aggression.

> **"The lights are going out all over Europe; we shall not see them lit again in our lifetime."**
>
> ATTRIBUTED TO SIR EDWARD GREY, BRITISH FOREIGN SECRETARY, 3 AUGUST 1914

Naval review
In July 1914, Britain's Royal Navy conducted a test mobilization, followed by a review at Spithead. Submarines were among the ships on show.

DEUTSCHLAND — AUGUST · 1914

Through 1914, there were more declarations of war as the conflict took on a global scale. Other countries asserted neutrality.

THE WIDENING WAR

Britain and France also **brought their empires into the war 118–19 »**. In Britain's case, this included the British dominions of Australia, New Zealand, Canada, and South Africa – although in South Africa entry into the war was contested by anti-British Boers. **Japan**, an ally of Britain since 1902, **declared war on Germany** on 23 August 1914 **84–85 »**. The **Ottoman Empire** entered the war as an **ally of Germany** at the end of October **74–75 »**.

NEUTRALITY

Italy opted to **stay neutral**. It had been a member of the **Triple Alliance** with Germany and Austria-Hungary since 1882 but, with the Italian people in equal measure **hostile to Austria-Hungary** and hostile to going to war, in August 1914 neutrality seemed the best policy. The **USA** also **declared neutrality 130–31 »**.

PUBLIC UNITY

Combatant countries experienced a wave of **social solidarity** and **patriotic fervour** at the outbreak of war **32–33 »**.

FRENCH MEDAL OF HONOUR

Rallying the nation
Germania, the personification of the German nation, stands ready for war in Friedrich August von Kaulbach's 1914 painting of the same name. The German government presented itself as the armed defender of civilization against tsarist Russia in the East.

On 31 July, German Chancellor Bethmann-Hollweg asked Moltke: "Is the fatherland in danger?". Moltke answered in the affirmative. On 1 August, Germany declared war on Russia. The Kaiser made a last-ditch bid for peace by sending a telegram to his cousin, Tsar Nicholas II, but the two heads of state were not in control. When the Kaiser ordered Moltke to limit the war to Russia, he was told that mobilization for a war on two fronts could not be changed. A German declaration of war on France followed on 3 August.

Enter the British

For the Germans, a crucial but unknown factor in the crisis was the reaction of Britain. The British Liberal government was horrified by the prospect of war. An inner circle of ministers had gone much further than was publicly known in committing British military support to France in case of war. As fighting broke out on the continent, they could not carry the rest of the government with them. More clear-cut than Britain's ententes with France and Russia, however, was its commitment to Belgium. Britain was a guarantor of Belgian neutrality under the terms of the 1839 Treaty of London. In order to implement the Schlieffen Plan, the German army had to cross Belgium. On 2 August, Germany demanded right of passage for its troops.

The Belgians opted to fight. When German troops entered Belgium on 3 August, Britain responded with an ultimatum demanding their withdrawal. A British declaration of war on Germany followed on 4 August. Chancellor Bethmann-Hollweg, appalled at this turn of events, told the departing British ambassador, Edward Goschen, that Britain had gone to war "just for a scrap of paper".

Pulling Together

The outbreak of war in August 1914 produced a remarkable show of solidarity in deeply divided societies. As the mobilization of mass citizen armies proceeded smoothly, revolutionary aspirations and anti-war sentiments drowned in a flood of patriotism.

Before 1914, war was a divisive issue in Europe. Nationalists and imperialists praised war as a healthy struggle for survival. Liberals and socialists denounced it as an offence against civilized values or an evil product of capitalism and autocracy. Although newspapers were often aggressively jingoistic, most ordinary people were not, as their voting patterns showed.

A general election in France in spring 1914 brought a landslide victory for radicals and socialists opposed to the country's virulently anti-German president, Raymond Poincaré.

In Germany, the Social Democrats, outspoken critics of Prussian militarism, were the largest party in the Reichstag. European socialists took the slogan "Workers of the world, unite!" seriously. The Second International, to which the socialist parties of all the major European countries belonged, believed it could make war impossible through coordinated working-class resistance.

On 31 July 1914, France's most prominent antiwar socialist, Jean Jaurès, was killed by a nationalist extremist in a Parisian café. This act of violence might have been expected on a wider scale – a struggle between those in favour of the war and those against it. Instead, the outbreak of war was followed by an extraordinary social and political solidarity.

Growing patriotism

In every country, the vast majority of people were convinced that their nation's cause was just, a necessary act of defence or the fulfilment of an obligation. Accepting the need to defend their country against tsarist Russia, the most reactionary regime in Europe, the German Social Democrats voted in support of the war. Surprised and elated, Kaiser Wilhelm stated that he "no longer saw parties, but only Germans". In Austria-Hungary, to general astonishment, even the empire's Slav minorities showed initial enthusiasm for the war.

In France, squabbling politicians buried their differences in response

Called to war
German reservists, some in uniform and others still in civilian dress, are mobilized at the start of World War I. Part-time, non-professional troops, reservists were soon to be thrown into battle.

« BEFORE

If the slide to war took Europe by surprise in summer 1914, it was partly because other crises and scandals were holding governments' attention.

INTERNAL UNREST
Russia faced widespread strikes that threatened to develop into revolutionary upheaval. In France, the public was preoccupied with the sensational trial of Henriette Caillaux, wife of a former prime minister. She had shot a French newspaper editor for publishing her love letters. The British were wrestling with a grave crisis over **Irish Home Rule 106–07 »**, which threatened civil war between Irish Protestants and Catholics, and an arson campaign by **suffragettes** seeking voting rights for women.

SUFFRAGETTE BANNER

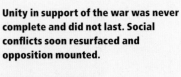

DISSENTING VOICES

Socialists who opposed the war from the start included Kier Hardie in Britain, Karl Liebknecht in Germany, and Russian Bolshevik leader **Vladimir Ilyich Lenin**. In 1915, Liebknecht and Rosa Luxemburg formed the revolutionary **Spartacus League** to oppose the war.

HONOURING THE SPARTICUS LEAGUE, BERLIN

to President Poincaré's appeal for a *Union sacrée* (Sacred Union) in defence of the Fatherland. French socialists redirected their hostility against German militarism. In Russia, widely believed to be on the brink of a revolution in the summer of 1914, a vast crowd assembled with banners and icons in St Petersburg to pledge their support to Tsar Nicholas II.

Britain was similarly swept by a wave of patriotism. This was stimulated by fear of an increasingly powerful Germany and widespread sympathy for the plight of Belgium. Suffragettes negotiated a halt to their violent campaign for women's voting rights, with the government freeing suffragette prisoners in return for the movement's support in the war.

Reviewing the Ulstermen

The Ulster Volunteers are reviewed by their founder, Edward Carson. On the outbreak of war, this Protestant militia, set up to fight Irish Home Rule, formed the basis of the British 36th (Ulster) Division.

Rule when it ended. Somewhat reluctantly accepted by the British Army, Redmond's Irish Volunteers formed the basis of the 16th (Irish) Division. Some Volunteers refused to follow Redmond and continued their campaign against British rule.

Conscript armies

Mobilization of Europe's conscript armies – a complex operation on a vast scale – mostly proceeded smoothly. Millions of men and horses were assembled, equipped, and sent by train to the front. Before the war, French military authorities had estimated that up to 13 per cent of those called up might not appear; in fact, only 1.5 per cent failed to present themselves as instructed. There were anti-draft riots in some Russian towns and country districts, but they were the exception. Nonetheless, the popular image of smiling soldiers leaving for the front cheered by crowds is deceptive. There were tears, anxiety, and resigned acceptance, as well as enthusiasm.

The large number of those not liable for military service who volunteered to fight in August 1914 is evidence of the war fever gripping European nations. Britain was the only combatant country that did not conscript. Responding to an appeal for volunteers launched by the newly appointed Minister for War, Lord Kitchener, over 750,000 men had enlisted by the end of September. World War I was, at least initially, a people's war.

> ## "A **fateful hour** has fallen upon **Germany...** The sword is being forced into our hands."

KAISER WILHELM II, IN A SPEECH IN BERLIN, 31 JULY 1914

British trade unions also rallied behind the call for war, cancelling a planned series of strikes.

Irish support

Most remarkably, a perilous situation in Ireland was transformed. The war broke out as Britain was about to grant the Irish a measure of self-government, known as Home Rule. This was opposed by the Protestants in Ulster, who had formed an armed militia, the Ulster Volunteer Force (UVF), to resist such moves. Pro-Home Rule Catholics had responded by arming a militia of their own, the Irish Volunteers.

The outbreak of the European war prevented a civil war in Ireland. UVF leaders offered the services of their militia to the British Army, which readily accepted them. Irish nationalist leader John Redmond also supported Britain in the war, calculating this would ensure implementation of Home

| **715,000** | **The number** |
of horses mobilized by Germany in 1914.

EMMELINE PANKHURST

Born in Manchester, Emmeline Pankhurst was the founder of the Women's Social and Political Union (WSPU) suffragist movement. From 1903, she adopted militant tactics, including attacks on property and hunger strikes, in pursuit of women's right to vote. On the outbreak of war in 1914, she dedicated her organization to support of the war effort. She called on women to "fight for their country as they fought for the vote". Pankhurst felt her stance was vindicated by the British parliament's partial extension of voting rights to women in 1918.

The **Declaration** of **War**

The outbreak of war in the summer of 1914 was greeted with a range of emotions from the people of Europe. Most imagined it would be a brief conflict, with short, murderous battles and a clear result. Thousands of young men immediately rushed to take part in the glory, while mobilization papers soon took others – fathers, brothers, and sons – away from their worried families.

"Up and down the wide road… crowds paced incessantly by day and night, singing the German war songs: 'Was blasen die Trompeten?', which is the finest, 'Deutschland, Deutschland über Alles', which comes next, and 'Die Wacht am Rhein', which was most popular. As I walked to and fro among the patriot crowds, I came to know many of the circling and returning faces by sight… Sometimes a company of infantry, sometimes a squadron of horses went down the road westward, wearing the new grey uniforms in place of the familiar Prussian blue… Sometimes the Kaiser in full uniform swept along in his fine motor, cheered he was certainly… [But] the most mighty storm of cheering was reserved for the crown prince, known to be at variance with his father in longing to test his imagined genius in the field."

MR H.W. NEVINSON, A CORRESPONDENT FOR THE "LONDON DAILY NEWS", IN BERLIN DURING THE FIRST DAYS OF AUGUST 1914

"'The tocsin!' cried someone in the field. 'There's a fire in the fields!' Then we saw men running… Soon the field was swept with a wave of agitation. My husband and I stared without understanding before we heard, right in our faces, the news that a neighbour, in his turn, was yelling, 'War! It's war!'

Then, we dropped our tools… and joined the crowd, running as fast as our legs could carry us, to the farmhouse. The men usually so calm… were seized with frenzy. Horses entered at quick trot, whipped by their drivers, while the oxen, goaded until they bled, hurried in reluctantly. In this coming and going of wagons and animals, I could hear disjointed phrases: 'General mobilization…', 'What a misfortune, what an awful misfortune!', 'I'll have to leave right away!', 'It was all bound to come to this.'"

MÉMÉ SANTERRE, A WEAVER FROM A FRENCH VILLAGE NEAR THE BELGIAN BORDER

War is declared
News of the much-anticipated announcement of war in August 1914 drew huge crowds on to the streets of Berlin. It was greeted with a mixture of solemnity and excitement, for a swift victory was expected.

2
NOT OVER BY CHRISTMAS
DECEMBER 1914

When Europe went to war in summer 1914, most people expected a decisive victory for one side or the other by the year's end. In fact, although battles were fought on a vast scale, costing hundreds of thousands of lives, the outcome of the war remained undecided.

NOT OVER BY CHRISTMAS

Britain's naval supremacy allows it to impose a blockade on Germany from the start of the war. Its warship HMS *Queen Elizabeth*, launched in 1913, was a super-dreadnought, at the time the world's most advanced battleship.

King Albert I of Belgium leads his nation's defiance of German military might. Belgium is overrun by the German army and subjected to brutal reprisals for alleged acts of resistance.

VIVE LA BELGIQUE
LIÉGE

At the Battle of Tannenberg on the Eastern Front in August 1914, cavalry play an important role in the fighting between Russia and the Central Powers.

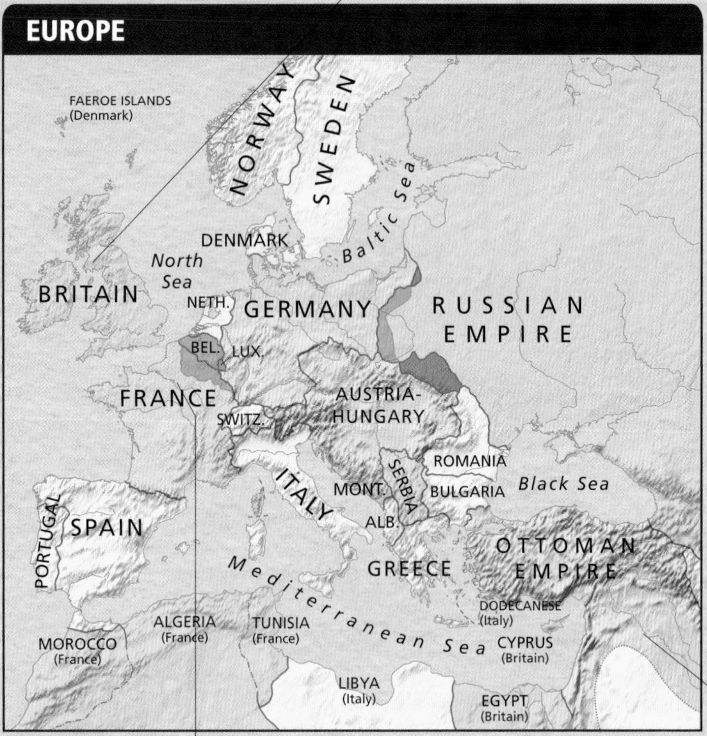
EUROPE
FAEROE ISLANDS
(Denmark)
NORWAY
SWEDEN
Baltic Sea
DENMARK
North Sea
BRITAIN
NETH.
GERMANY
RUSSIAN EMPIRE
BEL.
LUX.
FRANCE
SWITZ.
AUSTRIA-HUNGARY
ROMANIA
SERBIA
MONT.
BULGARIA
Black Sea
ITALY
ALB.
PORTUGAL
SPAIN
GREECE
OTTOMAN EMPIRE
Mediterranean Sea
DODECANESE
(Italy)
ALGERIA
(France)
TUNISIA
(France)
CYPRUS
(Britain)
MOROCCO
(France)
LIBYA
(Italy)
EGYPT
(Britain)

ICELAND
NORWAY
SWEDEN
BRITAIN
GERMANY
ATLANTIC OCEAN
FRANCE
AUSTRIA-HUNGARY
RUSSIAN EMPIRE
ITALY
Black Sea
Caspian Sea
PORTUGAL
SPAIN
OTTOMAN EMPIRE
SPANISH MOROCCO
MOROCCO
TUNISIA
CYPRUS
PERSIA
AFGHANISTAN
TIBET
(autonom
NEPAL
ALGERIA
LIBYA
EGYPT
KUWAIT
BAHRAIN
QATAR
RIO DE ORO
HEJAZ
NEJD
(Saudi)
TRUCIAL OMAN
OMAN
INDIA
ANGLO-EGYPTIAN SUDAN
(British mandate)
FRENCH WEST AFRICA
HADHRAMAUT
ADEN PROTECTORATE
GAMBIA
PORTUGUESE GUINEA
TOGO
FRENCH EQUATORIAL AFRICA
ERITREA
FRENCH SOMALILAND
SIERRA LEONE
LIBERIA
NIGERIA
ABYSSINIA
BRITISH SOMALILAND
CEYLO
GOLD COAST
CAMEROON
ITALIAN SOMALILAND
BRITISH EAST AFRICA
INDIAN OCEAN
RIO MUNI
(Spain)
FRENCH CONGO
BELGIAN CONGO
GERMAN EAST AFRICA
ANGOLA
NORTHERN RHODESIA
MADAGASCAR
SOUTHERN RHODESIA
GERMAN SOUTHWEST AFRICA
BECHUANALAND
PORTUGUESE EAST AFRICA
UNION OF SOUTH AFRICA

General Joseph Gallieni is entrusted with the defence of Paris in 1914. He leads the counterattack against the flank of invading German forces in September, using taxis to move troops from Paris to the front.

Ottoman Turkey joins the war on the side of the Central Powers in late October 1914. Russia declares war on Turkey after it bombs Russian Black Sea ports.

The King's African Rifles, a British colonial force, fight the Germans in East Africa. German colonial troops sustain a guerrilla campaign throughout the war, led by Colonel Lettow-Vorbeck.

In August 1914, Germany implemented the Schlieffen Plan. German leaders intended to defeat France in six weeks before turning to fight the Russians on the Eastern Front. Courageous resistance from the Belgians, although soon swept aside, slowed the advance of the main German armies into northern France. The French suffered tremendous losses attacking Germany's western border but, aided by the British Expeditionary Force (BEF), turned the tide with a counter-offensive at the Battle of the Marne. Germany was denied its swift victory and a series of battles progressing northwards to Ypres and the Yser river left both sides dug into trenches by December 1914. Meanwhile, on the Eastern Front, a Russian invasion of Germany was halted at Tannenberg. In warfare involving large-scale manoeuvres, the Russians generally had the better of Austria-Hungary but lost when fighting German forces.

By the third week in August, British and French troops were beginning to engage with the Germans on Belgian soil. As the next phase of the war opened, however, there was a final paroxysm of German rage against the Belgian nation. On 25 August, German troops occupying the historic city of Louvain, 30 km (19 miles) east of Brussels, fired on one another in a confused night-time incident. Convinced they had

5,521 The number of Belgian civilians who were massacred by advancing German forces during their invasion of Belgium. According to official figures, at least 14,000 buildings were deliberately destroyed.

been attacked by civilians rather than by friendly fire, German soldiers reacted ruthlessly, looting and burning the town's buildings (including its famous medieval library), executing more than 200 people, and emptying the town of its population.

The destruction of Louvain proved to be a propaganda disaster for Germany, confirming an image of the brutal "Huns" that would sustain its enemies in war for four years.

KING OF BELGIUM (1875–1934)

ALBERT I

Albert I had come to the Belgian throne in 1909 and was a popular king. As a constitutional monarch, he had no control over military matters until the outbreak of war, when the constitution made him commander-in-chief. His resistance to Germany was motivated by a determination to preserve Belgium as an independent nation. He kept his army intact in 1914, first in Antwerp and then through withdrawing westwards along the Flanders coast. He headed a government-in-exile in Le Havre, France. In October 1918, he commanded Allied forces in the Courtrai Offensive, in Belgium, re-entering Brussels in triumph in November 1918.

Pickelhaube

M1898 bayonet

Cartridge pouch

Scabbard

German infantry uniform
The uniform of a German noncommissioned officer at the start of World War I included a Pickelhaube (spiked helmet), made of boiled leather (no army used steel helmets in 1914). The cloth cover prevented the helmet from glistening in the sun.

Model 1866 boots

AFTER »

The Germans occupied almost the whole of Belgium. Antwerp fell in early October, but Belgian forces held on to a strip of the Flanders coast in the Battle of the Yser later that month.

PLUNDERED NATION
The Germans placed **Belgium under military government**. In 1916–17, Belgians were deported to work in German factories. **Belgian resistance workers** who spied on German troop movements or aided escaping Allied prisoners of war were **executed**. Many Belgians also suffered from malnutrition, despite food aid from the USA. Flemish separatism was encouraged by the Germans, and the **annexation of Belgium** became a **German war aim 202–03 »**.

The French Offensive

France's attacking strategy at the start of the war, flawed in conception and naively executed, led to heavy losses in Alsace, Lorraine, and the Ardennes. Despite the scale of the casualties, this military disaster did not break French resolve.

Celebrating victory
French propaganda shows Alsace-Lorraine as a woman carried off by a Prussian in 1870 but returned to her true French lover in 1914. Optimism about the recovery of the lost provinces proved to be premature.

BEFORE

In the first week of August 1914, five French armies mobilized on the country's eastern borders, ready to implement General Joffre's Plan XVII.

FAST FORWARDS
French mobilization was efficiently conducted. The French First and Second armies faced **Alsace and Lorraine**, the provinces lost by France to Germany in 1871. The other three armies took up positions from **Verdun** northwards. The **British Expeditionary Force (BEF)** was stationed to their left at **Maubeuge**.

FRENCH CONFIDENCE
The French anticipated a **German move through southern Belgium**, but not the large-scale sweeping movement planned by Alfred von Schlieffen **<< 22**. By 14 August, **German troops were pouring into Belgium << 42–43**, but General Joffre remained confident of success, dismissing fears expressed by **General Charles Lanrezac**, who was commanding troops on the left of the French line.

VON SCHLIEFFEN

On 8 August, French commander-in-chief General Joseph Joffre issued General Instruction No. 1, ordering a general offensive to open on 14 August. Two armies were to advance into Lorraine and three into the Ardennes forest and southern Belgium. By the time the order was issued, one French force had already crossed the German border. An army corps and a cavalry division under General Louis Bonneau was sent into Alsace on 7 August to take the city

84 **PER CENT of eligible French men were called up for military service. From 1913, the service period was three years.**

of Mulhouse. The Alsatians, supposedly groaning under German rule since 1871, were expected to rise up against their oppressors. Overcoming light German resistance, Bonneau entered Mulhouse, triggering a fanfare from French propagandists euphorically celebrating the liberation of Alsace.

The Germans quickly counterattacked and Bonneau embarrassingly scampered back across the French border, where he became the first of many French generals in the war to be sacked by Joffre. A hastily organized Army of Alsace retook Mulhouse, but the French effort in Alsace was overtaken by events further north and soon abandoned.

Attempt on Lorraine

The main French offensive opened in Lorraine on 14 August. The French First and Second armies crossed the border, advancing with banners and bands playing. The German Sixth and Seventh armies withdrew, fighting stiff delaying actions in which their machine-guns took a heavy toll of the brightly clad French

Royal commander
Crown Prince Rupprecht of Bavaria, depicted on this medal, commanded German forces in Lorraine in August 1914. Bavaria was part of the German Empire but had its own monarchy.

infantry. The Schlieffen Plan dictated that the Germans should hold prepared defensive positions at Morhange and Sarrebourg, but Crown Prince Rupprecht of Bavaria, commanding in Lorraine, obtained permission from German General Staff to launch a counteroffensive.

Forced back

On 20 August, German infantry moved forward after a concentrated artillery bombardment. Stunned by the power of the German heavy guns, the French Second Army reeled back from Morhange, forcing the First Army to fall back as well. By 23 August, the French troops, much depleted in numbers, had been thrown back to their starting points on the Meurthe river.

By then, the French Third and Fourth armies were engaged further north, with similarly disastrous results. They marched into the heavily wooded Ardennes expecting to achieve surprise and find it lightly held. For the Germans, this sector formed the innermost part of their great wheeling movement through Belgium. Their Fourth and Fifth armies, respectively commanded by Albrecht, Duke of Württemberg, and German Crown Prince Wilhelm, were advancing in the opposite direction to the French. German reconnaissance aircraft reported the presence of French troops, alerting the Germans to the imminence of battle. Depending on cavalry for reconnaissance, the French plunged forward, believing that, as Joffre's headquarters informed them, "no serious opposition need be anticipated". On 22 August, the opposing armies collided in morning fog. Both sides suffered heavy casualties. The rapid fire of the French 75 mm

Uncovered kepi

Tunic

Bayonet

Hobnailed boots

Regimental markings

Cartridge pouch

Haversack

Scabbard

Trousers

French infantry uniform

The French army entered the war with uniforms that made little concession to the need for camouflage. Dark blue overcoats and bright red trousers offered a clear target for enemy fire, although the red kepi was hidden by a cloth cover.

> **"** In an instant it had become clear that **all** the **courage** in the world **could not withstand** this **fire."**

CHARLES DE GAULLE, A PLATOON COMMANDER IN THE FRENCH FIFTH ARMY, AUGUST 1914

field guns slaughtered German troops caught on open ground, but the French came off worst. They were too often thrown forward in futile bayonet charges and reluctant to dig trenches, the only effective protection against artillery and machine-gun fire.

> **140,000** The estimated number of French casualties in the Battle of the Frontiers, 14–24 August, out of some 1.25 million troops deployed.

The French Third Colonial Division lost 11,000 of its 15,000 men in a day. Despite receiving orders from Joffre to resume their advance in the Ardennes, the French armies fell back in disarray behind the Meuse river.

End of the offensive

By 24 August, the French offensive laid down in Plan XVII had clearly failed. On the attack, French forces had proved naive, launching infantry assaults without artillery support and without adequate reconnaissance. Lack of heavy guns and entrenching equipment had proved fatal defects.

At the same time that French offensives failed in Lorraine and the Ardennes, French and British forces encountered the main German armies advancing through Belgium.

SAMBRE AND MONS

The **French Fifth Army**, under General Charles Lanrezac, fought the **German Second Army** at the Battle of the Sambre. On Lanrezac's left, the British Expeditionary Force confronted the German First Army at **Mons 46–47 »**. **Overwhelmed by the German forces**, the French and British began a **retreat** from Belgium that took them south of Paris **52–53 »**.

FRENCH RECOVERY

Departing from the **Schlieffen Plan**, Chief of the General Staff Helmuth von Moltke provided **reinforcements** to continue the German offensive in Lorraine. In **desperate fighting** in early September, France's eastern line held in front of Nancy and Verdun. Meanwhile, Joffre set about **rearranging his armies**. On 5 September, he launched a **major counteroffensive** at the **Battle of the Marne 54–55 »**.

Forced on the defensive, however, the French troops fought like tigers. The Germans, in their turn, discovered how difficult it was to assault determinedly held defensive positions. By 26 August, the French had halted their enemy in front of the town of Nancy.

African soldiers

Arab and Berber troops of the French Army of Africa were brought to France from Algeria, Morocco, and Tunisia on the outbreak of war. These colonial soldiers soon moved into frontline positions.

« BEFORE

Britain declared war on Germany on 4 August 1914. By the time the British Expeditionary Force (BEF) had deployed to France, the fighting was already well under way.

BRITAIN JOINS FRANCE

First organized in 1907, the BEF consisted of **six infantry divisions** and a **cavalry division**. Under plans discussed with the French army from 1911, the BEF was to take up position on the left of the French line. Home defence was to be entrusted to the Territorial Army and reserves. At the outbreak of war,

BRITISH FORCES ARRIVE AT BOULOGNE

however, the nervous British government insisted on two infantry divisions remaining at home. **Mobilization was punctual and efficient**, with large numbers of horses also sent to the front. The BEF was in position around Maubeuge in France by 20 August. By then, the **Lorraine offensive was in trouble « 44–45**, and **Belgium** was being **put to the sword « 42–43**.

« 44–45 « 42–43

BRITISH GENERAL (1852–1925)

JOHN FRENCH

The first commander of the British Expeditionary Force, Field Marshal Sir John French made his reputation as a dashing cavalry officer fighting the Boers in South Africa.

Appointed Chief of the Imperial General Staff in 1912, he resigned in April 1914 over government policy on Ireland. His seniority made him a natural choice to lead the BEF, but he soon proved to be out of his depth. He was reluctant to liaise with the French and, after initial setbacks in August, was persuaded only with great difficulty to return to the fight at the Battle of the Marne. Considered ill-equipped to cope with the challenges of trench warfare, he was replaced by Sir Douglas Haig in December 1915.

The **British** Go into **Action**

The regular professional soldiers of the British Expeditionary Force arrived in France in August 1914 to find themselves directly in the path of the main German offensive through Belgium. They received their first taste of war at the Battle of Mons.

Placed in command of the British Expeditionary Force (BEF), Field Marshal Sir John French was given written instructions by the newly appointed Secretary of State for War, Lord Kitchener. These told him to "support and cooperate with the French army", while at the same time stressing that he would "in no case come under the orders of any Allied general". The field marshal was also instructed to take the greatest care to minimize "losses and wastage".

How the BEF was to remain independent and intact while wholeheartedly supporting the French was not explained. Kitchener also sent a personal message to the troops in which they were advised, among other things, to behave courteously in foreign lands and resist "temptations both in wine and women".

The BEF's position on the Belgian frontier at the extreme left of the French line was considered a quiet sector. By 16 August, when Field Marshall French went for his first meeting with General Charles Lanrezac, commander of the French Fifth Army, it was becoming apparent this would not be the case.

100,000 The number of British soldiers deployed by the BEF in August 1914. By the end of the year, 90 per cent were killed, wounded, or missing.

Mutual incomprehension

Ordered by a complacent General Joffre to advance into southern Belgium, Lanrezac was convinced he was about to be overwhelmed by German forces. He did not trust the British to protect his left flank, especially as they had arrived with only four divisions instead of the promised six. The meeting between French and Lanrezac ended in mutual incomprehension.

The British advanced into Belgium, reaching the Condé-Mons canal on 22 August, a day ahead of General Alexander von Kluck's German First Army, which was advancing from the east. Under orders to maintain the pace of the advance through Belgium, Kluck mounted a frontal assault on the British, who were in defensive positions along the far bank of the canal. The Battle of Mons, as it became known, was a fierce skirmish.

Gunned down

The British were short of machine-guns but the rapid rifle fire of the regular soldiers mowed down the massed columns of German infantry. British field artillery was pushed dangerously forward, because the gunners were unpractised in firing beyond line of sight, but its shrapnel was brutally effective against soldiers advancing in the open. By the end of the day, the BEF had suffered 1,600 casualties, and the Germans 5,000. Outnumbered two to one in soldiers and guns, the British had been forced to pull back, but they were ready to resume the next day.

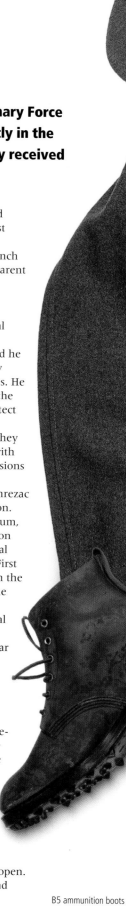

Peak cap

B5 ammunition boots

Knapsack

Tunic

Cartridge pouch

British uniform
The British army adopted khaki as its campaign uniform in 1897, replacing the traditional red coats. This camouflage increased soldiers' chances of survival, but the cloth and leather headgear gave no protection against shrapnel.

Pattern 1907 bayonet

Scabbard

The Battle of Mons was a minor engagement, but because it was the first entry of British troops in the war it was portrayed as an epic battle to the British public.

THE MONS MYTH
Mons was soon being compared to historic examples of British forces defying much larger enemy armies, such as the **Battle of Agincourt**. A popular myth developed in 1915 that **angels** had intervened to protect British soldiers. The "angel of Mons" became a standard theme of British **propaganda**.

THE GREAT RETREAT
Mons was the starting point for the **Great Retreat 52–53 ≫**, in which **French and British troops** marched **from Belgium to south of the Marne river**, with German armies advancing behind them. Joffre struggled to **reorganize French forces**. With some difficulty he revived cooperation with the British, convincing their commander to **resume the fight**.

MUSIC SCORE MARKING BRITISH SUCCESS AT MONS

To the right of the British position, however, Lanrezac's army was in serious trouble. The French faced a large-scale attack by General Karl von Bülow's German Second Army, which had established bridgeheads across the Sambre and Meuse rivers.

Retreat and pursuit
Lanrezac needed to extricate his army from potential encirclement and destruction. On the night of 23 August, he sent Joffre the unwelcome news that he was going to withdraw the following day. The BEF had no choice but to follow Lanrezac's example. Beginning on 24 August, there was

38 The number of British field guns that were lost to the Germans at the Battle of Le Cateau during the British retreat.

a series of hard-fought actions as the British sought to disengage from an enemy in close pursuit. Getting the field guns away before they were seized was often a hazardous operation, as batteries kept firing until the very last moment, covering the infantry as it fell back from the German advance.

The largest engagement was at Le Cateau, northern France, where the Germans caught up with the BEF's II Corps, commanded by General Sir Horace Smith-Dorrien, on the night of 25 August. Disobeying an order

from French to continue the withdrawal, which he considered impossible, Smith-Dorrien turned to fight. On the morning of 26 August, the British delivered a sufficient check to the Germans to allow an orderly withdrawal later in the day, but this was achieved at the cost of some 8,000 men, including a battalion of Gordon Highlanders who, failing to receive the order to retreat, fought on until all were dead or captured.

The war had hardly begun and the BEF had already lost about 10 per cent of its original strength.

Retreating troops
A British officer with a head wound is aided to walk in the retreat from Mons. Combat against the odds, followed by a long retreat, placed immense strain upon British morale and physical endurance.

"You'd have to load your rifle and fire, tip the case out, fire, fire, fire, fire."
CORPORAL BILL HOLBROOK, ROYAL FUSILIERS, AT THE BATTLE OF MONS

Retreat from Mons
Richard Caton Woodville's painting *Charge of the Ninth Lancers* shows British troops fighting to save a battery of field guns on 24 August 1914, the first day of the retreat from Mons. Captain Francis Grenfell of the Ninth Lancers won a Victoria Cross for his part in the incident.

Artillery

At the start of the war, field artillery was relatively mobile and often loaded with shrapnel to scythe down advancing infantry. Trench systems demanded heavier guns that could saturate enemy defences with shellfire.

[1] **18-Pounder field gun (British)** The standard British field gun lacked the power or angle of fire to be effective against trenches. [2] **149 mm Obice Krupp M14 Howitzer (Italian)** This German design was built in Italy under licence. Howitzers were used to fire heavy shells on a high trajectory, enabling them to reach concealed targets. [3] **2.75 in mountain gun (British)** This weapon saw service in Mesopotamia (Iraq) and on the Macedonian front. [4] **75 mm field gun (French)** The hydraulic recoil mechanism of this gun enabled accurate and rapid fire, without the need to reposition the gun after each shot. [5] **Gas shell (German)** The first use of artillery fired chemical shells was at Neuve-Chapelle in October 1914. [6] **77 mm shrapnel shell (German)** Packed with a large number of bullets, shrapnel shells were effective against massed troops in open terrain. [7] **Munitions carriage with 38 cm shell (German)** Some shells were so large that they had to be transported by carriage. [8] **75 mm shells (French)** Shells for the 75 mm field gun contained either shrapnel or high-explosives. [9] **Schneider mortar (French)** Designed to fire at a steep angle, mortars were useful in trench warfare. [10] **Fahrpanzer (German)** This gun was mounted on narrow gauge railway tracks and operated by a two-man crew. [11] **149 mm Howitzer M14/16 (Austro-Hungarian)** This howitzer was built by Skoda, the largest industrial enterprise in the Austro-Hungarian Empire. [12] **21 cm Mörser 16 (German)** This howitzer, here packed for transportation, was used by the German army until 1940.

[1] 18-POUNDER FIELD GUN
(BRITISH)

[4] 75 MM FIELD GUN (FRENCH)

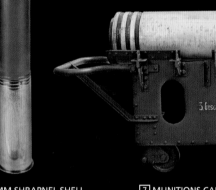

[5] GAS SHELL
(GERMAN)

[6] 77 MM SHRAPNEL SHELL
(GERMAN)

[7] MUNITIONS CARRIAGE
WITH 38 CM SHELL (GERMAN)

[11] 149 MM HOWITZER M14/16
(AUSTRO–HUNGARIAN)

A series of attempted outflanking moves by armies on both sides carried the fighting from the Aisne north to the coast, where Belgian troops retreating from Antwerp held the line at the Yser.

5 21–29 Oct
Belgians open sluices along Yser Canal to let in seawater at high tides. The resulting floods thwart the German attempt to cross the Yser.

3 6–13 Oct
Belgian Army retreats from Antwerp via Ghent to a line along the Yser

16–30 OCT
Yser

4 19 Oct–11 Nov
Hardest fighting of the "Race to the Sea". British and French hold on to salient around Ypres, which remains in Allied hands throughout the war

19 OCT–22 NOV
First Ypres

2 27 Sept–12 Oct
French 10th Army holds off attempted German breakthrough

27 SEPT–12 OCT
First Artois

1 22–26 Sept
French 2nd Army attempts to outflank German right wing

22–26 SEPT
First Picardy

12–28 SEPT
Aisne

KEY

Major French attack (with date)

Major German attack (with date)

Major battle (with date)

Allied front line November

Belgian sector

British sector

French sector

German front line November 1914

Belgian fortified town/city

French fortified town/city

AFTER

The **Race to the Sea** culminated in the **First Battle of Ypres, fought from mid-October to late November.**

APPROACHING STALEMATE
Beginning while fighting raged to the north at the Battle of the Yser and to the south at La Bassé, **intensive combat at Ypres 60–61 »** continued until the third week in November. With neither side able to make a breakthrough, **this ended the first mobile phase of the war** on the Western Front. Joffre launched another **offensive in Champagne** in December, but **no further substantial movement** could be achieved by either side. The trenches that were dug by troops at various points in these battles were gradually joined together to **create a continuous trench line.**

---

along France's eastern border – and flung them forward in a series of offensives, each of which met the enemy head on.

Clashes in northern France

Once troops entrenched, no progress could be made and a new flanking manoeuvre had to be attempted further north. The French came close to a major defeat at Arras, but held firm after General Foch, put in overall command in the northern sector, issued the order: "No retirement; every man to the battle."

Making aggressive use of massed cavalry divisions, the Germans captured Lille in early October. Meanwhile, the British Expeditionary Force (BEF) was moved by train to the far left of the Allied line. Advancing towards Lille, it ran into German cavalry at La Bassée.

Driving to battle

In 1914, the Belgian army fitted a number of Minerva automobiles with steel plate and mounted guns on top, creating the first armoured cars. They were used as rescue vehicles and for reconnaissance.

"We established a rough firing line and there we stayed... We bogged down."

DRUMMER E.L. SLAYTOR, COLDSTREAM GUARDS, AT THE AISNE, 16 SEPTEMBER 1914

While infantry and cavalry clashed in northern France, the Belgians, led in person by King Albert I, were engaged in a desperate defence of Antwerp. From 28 September, the Germans mounted a major attack on the fortified city. Their array of heavy siege guns had the same effect as at Liège, Namur, and Maubeuge, and battered Antwerp's fortresses to destruction.

As the defence wavered, Britain sent the Naval Division to Antwerp to bolster Belgian morale, and a British infantry division landed at the Belgian port of Zeebrugge. The First Lord of the Admiralty, Winston Churchill, travelled to Antwerp to persuade the Belgians to continue resistance. It was in vain. The city's defences were penetrated and on 9 October the king and his government left for the coastal town of Ostende. Antwerp surrendered to the Germans the following day. Most of the Belgian army escaped to continue the fight at the Yser river.

KEY MOMENT

THE BATTLE OF THE YSER

Abandoning the defence of Antwerp on 9 October, Belgian troops withdrew along the coast to the Yser Canal between Nieuport and Dixmude, where they took up position on high embankments dominating low-lying land. The German Fourth Army attacked, hoping to break through to the vital Channel ports of Boulogne and Calais. With battle raging, on 25 October King Albert ordered engineers to open the locks. As water flooded a wide area, German troops were forced to retreat or drown. The Belgians were left in possession of a coastal strip of their national territory that they held throughout the war.

Fighting to a Standstill

The collision of Allied and German forces in Flanders at the First Battle of Ypres was a bloody climax to the opening mobile phase of the war on the Western Front. After the battle proved indecisive, the armies settled into trench warfare.

French commander-in-chief, General Joffre, regarded the area around the Belgian city of Ypres as the gateway through which Allied forces would advance to liberate northern France and Belgium from German occupation. To German Chief of the General Staff Erich von Falkenhayn, it was the route by which his forces could seize the Channel ports of Dunkirk, Calais, and Boulogne – Britain's links to the battlefields.

‹‹ BEFORE

Between August and September 1914, it became clear that plans drawn up before the war had failed to work. Fresh offensives were improvised by generals still seeking a quick victory.

INSPECTION OF INDIAN TROOPS, 1914

BATTLE MOVES NORTH
A series of attempted outflanking movements known as the **Race to the Sea ‹‹ 58–59**, carried the fighting northwards from the Aisne to **Flanders**. The BEF was moved by train to Flanders, where it fought the Germans at **La Bassée** from 10 October. The Belgian army, retreating from Antwerp, defended a coastal strip at the **Yser**. The British rushed troops to Flanders, including elements of the Indian army.

The Indian troops who took part in the "Race to the Sea" had only been in Europe for six weeks. Their first engagement was at the Battle of La Bassée in October 1914.

Falkenhayn succeeded in assembling superior forces to the Allies, partly through calling on corps of enthusiastic young volunteers, many of them still students, who had joined up in the early days of the war. These reservists – whose numbers included the young Adolf Hitler, an Austrian enrolled in the Bavarian forces – had received only two months of military training.

By this stage in the war, the British were able to field seven infantry divisions plus three cavalry divisions, which fought dismounted, alongside the foot soldiers. After some initial fighting, the first major German offensive was launched on 20 October. Because of Allied inferiority, the battle turned into a desperate Anglo-French defence of a salient around Ypres, with British troops holding positions in front of the town and the French defending the flanks.

360,000 The number of French, British, and Belgian troops killed in action by the end of 1914. The majority (300,000) were French.

240,000 The number of German troops who were killed during this period.

Heavy losses on both sides
The British and French improvised defensive positions, digging shallow trenches and exploiting the protection of stone walls, ditches, and village houses. The British were chronically short of heavy artillery and machine-guns, but their rapid rifle fire, which the Germans persistently mistook for the fire of machine-guns, imposed heavy losses on the massed German infantry.

The slaughter of German troops marching into gunfire while singing patriotic songs at Langemarck, near Ypres, on 22 October became one the best-known German stories of the war. In fact, this was a half-truth, since the troops were singing only to identify themselves in the morning mist.

By late October, the Allies had ceded ground, but the initial German offensive had stalled.

German commemorative bayonet
The Iron Cross on this bayonet is a reference to Germany's most common military decoration. Four million Iron Crosses were awarded in the war, including one to Adolf Hitler at First Ypres.

Falkenhayn then launched a fresh attack towards Ypres along the Menin Road. His expectations of success were high, for the British forces had been severely depleted. When Kaiser Wilhelm came to forward headquarters on 31 October, it was in the hope of celebrating a major victory. In fact, the Germans did achieve a potentially important breakthrough at the village of Gheluvelt on the outskirts of Ypres. Their heavy guns hit a British divisional headquarters at Hooge Château, just east of the village, unusually adding staff officers to the lengthening list of casualties.

The Allies lost the vital high ground dominating Ypres, but remnants of half-broken British battalions were assembled to mount a counterattack and, with the help of just a handful of French reinforcements, a line was held. The British were desperately short of soldiers and ammunition. The arrival of forces from India helped alleviate the problem, and a number of Territorial battalions were sent across the Channel for the first time.

Nonetheless, the German renewal of the offensive in the second week of November came perilously close to overwhelming the British line.

British counterattack
At the climax of the battle, on 11 November, elite Prussian Foot Guards were at one point resisted only by hastily armed British cooks and officers' servants. By the end of that day, however, a

TECHNOLOGY

BARBED WIRE

Invented in the US in the 1860s, barbed wire was originally designed to control cattle. It had seen extensive military use in the Russo-Japanese War of 1904–05. By the end of 1914, barbed wire attached to wooden or metal stakes was being planted in front of trenches to block infantry assaults or raiding parties. When attacking infantry found their path barred by uncut wire, they were stranded under the fire of enemy guns and massacred. Soldiers devoted perilous night hours to repairing their own wire and sabotaging the enemy's with wire-cutters.

Simple but effective

Barbed wire increased the dominance of defence over offence by entrapping the attacking troops. Later in the war, barbed wire entanglements in front of trenches could be up to 30 m (100 ft) deep.

Troops dig in

The original trenches on the Western Front were hastily dug temporary field fortifications. These hard-pressed British soldiers will have been grateful even for this primitive protection against enemy fire.

"We must... **strike** the decisive **blow against our** most **detested enemy.**"

GERMAN ORDER OF THE DAY, YPRES, 30 OCTOBER 1914

counterattack by British light infantry at Nonnebosschen succeeded in driving the Guards back, and Falkenhayn knew the Ypres offensive had ended in failure. Although some fighting continued around Ypres until 22 November, the official date of the end of the battle, the German armies no longer threatened a breakthrough.

For the British, First Ypres was the graveyard of the pre-war regular army – the "Old Contemptibles", so named

because of an alleged derisory reference by the Kaiser to their puny fighting strength. The original BEF troops that landed in France in August 1914 had suffered around 90 per cent casualties, with a large proportion of the losses at Ypres.

German setback

Strategically, the failed offensive at Ypres was a serious setback for Germany. Falkenhayn informed the

Kaiser that there was no further chance of achieving an early victory on the Western Front. The German high command eventually concluded that it was best to create a strong defensive trench system on the Western Front while taking the offensive against the Russians in the east. Irrepressible in his pursuit of the offensive, General Joffre continued to order his troops to attack in Champagne and Artois in December, but elsewhere on the Western Front the fighting subsided. Soldiers had dug themselves into trenches as best they could wherever the fighting had come to a halt. As time passed, these trench lines were gradually reinforced, joined together, and extended. Troops on both sides settled in.

As the final weeks of 1914 approached, it was apparent that there would not be a swift victory for the Allies or the Germans. War would certainly not be over by Christmas.

AFTER ≫

The First Battle of Ypres resulted in many casualties. But it was inconclusive, and fighting at Ypres continued for the next four years.

REMEMBERING THE DEAD

Germans remember First Ypres as the **Kindermord** ("massacre of children"), because of the heavy losses among young volunteers. One victim was the youngest son of sculptress Käthe Kollwitz, who made **grieving statues** for the war cemetery at Vladslo, Belgium.

HARD TO DEFEND

The battle left the Allies occupying an exposed salient. Over the next four years the fighting continued, including **Second Ypres 102–103 ≫** in 1915 and **Third Ypres 240–241 ≫** in 1917.

KOLLWITZ SCULPTURE

The **Christmas Truce**

The Christmas Truce was actually a series of ceasefires that took place along the Western Front in 1914. Although it was not an official truce, and in some areas the fighting continued, it is thought that up to 100,000 British and German troops took part. Troops sang carols across the trenches and met in No Man's Land to exchange gifts and souvenirs.

"On Christmas Eve the Germans entrenched opposite us began calling out to us… 'Pudding', 'A Happy Christmas' and 'English-means good'… so two of our fellows climbed over the parapet… and went towards the German trenches. Halfway they were met by four Germans, who said they would not shoot on Christmas Day if we did not. They gave our fellows cigars and a bottle of wine and were given cake and cigarettes.

When they came back I went out with some more of our fellows and we were met by about 30 Germans, who seemed to be very nice fellows. I got one of them to write his name and address on a postcard as a souvenir. All through the night we sang carols to them and they sang to us and one played 'God Save the King' on a mouth organ.

On Christmas Day we all got out of the trenches and walked about with the Germans, who, when asked if they were fed up with the war, said 'Yes, rather'… Between the trenches there were a lot of dead Germans whom we helped to bury. In one place where the trenches are only 25 yards apart we could see dead Germans half buried. Their legs and gloved hands sticking out of the ground. The trenches in this position are called 'The Death Trap' as hundreds have been killed there.

A hundred yards or so in the rear… there were old houses that had been shelled. These were explored… and we found old bicycles, top hats, straw hats, umbrellas, etc. We dressed ourselves up in these and went over to the Germans. It seemed so comical to see our fellows walking about in top hats and with umbrellas up… We made the Germans laugh.

No firing took place on Christmas night and at four the next morning we were relieved by regulars."

RIFLEMAN C.H. BRAZIER, QUEEN'S WESTMINSTERS, EXTRACT FROM A LETTER WRITTEN HOME, PUBLISHED IN THE *HERTFORDSHIRE MERCURY* ON 9 JANUARY 1915

A temporary peace
Among the many soldiers who participated in the truce were these British soldiers from the 11th Brigade, Fourth Division, and their German counterparts, gathered at Ploegsteert, Belgium, on Christmas Day 1914.

The **Battle** of **Tannenberg**

The war on Germany's Eastern Front opened in August 1914 with a Russian invasion of East Prussia. The defeat of a Russian army at Tannenberg was greeted by the German people as a miracle of deliverance, making national heroes of generals Hindenburg and Ludendorff.

BEFORE

At the start of the war, Germany intended to stand on the defensive against Russia until France had been defeated in the west.

PLANS FOR THE EAST

Germany assumed **Russian mobilization** would take at least 40 days to complete. The Russians, however, had promised the French that Russian forces would **launch an attack against Germany within 15 days** of the outbreak of war. Russia planned to begin its role in the war by taking the offensive against **Austria-Hungary**.

Russian prisoners
The Germans took over 90,000 Russian soldiers prisoner at Tannenberg. Remaining captives until 1918, they provided valuable labour for Germany's war effort, including building trench systems on the Western Front.

Following the dictates of the Schlieffen Plan, the Germans had sent seven of their eight armies to Belgium and France. The Eighth Army, commanded by General Maximilian Prittwitz, was to act as a holding force until troops could be transferred from the west. The Russians, their forces divided between the German and Austro-Hungarian fronts, had two armies available for an invasion of East Prussia, giving them considerable local superiority in manpower. Honouring their agreement with France, the Russians attacked on day 15 of the war, even though their mobilization was far from complete.

The advance of Russian troops on to German soil, preceded by marauding Cossack cavalry, sent a wave of panic through Germany. Roads were clogged with East Prussian refugees fleeing westwards. Abandoning prepared

> **EAST PRUSSIA The easternmost area of Germany, on the Baltic coast, which is now divided between Poland, Russia, and Lithuania.**

defensive positions, the German Eighth Army advanced towards the Russian First Army. Commanded by General Paul von Rennenkampf, the Russians repelled German attacks at Gumbinnen.

Role of intelligence

When reconnaissance aircraft reported the advance of the Russian Second Army to the south of the Masurian Lakes, Prittwitz panicked and ordered a general withdrawal to the Vistula, angering the German high command. Prittwitz was sacked and replaced by veteran General Paul von Hindenburg, with General Ludendorff – the hero of the recent siege of Liège – as his Chief of Staff.

Hindenburg and Ludendorff arrived in East Prussia to find a perfectly viable plan for a counter-offensive already in place, devised by Prittwitz's staff. Gambling that the fighting at Gumbinnen would have temporarily

Eye in the sky
This German pilot's badge shows a Taube monoplane, the main aircraft used by Germany for reconnaissance in August 1914. These frail machines had a decisive effect at the Battle of Tannenberg.

halted Rennenkampf, the Germans decided to concentrate their forces against the Russian Second Army, commanded by General Alexander Samsonov, which was blithely pushing forward almost unopposed through the forests to the south.

The German plan took advantage of aerial reconnaissance, by both primitive Taube aeroplanes and

airships. An intercepted Russian radio message, transmitted uncoded, confirmed that Rennenkampf was not intending to resume his advance.

Setting the trap

Leaving a thin screen of cavalry and reserves in front of the Russian First Army, an entire German corps under General Hermann von François was moved by train to the south of the Russian Second Army. Other German troops marched from Gumbinnen towards Samsonov's northern flank.

Samsonov was ignorant of the position of German forces and had no contact with the Russian First Army. Nonetheless, a spirit of optimism reigned. When German flank attacks began on 26–27 August, Samsonov pressed forward. By 29 August, the German pincers had closed behind him and most of the Second Army was trapped. Having lost control of his forces, Samsonov walked into the forest and shot himself. Claiming a great victory, the Germans named it Tannenberg after a 15th-century battle famed in Prussian history.

Fighting switches to the south, 24–26 August

Hindenburg and Ludendorff took command and ordered German 8th Army south to attack the Russian 2nd Army. While Rennenkampf's 1st Army dithered and Samsonov's 2nd Army advanced, by 26 August the Germans were ready to spring the trap and destroy Samsonov's army.

The Russian advance, 17–23 August

The Russian 1st and 2nd armies advanced with a wide gap between them. When the Germans moved against the Russian 1st Army, they were defeated at Gumbinnen. The Russian 2nd Army threatened to advance behind the German forces from south of the Masurian Lakes.

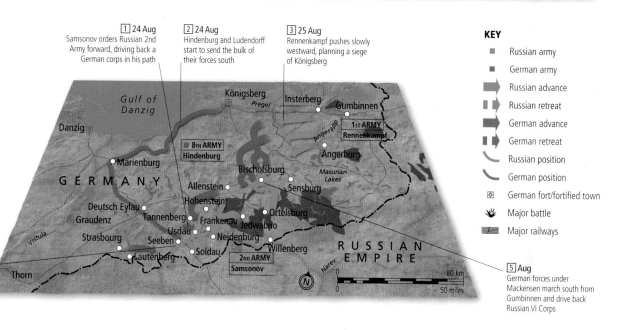

④ 20–23 Aug
Two German corps move by train to reinforce the line in front of Russian 2nd Army

② 20 Aug
German forces attack at Gumbinnen, despite some success they are forced to withdraw westwards

① 15–20 Aug
Russian 1st Army crosses the East Prussian border. Part of German 8th Army moves to block them

③ 20 Aug
Russian 2nd Army crosses the East Prussian border

① 24 Aug
Samsonov orders Russian 2nd Army forward, driving back a German corps in his path

② 24 Aug
Hindenburg and Ludendorff start to send the bulk of their forces south

③ 25 Aug
Rennenkampf pushes slowly westward, planning a siege of Königsberg

④ Night of 25 Aug
German I Corps under François reaches Seeben by train and prepares to attack Samsonov's southern flank

⑤ Aug
German forces under Mackensen march south from Gumbinnen and drive back Russian VI Corps

KEY

▪	Russian army
▪	German army
▶	Russian advance
◧▶	Russian retreat
▶	German advance
◧▶	German retreat
⌐	Russian position
⌐	German position
⊠	German fort/fortified town
✻	Major battle
▤	Major railways

A German victory, 27–31 August

The Russian forces were defeated in every major engagement. Outgunned and outmanoeuvred, they tried to retreat, but their route was barred by German I Corps.

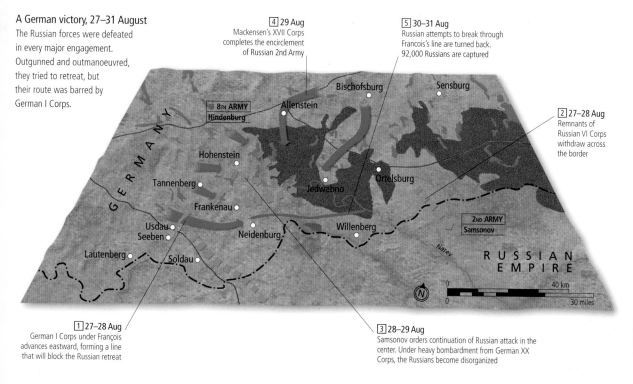

④ 29 Aug
Mackensen's XVII Corps completes the encirclement of Russian 2nd Army

⑤ 30–31 Aug
Russian attempts to break through Francois's line are turned back. 92,000 Russians are captured

② 27–28 Aug
Remnants of Russian VI Corps withdraw across the border

① 27–28 Aug
German I Corps under François advances eastward, forming a line that will block the Russian retreat

③ 28–29 Aug
Samsonov orders continuation of Russian attack in the center. Under heavy bombardment from German XX Corps, the Russians become disorganized

AFTER

Germany was to find no easy victory on the Eastern Front to compensate for its failure to win in the west.

RUSSIA RALLIES

The Russians recovered from Tannenberg. When the Germans turned their forces against the Russian First Army in September, Rennenkampf managed **a fighting withdrawal** at the **Battle of the Masurian Lakes 134 》**, and then mounted a successful counter-offensive. Russia was also scoring successes against the **Austro-Hungarians in Galicia 68–69 》**, and fighting on the **Eastern Front continued in Poland 70–71 》**. Hindenburg and Ludendorff took the credit for saving Germany from the Russian hordes, and were endowed the two generals with almost magical prestige. Their rise to power had begun.

GERMAN GENERAL Born 1847 Died 1934

Paul von Hindenburg

"With clean hearts we **marched** out **to defend** the **Fatherland.**"

PAUL VON HINDENBURG, SPEECH AT THE OPENING OF THE TANNENBERG MEMORIAL, SEPTEMBER 1927

If Paul von von Hindenburg had died at the age of 65, no one in the world would have heard of him. Born a Junker – a member of the landed aristocracy who formed the social, political, and military elite of the Prussian state – he adopted the conservative values of his class and pursued a military career. Joining the elite Prussian Foot Guards as a junior officer in 1865, he swore the standard oath to behave as "an upright, fearless, dutiful, and honourable soldier".

Prussian wars

That is no doubt how Hindenburg saw himself throughout his life. He experienced at first hand the dramatic events that created the German Empire, serving in Prussia's victorious wars against Austria and France, and witnessing the proclamation of the king of Prussia as emperor (Kaiser) of Germany in Versailles in 1871, at the end of the Franco-Prussian War. Recognized as solid, able, and reliable, he made a successful career through four decades in the peacetime army,

but always fell short of the highest appointments. In 1911, he retired – not, he later claimed, because of "professional or personal friction", but in fulfilment of "the duty to make way for younger officers".

Call of duty

After the outbreak of war in August 1914, all recently retired officers expected the call to return to arms. For Hindenburg, it came three weeks into the war. The German General Staff had decided that Erich Ludendorff, who had distinguished himself at the siege of Liège, was the man to handle a threatening situation on the Eastern Front. Ludendorff was ordered to East Prussia, where he would take over as Chief of Staff. He needed an army commander to serve under.

Hindenburg was living in Hanover, on the rail route Ludendorff would take from Belgium. On the evening of 22 August, he was informed that he was to take command of the Eighth Army. At 4am the next morning, he joined Ludendorff's train at Hanover

Hero of Tannenberg

Painted after the victory at Tannenberg, this portrait shows Hindenburg as the stern, paternal embodiment of the Prussian military tradition. Germans were reassured by his air of calm strength and simplicity.

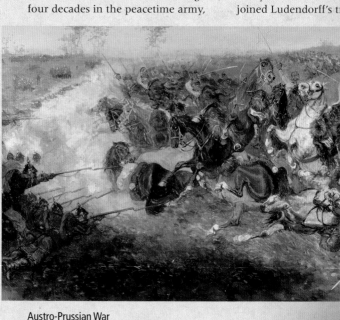

Austro-Prussian War

As a young officer, Hindenburg was commended for his bravery against the Austrians at the Battle of Königgrätz. He was one of a few German commanders old enough to have fought against European powers.

troops engaged in combat. The weather was freezing, daytime temperatures dropping to -13°C (9°F). Ludendorff was in effect attempting to repeat the encirclement of Tannenberg, but Russian commanders had learned their lesson. They cancelled the advance on Silesia and pulled back at high speed through forced marches – some units covered as much as 100 km (60 miles) in two days.

Mackensen smashed through the Russian flank but then found his army caught by a flanking attack from the Russian Fifth Army. By the time the Germans extricated themselves, the Russians had entrenched in front of Lodz. Ludendorff demanded and

received reinforcements from the Western Front, while launching frontal assaults in an attempt to take the city.

By 6 December, the men were near exhaustion. The Russians decided upon a strategic withdrawal towards Warsaw and left Lodz to the Germans. Within a week the fighting ran down, as both sides dug in for the rest of the winter in trench lines.

The fighting of 1914 had an unexpected conclusion in Galicia. In the first week of December, Austria-Hungary achieved a successful offensive at Limonova, south of Cracow. The Russians were forced into a withdrawal that ended the threat to the Carpathian passes, although the

1.5 MILLION **The number of Russian casualties.**

1 MILLION **The number of Austro-Hungarian losses on all fronts by the end of 1914.**

fortress at Przemysl remained under Russian siege. This was not enough to restore German faith in Austro-Hungarian Chief of Staff Conrad, but it enabled him to fight off a German bid to place all the forces of the Central Powers on the Eastern Front under unified command.

The human impact of the fighting had been immense, with more than two million troops killed, wounded, or taken prisoner. The fate of civilians in the territory was dismal. Cholera and typhus, the traditional companions of war, had made their appearance. No end to the war between the three empires was in sight.

Entrenched and ready for action
German troops with MG 08 machine-guns and Mauser rifles wait for the enemy in a hastily dug trench on the Eastern Front. Their combined firepower could repel almost any infantry assault.

The situation in late 1914 provoked a bitter debate between German commanders over priorities while fighting continued through winter.

THE BATTLE RESUMES
Generals Hindenburg and Ludendorff were **convinced that they could defeat Russia**. German Chief of the General Staff Erich von Falkenhayn was not prepared to focus exclusively on the Eastern Front, but did support major German operations there in 1915. Meanwhile, Austria-Hungary faced **successful resistance by Serbia**. In March 1915, the besieged Austrian fortress at Przemysl **fell to the Russians**, entailing the surrender of 120,000 men.

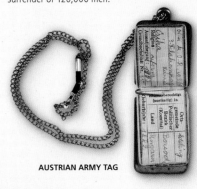

AUSTRIAN ARMY TAG

Cavalry

"**The rifle...** cannot replace the effect produced by the **speed of the horse** ... and the **terror of cold steel.**"

BRITISH ARMY CAVALRY TRAINING MANUAL, 1907

Italian carbine
Cavalry were mostly issued with carbines such as this Carcano, a shorter-barrelled but less accurate version of the Italian infantry rifle.

Before 1914, cavalry formed a social elite in all European armies, their colourful uniforms and dashing appearance a striking feature of military parades and state ceremonies. They were also an essential element in fighting wars. In the absence of motor vehicles, still in their infancy, cavalry offered speed of movement. Their roles included reconnaissance, direct frontal charges to overrun enemy infantry (foot soldiers) and capture guns, the pursuit of retreating troops, and rapid advance through undefended territory.

Army commanders were well aware of the problems that cavalry faced when confronted with modern firepower – a man on a horse was a large target and could not easily exploit cover – but cavalry had adapted to the firepower revolution of the period, equipping their formations with machine-guns and field artillery.

There were undeniably archaic aspects to European cavalry. Most uniforms were designed for show rather than camouflage – German and Austrian Uhlans, for example, wore unusually tall headgear, while French cuirassiers donned shiny breastplates and plumed helmets. Many regiments carried lances decorated with brightly coloured pennons. In contrast, the British, with recent experience of fighting in the Boer War, wore khaki.

Armies differed in the extent to which their cavalry were trained to fight dismounted with their carbines or rifles. The need for this was widely acknowledged, but the tradition of the charge, with drawn sword, still held its grip on the military imagination.

World War I was in many ways a disappointment for cavalry. Even in the mobile campaigns of 1914, aircraft proved superior at reconnaissance. On the Eastern Front, the Russians,

Cossack cavalry
A column of Russian Cossack horsemen rides towards battle in their traditional fur hats. Feared for their raiding tactics, they also knew how to form a dismounted firing line when defence was needed.

deploying some 30 cavalry divisions, sent masses of horsemen charging across Galicia. On the Western Front, German cavalry swept across northern France during the "Race to the Sea". But problems quickly grew. Cavalry strained supply systems, because of the horses' need for fodder. Losses were heavy from the start. Mostly obliged to dismount to fight, cavalrymen often proved second-rate infantry, their carbines less accurate than rifles and their shooting inferior.

Cavalry and the trenches

In the trench warfare of the Western Front from 1915, there were no spaces in which cavalry could operate. The British, in particular, continued to believe that by charging through a gap

> "In order to **shorten the war...** we must **make use** of the mobility of the **cavalry.**"

GENERAL DOUGLAS HAIG, JUNE 1916

in the German trench lines opened up by infantry and artillery, their cavalry could turn a defeat into a rout, but it did not work. Advancing on horseback under machine-gun and artillery fire, across terrain made treacherous by mud, shell holes, trenches, and barbed wire, was simply too difficult.

In all European armies, the ratio of cavalry to infantry declined sharply in the course of the war, and many cavalrymen ended up serving their turn in the trenches as infantry.

However, cavalry did have something to offer in World War I. Even on the Western Front, cavalry occasionally carried out successful charges against entrenched infantry and machine-gun posts. Away from the main European theatres, especially in Russian operations in the Caucasus and British campaigns in Palestine, well-handled cavalry forces were frequently decisive.

General Edmund Allenby, commanding on the Palestine front from 1917, had an army with more than 20 per cent cavalry. The Desert Mounted Corps, including Light Horse regiments from India, Australia, and New Zealand, and the Territorials of the British Yeomanry, carried out sweeping manoeuvres and successful cavalry charges against entrenched Turkish infantry and artillery.

Last charge

By 1918, in the crucial European theatres of operations, cavalry was no longer a potentially decisive arm. The Russian Civil War, from 1918–21, was the last major conflict in which cavalry played a prominent role. The growth of motorized forces in the 1920s and '30s finally spelled the end of the long tradition of the mounted warrior in Europe.

Horse gas mask
Gas masks were designed for horses as well as for their riders. The mask protected the animals against poison gasses such as chlorine and phosgene.

TIMELINE

■ **August 1914** All European armies start the war with large bodies of cavalry, constituting between 10 and 30 per cent of their total forces. The advance of Russian Cossacks into East Prussia and Galicia provokes panic among the populations of Germany and Austria.

■ **August–September 1914** French and British cavalry fight fierce rearguard actions against the Germans during the Great Retreat.

GERMAN UHLAN HAT

■ **September 1914** Six German cavalry divisions take the offensive around Lille in northern France, probably the largest body of horsemen ever to fight in Western Europe.

■ **October 1914** Dismounted to form a firing line, the British Cavalry Corps fights a famous action to defend Messines Ridge during the First Battle of Ypres.

■ **1915** Large numbers of cavalrymen, especially on the Western Front, are made to serve as infantry in trench warfare.

■ **March–May 1915** South African cavalry carry out a successful campaign to occupy German Southwest Africa (now Namibia).

■ **January–April 1916** On the Caucasus front, Russian General Nikolai Yudenich captures Erzurum and Trebizond (now Trabzon) from Turkey, making bold use of massed cavalry.

■ **July 1916** Ordered to attack German positions at High Wood during the Battle of the Somme, an Indian cavalry division fails to exploit a brief opportunity for a breakthrough.

■ **April 1917** At Monchy-le-Preux, during the Battle of Arras on the Western Front, British cavalry suffer heavy losses attempting to exploit a gap in the German line created by the advance of tanks and infantry.

■ **October 1917** At Beersheba in Palestine, Australian cavalry execute a successful charge against Turkish defensive lines that contributes decisively to a British victory.

■ **November 1917** At the Battle of Cambrai on the Western Front, a Canadian cavalry brigade advances 13 km (8 miles) and captures 100 German machine-guns in one of the most ambitious of failed breakthrough attempts.

■ **October 1918** Australian Light Horse Regiment, serving with the British Desert Mounted Corps, occupies Damascus in Syria towards the end of the campaign against Ottoman Turkey.

■ **1918–21** All armies engaged in the Russian Civil War and the Russo-Polish War make extensive use of cavalry. The Battle of Komarow, fought between Polish and Soviet horsemen, in August 1920, is often considered the last significant cavalry battle.

« BEFORE

For over a century before World War I, the Turkish-ruled Ottoman Empire was in decline. Attempts at reform failed to restore its military strength.

DIMINISHING EMPIRE

Ottoman military weakness was revealed by the **Italo-Turkish War of 1911–12**, which enabled Italy to seize Libya, and the Balkan Wars of 1912–13, which deprived Turkey of almost all its remaining territory in Europe. The Ottoman Empire **lost a third of its area « 18–19** in the years leading up to World War I.

THE YOUNG TURKS

A revolt by **"Young Turk" military officers** deposed Ottoman Sultan Abdulhamid II in 1909 and **replaced him with Mehmed V**. Attempts at constitutional government were undermined by the strains of defeat in war. By 1914, the government was dominated by Interior Minister **Talaat Pasha** and War Minister **Enver Pasha**.

Turkey Enters the War

The decision of Ottoman Turkey to go to war as an ally of the Central Powers was a crucial moment in modern history. It not only shaped the course of World War I but also profoundly influenced the future of the entire region, including Iraq, Syria, Palestine, and Egypt.

Desperate to restore Turkey's status as a military power, Turkish governments before World War I sought foreign expertise and investment, without tying themselves to the European alliance system. The Turkish army established close links with Germany, which sent a military mission under General Liman von Sanders to modernize Turkish land forces. The Turkish navy, on the other hand, traditionally looked to Britain for ships and advisers.

As the war crisis erupted in Europe in July–August 1914, pro-German figures in the Turkish government signed a secret treaty with Germany aimed specifically against Russia, the historic enemy of the Ottoman Empire. Meanwhile, the Turkish people were eagerly awaiting delivery of two dreadnoughts, *Reshadieh* and *Sultan Osman I*, paid for by public subscription and being built at shipyards in Britain. Possession of such warships was the mark of great power status.

At the start of August, the British Admiralty, facing war with Germany, seized the dreadnoughts for the Royal Navy. In response, a wave of anti-British feeling swept through Turkey.

On 10 August, the German warships *Goeben* and *Breslau* sailed through the Dardanelles and were handed to the Turks. With this action, Turkish commitment to Germany was sealed.

Enver Pasha
Turkey's war minister, Enver Pasha, played a leading role in bringing Turkey into World War I on the side of Germany. Also commander of the Ottoman forces, Enver was virtually a military dictator during the war.

British naval advisers were asked to leave, and German Rear Admiral Wilhelm Souchon took command of Turkish naval operations.

Shelling Russian ports

On 29 October, sailing aboard *Goeben*, renamed *Yavuz Sultan Selim*, Souchon took his fleet and bombarded Russian Black Sea ports, including Odessa and Sebastopol. Russia responded by declaring war on Turkey, followed in the first week of November by France and Britain.

The Ottoman Sultan, Mehmed V, was also the caliph – the head of the worldwide

Turkish troops on the march

Although Turkish forces fought with determination, they were often let down by the misjudgements of their senior commanders. At the Battle of Sarikamish, only 18,000 out of an intial force of 95,000 survived.

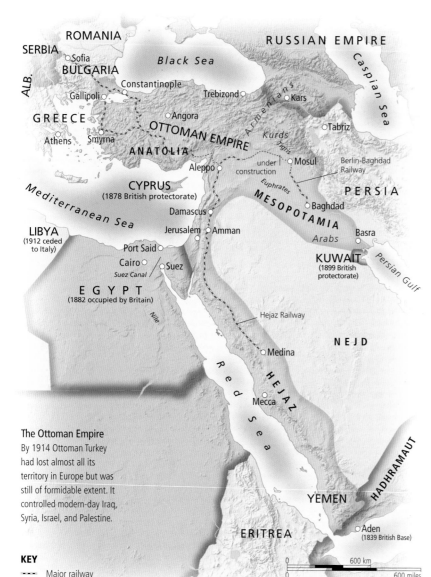

The Ottoman Empire
By 1914 Ottoman Turkey had lost almost all its territory in Europe but was still of formidable extent. It controlled modern-day Iraq, Syria, Israel, and Palestine.

KEY
---- Major railway

TECHNOLOGY

DESTROYERS

The workhorses of every navy, destroyers were built in large numbers in 1914–18. Small, fast, and versatile, they fulfilled a wide range of functions from coastal defence to minelaying and anti-submarine warfare. No battleships or battlecruisers would go to sea without destroyers to defend them against submarine attacks. Later in the war, they defended merchant convoys.

Destroyers' guns were too light to exchange salvoes with the heaviest vessels in an enemy's fleet, but destroyers were often highly effective in other ways, such as attacking with torpedoes. Destroyer commanders earned a reputation for acting with bold aggression and independence.

Rapid advances in technology transformed naval warfare at the end of 1914.

NEW DEVELOPMENTS

The German navy deployed **airships for reconnaissance** and the Royal Navy used **float aircraft**, winched over the side of a ship to take off from the sea. The first raid by seaplanes on a shore target was the Royal Naval Air Service's attack on airship sheds at the **German port of Cuxhaven** on Christmas Day 1914. Meanwhile, another sortie by German battlecruisers led to the **Battle of Dogger Bank 124–25 ›› ** in early 1915.

U-BOAT ATTACKS

In February 1915, Germany initiated its first phase of **unrestricted submarine warfare**, leading to the **sinking of the cruise liner *Lusitania* 126–27 ›› ** in the following May, **antagonizing the USA**.

---

contact mine off the coast of Ireland. It was clear that the Royal Navy was not equipped to deal with minesweeping or anti-submarine warfare.

British blockades

The threat posed to his most important warships by mines and submarines forced Jellicoe to curtail operations in the North Sea. He could still impose a naval blockade on Germany from a distance by controlling the entrance to the English Channel and the passage between Scotland and Norway. These distant blockades, however, allowed the German fleet to attempt surprise sorties into the North Sea.

On 16 December, a German battlecruiser squadron under Rear Admiral Franz von Hipper bombarded the English east coast towns of Scarborough, Whitby, and Hartlepool. British naval intelligence had given warning of the sortie but the Grand Fleet failed to intercept Hipper's raiders. The bombardment caused more than 700 casualties, including 137 people killed, mostly civilians. In Britain, it aroused public indignation against German brutality, but also outrage at the failure of the Royal Navy to defend the country.

By the end of 1914, it was clear that naval enthusiasts, especially British ones, were not going to have the war they had expected.

AMERICAN NAVY RECRUITMENT POSTER, 1917

British quick-firing naval gun
The 100 mm Mark IV, introduced in 1911, armed most Royal Navy destroyers in World War I. On 5 November 1914, this Mark IV gun mounted on HMS *Lance* fired Britain's first shot in the war, aimed at a German minelayer.

Queen of the Royal Navy
The HMS *Queen Elizabeth* was one of Britain's first super-dreadnoughts. Entering service in 1915, it was fuelled by oil instead of coal and armed with eight 381 mm (15 in) guns, which could hit an enemy ship at a range of 25 km (16 miles).

Coronel and the Falklands

In the early months of the war, the Allies faced a potential threat to seaborne trade from enemy cruisers. It was defused, but only after serious setbacks and through the deployment of large-scale naval forces to track down and destroy German warships.

Almost half the world's merchant shipping was owned by Britain and its dominions. Britain depended on seaborne imports for 60 per cent of its food, as well as essential strategic goods such as rubber and oil. Worldwide sea lanes were potentially hard to defend, and attacks on them by German warships posed a serious threat to Britain's ability to wage war. The only significant force of German warships at large on the

world's oceans was the East Asiatic Cruiser Squadron, commanded by Admiral Graf Maximilian von Spee. The squadron consisted of the powerful armoured cruisers SMS *Scharnhorst* and *Gneisenau* and the light cruisers SMS *Emden*, *Leipzig*, and *Nürnberg*. Its base was at Tsingtao in China, but when war broke out the cruisers were scattered across the Pacific. Assembling his ships in the German-ruled Mariana Islands, Spee decided to head east towards South America, away from the Japanese navy, Britain's ally. The *Emden*, commanded by Captain Karl von Müller, was sent to the Indian Ocean.

The unexpected appearance of the *Emden* in an ocean rich in Allied merchant shipping caused mayhem. Operating with scrupulous respect for the rules of war, Müller stopped and sank 16 British merchant

Australian cap
This cap was worn by stoker John Robb of the Royal Australian Navy. Robb was one of the crew of the HMAS *Sydney* when it captured the German cruiser *Emden* at the Cocos Islands on 9 November 1914.

Gun damage
Emden's bell shows the effects of the bombardment from *Sydney*'s guns. *Emden*'s captain beached the ship to avoid sinking, but its sailors suffered almost 200 casualties.

« BEFORE

Britain was well aware that its dominant position in world commerce and its heavy dependence on imports made its merchant ships a target for Germany.

ROYAL NAVY BLOCKADES
The **German navy** faced problems in mounting a commerce-raiding campaign. The Royal Navy established a **blockade of the English Channel and North Sea** **« 78–79** from the first day of the war. German ships at loose elsewhere had difficulty obtaining coal, which was readily available to Britain and France through their empires.

GERMAN THREATS
Britain had already been **threatened by two German light cruisers**. In the Indian Ocean, the SMS *Königsberg* had been troublesome until trapped by the Royal Navy in the East African Rufiji delta in late October 1914 **« 76–77**. In the Caribbean, the SMS *Karlsruhe* had **sunk 16 merchant ships**. German hopes for the *Karlsruhe* were dashed, however, when it suffered a catastrophic internal explosion off Barbados on 4 November.

> **"** Enemy **cruisers** cannot **live** in the ocean for any length of time. **"**
>
> WINSTON CHURCHILL, FIRST LORD OF THE ADMIRALTY, 1914

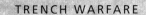

dawn, often the occasion for a ritualistic exchange of fire expected to hurt no one. Then rations were brought up from the rear. Tasks such as cleaning weapons and maintaining or extending trenches filled the day until "stand down" at dusk. Night was a time for repairing barbed wire or moving troops and equipment.

On an active front, commanders insisted on constant harassment of the enemy. Front line units suffered

5,000 The average number of British casualties per month in the trenches of the Ypres salient in 1916, when no major battle was fought.

a grinding attrition of casualties from sniper fire, mortars, or artillery. At night, patrols were sent out into No Man's Land or raids were mounted against enemy trenches, producing heavy casualties for both sides.

Few soldiers went "over the top" in a major offensive more than once or twice. When they did, it was an experience they would never forget.

Observation of the enemy, either through periscopes or at advanced listening posts thrust forward into No Man's Land, was a 24-hour-a-day task, and any soldier who fell asleep on sentry duty was severely punished. Soldiers on the Western Front would typically spend less than a week on the front line, before being rotated to the reserve line or the rear, where they laboured on exhausting tasks such as carrying ammunition to the front line.

Lice, rats, and "trench foot"

Infestation with lice was almost universal in the trenches, which also swarmed with well-fed rats. Sometimes corpses and body parts became embedded in trench walls, as it was often too dangerous to retrieve them. Latrine facilities could be primitive. On the Western Front, troops were usually adequately clothed and fed, but such was not the case on other fronts. Extreme weather could turn the trench experience into a nightmare. In the summer heat at Gallipoli, troops were tortured by thirst and racked by disease. In Flanders, heavy rain flooded trenches, turning the battle area into a quagmire; troops standing for days in deep water suffered "trench foot", which could lead to gangrene and amputation.

German trench

This trench has been dug into soft earth, so the walls are "revetted" with wattle to hold them firm. A duckboard of wooden slats has been laid to provide a mud-free walkway.

TIMELINE

- **September 1914** German Chief of the General Staff General Helmuth von Moltke orders forces retreating from the Marne to "fortify and defend" a line at the Aisne river. Entrenched German troops halt the advance of British and French forces, who dig their own improvised trenches.

- **December 1914** With armies entrenched across the Western Front, there is widespread fraternization between German and Allied troops on Christmas Day.

- **January 1915** German Chief of the General Staff General Erich von Falkenhayn orders troops on the Western Front to make their trench lines defensible against superior forces, leading to stalemate.

- **April 1915** The Germans introduce poison gas during the Second Battle of Ypres. Gas becomes a fixed feature of trench warfare on the Western Front.

- **April 1915** Allied troops landing at Gallipoli, Turkey, find themselves forced to entrench under unfavourable conditions. They are unable to make significant progress against Turkish defensive positions.

BISCUIT RATIONS TURNED INTO A FRAME

- **June 1916** Russian General Alexei Brusilov drives Austro-Hungarian forces out of their trench lines and advances 80 km (50 miles).

- **July 1916** German troops in concrete bunkers survive a prolonged Allied bombardment to emerge and cut down attacking soldiers on the first day of the Somme offensive.

- **February–March 1917** German forces on the Western Front between Arras and Soissons withdraw to newly prepared defensive positions (the Hindenburg Line).

- **September 1917** A German offensive against the Russians at Riga shows the effectiveness of using specialist assault troops to penetrate trench systems in depth.

- **November 1917** A British offensive at Cambrai uses massed tanks to overcome soldiers in German trenches, but without decisive effect.

- **March 1918** The German Spring Offensive ends the stalemate on the Western Front.

- **September–October 1918** Allied forces break through the Hindenburg Line.

Life in the Trenches

Life in the trenches varied according to sectors, fronts, the time of year, and local weather conditions. It was, however, far from pleasant. Soldiers on all sides lived under the threat of death from either sniper or shell. Vermin, such as rats and lice, were numerous; trenches would flood in wet weather; and men suffered frostbite in the freezing cold. Those serving also had to contend with the extreme tedium of trench warfare, which was largely static.

"I am still stuck in this trench and so far as I know not likely to be relieved for some days, as I've had a week of it and the regulation dose is four days... I haven't washed or had my clothes off at all, and my average sleep has been two and a half hours in the twenty-four. I don' think I've started to crawl yet, but I don't suppose I should notice if I had... My men are awfully cheery; they are the best souls in the world... although I've lost a good many lately... But there are points in the life that appeal to me vastly, the contrast for instance: the long, lazy, hot days, when no work is done, and any part of the body that protrudes above the trench is most swiftly blown off; the uncanny, shrieking, hard-fought nights with their bizarre and beastly experiences, their constant crack and thunder, their stealthy seeking for advantage, and regardless seizure of it, and in the middle of it all perhaps a song sang round a brazier, a joke or two yelled against the noise of shells and rifles until the sentries' warning.**"**

CAPTAIN EDWIN GERALD YENNING, ROYAL SUSSEX REGIMENT, LETTER TO HIS SISTER, 20 JUNE 1915

"There is something inexpressibly sad and full of renunciation in this stationary warfare. Life would be so easy if we could march, as they do in Russia, march along into the blue distance in the morning light... But here we burrow deep into the earth. There is a candle burning even now in our dug-out, though it is bright daylight outside. Close by, the lads are filling sandbags with which tonight they will stop in our parapets. Everything is quiet just now. The enemy is waiting for nightfall; because he knows that then we shall be working at our farthest-forward position. So there is no real activity except in the dark.**"**

LETTER FROM ALFRED VAETH, 12 SEPTEMBER 1915

The tedium of the trenches
German soldiers read and write letters in a trench in June 1915. Stalemate on the Western Front meant there were often long lulls in the fighting, and soldiers frequently complained of boredom.

Failure on the Western Front

In early 1915, Allied operations – the First Champagne Offensive and the Battle of Neuve Chapelle – revealed the problems generals would face in trench warfare on the Western Front. Taking the offensive resulted in heavy losses but minimal gains.

The fighting of 1914 left the opposing armies on the Western Front entrenched from the north coast of Belgium to the Swiss border.

LINES ARE DRAWN
The **Allied side of the line** was manned along most of its length by the French. A sector in Flanders and northern France was held by British troops. The **British First Army** was opposite **Neuve Chapelle** and the **Second Army** was at Ypres ≪ 60–61.

KING ALBERT I OF BELGIUM

Belgian and French forces held the sector nearest to the coast. The French and Belgian desire to liberate their territories influenced the Allies in favour of an **offensive strategy**.

By the end of 1914, a new phase had opened on the Western Front – the stalemate of the trenches. But that is not how it appeared to French commander General Joseph Joffre at the time. Joffre was still planning strategic manoeuvres. He envisaged the German armies, which were pushed forwards in a great arc between Verdun and Lille, being forced to withdraw by Allied advances from Champagne to the south and Artois in the north. He planned for his armies to break through into Belgium, threatening the Germans with encirclement.

Joffre began the campaign against German trenches on the Champagne front in late December 1914. Known as the First Champagne Offensive, it lasted into March 1915. German trench lines were primitive compared with what they would later become. Usually, a single, narrow front-line trench was packed with troops under orders to hold their position at all costs. If the trench was lost, German reserves counterattacked with ferocity to retake the position.

In almost continuous fighting at Champagne, the French army suffered about 90,000 casualties. German losses were probably similar. In the small strips of ground that were fought and refought over, villages were shelled to obliteration. The French advance gained a maximum 3 km (2 miles) of territory.

The Western Front in 1915

A line of trenches snaked across Belgium and northeast France. The key battles of 1915 occurred in Flanders and Artois in the north and Champagne further south, with the French and British mostly on the offensive.

Joffre was already planning an offensive in Artois while the fighting in Champagne raged on. Artois was the junction between the French and British sectors, and British commander Field Marshal Sir John French, eager to shake his troops out of the morale-sapping routines of the trenches, agreed to a joint offensive. Conditions were ripe: the Germans had begun moving large numbers of their best troops to the Eastern Front for an attempt at a decisive blow against Russia.

However, Britain had also begun to think there might be better military opportunities elsewhere. In mid-February, British troops intended for France were diverted to the attack on Turkey at Gallipoli. Joffre had been promised that British forces would take over French responsibilities along the line from Ypres north to the coast. Now that this offer was withdrawn, Joffre cancelled the joint operation at Artois. Perhaps eager to show his Allies what he could do on his own, French decided to go ahead with a limited British attack at Neuve Chapelle.

The Battle of Neuve Chapelle

Well planned and prepared, the Neuve Chapelle operation's aim was to capture Aubers Ridge, a modest eminence in mostly flat country that gave a distinct advantage to the side

> **In the initial attack at Neuve Chapelle, British and Indian forces outnumbered the opposing German troops by five to one.**

that held it. The route to the ridge passed through the ruined village of Neuve Chapelle. The attack was entrusted to the First Army under General Douglas Haig, a rising star who had performed well as a corps commander in the First Battle of Ypres.

The British made innovative use of aerial photography to map the German defences, which were thinly manned and poorly constructed – the wet ground had forced both sides to build parapets upwards rather than dig downwards for shelter.

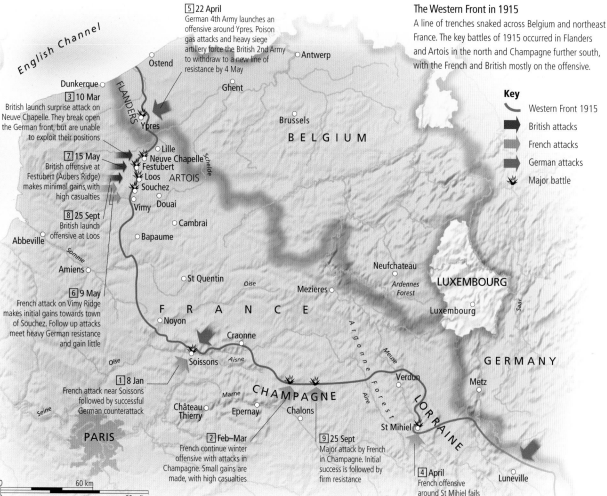

and his foreign minister, Giorgio Sonnino, to sign the Treaty of London with the Allies on 26 April.

Under the terms of the treaty, which remained secret, Italy had to declare war on the Central Powers within a month. This was not easily done. In early May, neutralists in the Italian parliament voted Salandra out of office, but King Victor Emmanuel III, who was pro-war, reinstated him. Italian nationalists, including the prominent poet Gabriele d'Annunzio, mounted a passionate propaganda campaign in favour of joining the war.

On 23 May, Italy declared war on Austria-Hungary. Despite Italy's promise in the Treaty of London, its declaration of war on Germany did not follow until 1916. Austria-Hungary was faced with the task of sustaining a war on three fronts – against Russia, Serbia, and Italy – which could have quickly proved disastrous. But the timing of Italy's declaration of war was fortuitous for Austria-Hungary because at that very moment the successful

Distinctive headgear
The Italian Bersaglieri Corps was a highly regarded light infantry formation. Their wide-brimmed hats were decorated with black capercaillie feathers.

Gorlice-Tarnow Campaign was relieving the pressure on Austro-Hungarian forces fighting the Russians on the Eastern Front.

The Isonzo Campaign

Defending their 600 km (370 mile) border with Italy would have been difficult for the Austro-Hungarian army had it not been for the terrain. Most of the frontier consisted of impassable mountain peaks, except in the Trentino, where the mountain barrier was traversed by a number of passes. Italian Chief of Staff Luigi Cadorna chose to concentrate his forces at the eastern end of the border, where the Isonzo valley offered a corridor into Austro-Hungarian territory.

The Isonzo was no easy option for the Italians, however, for the Austro-Hungarian forces occupied defensive positions – some blasted out of rock with dynamite – on the ridges, blocking progress from the coastal plain and at the northern end of the valley.

Cadorna opened the First Battle of the Isonzo with an offensive on 23 June. The Italian armies were short of heavy artillery. Their best troops, such as the Alpini and the Bersaglieri, were impressive, but many others were poorly trained peasant conscripts from southern Italy who had little emotional connection with the north of the country.

The initial Isonzo offensive failed, despite the Austro-Hungarians being outnumbered by the Italians, as did three more Isonzo offensives before the end of 1915. Italy lost around

> **217** The number of Italian generals sacked by Chief of Staff Luigi Cadorna between June 1915 and October 1917.

27,000 soldiers in the four battles, and the ground gained was minimal. Losses on the Austro-Hungarian side were also heavy. Shells exploding on the rocky terrain showered sharp rock fragments over a wide area, causing more casualties per shell than in the soft soil of France.

The Austro-Hungarians clung on to their defensive positions and were gradually reinforced. Cadorna, a much feared commander, dismissed many of his generals and imposed brutal discipline on troops, but he had no tactical or strategic solution to the stalemate on the Isonzo Front.

> **"** Blessed are those in their twenties… who are **hungry and thirsty** for **glory,** for they shall be fulfilled. **"**
>
> GABRIELE D'ANNUNZIO, PRO-WAR SPEECH IN GENOA, 4 MAY 1915

AFTER »

The deadlock on the Italian front lasted for almost two and a half years, until it was ended by a victory for the Central Powers at Caporetto (now Kobarid in Slovenia).

GAINS AND LOSSES
Austria-Hungary's position was strengthened by the **defeat of Serbia 140–41 »** in the winter of 1915–16. This allowed the Austro-Hungarians to mount an initially successful **offensive at Asiago** in the Trentino in May 1916, although without decisive results. The Italians achieved a limited victory at **Gorizia** (the Sixth Battle of the Isonzo) in August 1916 after Austria-Hungary diverted troops to respond to the **Russian Brusilov offensive 174–75 »**.

DEFEAT AT CAPORETTO
The Italians renewed their Isonzo Campaign in spring 1917, advancing to within 15 km (9 miles) of Trieste in June. They reached the **Eleventh Battle of the Isonzo** in September 1917. In October, a joint German and Austro-Hungarian offensive shattered the Italian line at **Caporetto 248–49 »**.

defeat of Serbia 140–41 »; Russian Brusilov offensive 174–75 »; Caporetto 248–49 »

ITALIAN POET (1863–1938)

GABRIELE D'ANNUNZIO

Italian poet and nationalist Gabriele d'Annunzio campaigned in favour of Italy going to war in 1915, and maintained a high profile throughout the conflict. He took part in a daring, if futile, naval raid on the Austro-Hungarian port of Bakar and, in August 1918, led an air squadron on a 1,100-km (700-mile) flight to Vienna, dropping propaganda leaflets on the Austrian capital. After the war, D'Annunzio protested against the treatment of Italy in the peace treaty and led a private army to occupy the disputed port of Fiume (now Rijeka in Croatia), which he held for over a year.

Anzac Troops

"You are going out to **fight for Australia... strive** to keep a **fit man** and **do your duty.**"

CHARLES GREENWOOD OF VICTORIA, LETTER TO HIS SON, AUGUST 1918

Turndown collar with bronze insignia of the rising sun

In 1914, Australia and New Zealand were self-governing colonies within the British Empire. At the outbreak of war, they unhesitatingly joined the war against Germany in solidarity with what most of their white population regarded as "the mother country".

An appeal for volunteers to serve in Europe met an enthusiastic response. Although the colonies' armies were tiny, all male Australians and New Zealanders had received basic military training.

Both countries were sparsely populated, with Australians numbering almost 5 million and New Zealanders about a million – yet they provided a remarkably high number of soldiers in the course of the war, with some 416,000 enlisting in Australia and 124,000 in New Zealand, including a Maori contingent. In October 1914, the first convoys of the Australian Imperial Force and the New Zealand Expeditionary Force assembled on Australia's west coast, from where they sailed to Egypt.

60 PER CENT of Australians serving on the Western Front were killed or wounded.

53 PER CENT of New Zealand troops serving on the Western Front were killed or wounded.

Fearsome reputation

The New Zealanders were primarily farmers, the Australians a more mixed group, with city dwellers as numerous as men from the outback and miners. They had in common a tough spirit of independence and a distinct distaste for formal discipline and normal military etiquette. Lodged in training camps alongside the Egyptian pyramids, the Anzac troops soon developed a fearsome reputation among British officers and the Egyptian civilian population.

It was in Egypt that they were designated the Australian and New Zealand Army Corps, soon conveniently abbreviated to Anzac. A British officer, General Sir William Birdwood, was given command of the corps. It was a good appointment because he won the enduring respect of the Anzac soldiers, a unique achievement for a senior British commander. In contrast, General Sir Alexander Godley, who led the New Zealanders throughout the war, was savagely disliked. Friction over the quality of British generals and their perceived carelessness with the lives of colonial troops became acute after Anzac soldiers entered action for the

General Sir John Monash

One of the most respected Allied generals of the war, Monash was an Australian of German Jewish origin. From May 1918, he commanded the Australian Corps, the largest corps on the Western Front.

first time at the Gallipoli landings in April 1915. From the start, the Australians and New Zealanders showed themselves to be resourceful, dauntless fighters under some of the worst conditions experienced anywhere in the war.

But frustration and discontent soared as the campaign became bogged down in stalemate. News of heavy casualties suffered in ill-conceived attacks, such as the bayonet charges ordered by Godley at the Nek in August, fed back to Australia despite censorship, and enthusiasm for volunteering faltered. New Zealand introduced conscription in mid-1916, but Australians rejected it in two referendums.

The Gallipoli Campaign would ever after define World War I for Australians and New Zealanders, yet it was merely the beginning of their soldiers' contribution to the war.

After Gallipoli, some Anzac troops stayed in the Mediterranean, forming a mounted division to fight the Turks

Australian service tunic

Soldiers were issued with a distinctive khaki tunic made of Australian wool. A thoroughly practical garment, it was a looser fit than the standard British tunic and had four large external pockets at the front.

Arm patch with Australian insignia

Khaki twill weave cloth tunic

in the Sinai and Palestine. Because they did not correspond to the British notion of proper cavalry, these troops were designated as "mounted infantry", carrying only rifle and bayonet and denied the cavalryman's sword until nearly the end of the war. Their performance was eventually recognized as outstanding and they enjoyed the satisfaction of riding into both Jerusalem and Damascus by the war's end.

Most Australian and New Zealand troops transferred to the Western Front, serving in France from spring 1916. Fighting in some of the fiercest actions of the trench war, they earned a reputation as elite troops, especially feared and respected by the Germans, while remaining critical of the British high command's acceptance of the need for heavy losses.

Peaceful penetration

By spring 1918, the now independent Australian Corps had become a focus for the development of new battle tactics, dubbed "peaceful penetration", which were designed to exploit the potential of artillery and tanks as offensive weapons and minimize infantry casualties.

Finally under Australian command, with General John Monash leading the corps from May 1918, they spearheaded

Recruitment poster

A wartime poster encourages young Australians to join the troops at Gallipoli. The Australian Imperial Force consisted entirely of volunteers, but it became more difficult to attract new recruits as the war went on.

key attacks in the Hundred Days Offensive that finally won the war on the Western Front.

Some 330,000 Australians and over 90,000 New Zealanders served in the war overseas. About 60,000 Australians and 17,000 New Zealand soldiers were killed. An experience that was never to be forgotten in the histories of the two countries, World War I accelerated a nascent sense of independent nationhood.

New Zealand hat

This khaki felt hat was worn by a soldier in the New Zealand Cyclist Corps. Bicycles were a useful source of mobility in World War I and Anzac cyclists made a significant contribution in a support role.

New Zealand Cyclist Corps badge

" Somewhere between the **landing at Anzac** and the end of the Battle of the Somme, **New Zealand** very definitely **became a nation.** "

ORMOND BURTON, NEW ZEALAND STRETCHER-BEARER AND INFANTRYMAN, LATER PACIFIST

TIMELINE

November–December 1914 Troops of the Australian Imperial Force and the New Zealand Expeditionary Force sail for Egypt, where they are trained and organized into the Anzac Corps under General Sir William Birdwood.

April–May 1915 The Anzac troops take a leading part in the landings at Gallipoli, Turkey, on 25 April, now celebrated as Anzac Day. They defend a foothold on Anzac Cove against fierce Turkish counterattacks.

August 1915 An attempted breakout from Anzac Cove leads to heavy Australian and New Zealand casualties at Lone Pine, the Nek, and Sari Bair.

December 1915 Australian and New Zealand forces are evacuated from Anzac Cove at the end of the failed Gallipoli Campaign and returned to Egypt, where I and II Anzac Corps are formed.

March 1916 The Anzac Mounted Division is formed in Egypt; the Australians and New Zealanders go on to serve with distinction as light cavalry in the campaigns against Turkey in Palestine and Syria.

March–April 1916 The two Anzac corps are transferred to Europe, and the first Australian and New Zealand troops take up position in the trenches on the Western Front.

LONE PINE ANZAC CEMETERY, GALLIPOLI

July–September 1916 Anzac troops participate in the Battle of the Somme. The Australians suffer heavy losses in the capture and defence of Pozières (23 July–7 August).

June 1917 New Zealand and Australian divisions are prominent in the successful Battle of Messines on the Flanders front.

September–October 1917 Australian and New Zealand soldiers suffer heavy casualties in the Battle of Passchendaele, fought in the rain and mud of Flanders.

December 1917 The five Australian divisions form the Australian Corps under General Birdwood and the New Zealand Division becomes part of British XXII Corps under General Alexander Godley.

July 1918 Under the command of General John Monash, the Australian Corps mounts a successful offensive on the Western Front at Le Hamel (4 July).

August–November 1918 The Australian Corps spearheads a British offensive at Amiens, beginning the war-winning Hundred Days Offensive.

BEFORE

Turkey's decision to enter the war on the side of Germany in October 1914 led Britain and France to consider ways of attacking the Turks.

TURKISH TARGETS

The narrow channel of the **Dardanelles** gave sea access from the Mediterranean to the Turkish capital, Constantinople, and from there to the Black Sea and Russia's southern coast. British Admiralty chief **Winston Churchill** sent ships to **bombard Turkish forts** at the mouth of the Dardanelles within days of **Turkey joining the war ≪ 74–75**.

DIVERSIONARY TACTIC

Churchill's suggestion for further attacks on the Dardenelles was blocked by the British War Council until the start of 1915, when the **Russians**, hard-pressed by Turkish forces in the Caucasus, asked their **Western allies** to mount a **diversionary attack**. The idea of attacking the Dardanelles was then revived, attracting support as an **alternative** to the **costly fighting** on the **Western Front**.

BRITISH POLITICIAN (1874–1965)

WINSTON CHURCHILL

At the start of World War I, Churchill was a prominent member of Britain's Liberal government. As First Lord of the Admiralty, in command of the Royal Navy, he took the blame for early setbacks in British naval operations and for the fiasco at Gallipoli. Relegated to a minor government post in May 1915, he resigned in November to serve as an infantry officer on the Western Front. In July 1917, he returned to government as an energetic Minister of Munitions. Gallipoli was continually cited against Churchill until it was overshadowed by his performance as British prime minister in World War II.

The Gallipoli Campaign

The Allies initially attempted a naval breakthrough in the Dardanelles straits. When this failed, they embarked upon a land campaign on Turkey's Gallipoli peninsula – a disastrous operation that was a harrowing initiation for Australian and New Zealand troops.

The idea for an attack on the Dardanelles appealed to British politicians, who wanted large gains at small cost. An Allied naval force, they thought, would break through to Constantinople (modern Istanbul), where the threat of its guns would force Turkey to surrender, opening up a sea route to Russia.

But Winston Churchill, the minister responsible for the Admiralty, the prime advocate of the operation, ignored one detail: the Royal Navy did not believe it could be done. The Dardanelles was blocked by minefields and defended by a series of forts and German mobile howitzers.

On 19 February, British Admiral Sackville Carden opened the naval attack. He had a sizeable Anglo-French fleet, including Britain's super-dreadnought HMS *Queen Elizabeth*, but the rest were "pre-dreadnoughts" – dating from before HMS *Dreadnought*, launched in 1906, set a new standard for warships. Their only minesweepers were trawlers fitted with mine-clearing equipment. By 25 February, the Turks had been driven from forts at the entrance to the straits, but beyond that progress had stalled.

In the second week of March, British Minister for War Lord Kitchener ordered landings on the Gallipoli peninsula. The

British 29th Division and the Australian and New Zealand Army Corps (Anzac) were to assemble, along with a French colonial division, at the Greek island of Lemnos, under General Sir Ian Hamilton.

Destroyed by mines

Meanwhile, the naval bid to breech the Dardanelles reached its climax. On 18 March, Admiral John de Robeck sent his battleships forward. Four French pre-dreadnoughts engaged in a close-range duel with forts flanking the Narrows, while the trawlers cleared the mines. After one of the French battleships was beached to avoid sinking, Robeck ordered the others to withdraw. In the process, the French battleship *Bouvet* struck

Shore bombardment

HMS *Cornwallis*, here bombarding Turkish positions, was present at Gallipoli from February 1915 to the evacuation of troops in December.

a mine and sank, taking 639 of its crew with it. Then a British battlecruiser and two British pre-dreadnoughts struck mines. There would be no further attempt at a naval breakthrough.

The task of the army landing force was to take the Turkish positions defending the straits, after which the mines could be cleared and the navy

Landing plans

The Allies intended Anzac troops to cut across the Gallipoli peninsula while other British troops advanced from Cape Helles. They expected to capture the peninsula in a few days.

Turkish hand grenade

The 73 mm (2.8 in) Tufenjieff hand grenade was much used by the Turkish army in trench warfare at Gallipoli. Activated by lighting the rope fuse, it was then lobbed at the enemy.

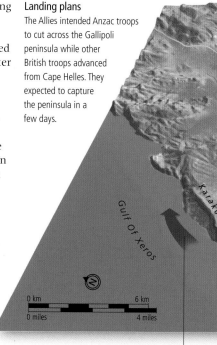

Diversionary attack by Royal Naval Division

"If the Fleet gets through, **Constantinople** will fall… and you will **have won** not a **battle,** but the **war.**"

LORD KITCHENER, MINISTER FOR WAR, MARCH 1915

sail through in peace. Hamilton had little information on the terrain of the area or on Turkish defensive positions.

Allied landings

A plan was hastily put together for the British 29th Division to land on beaches, coded S, V, W, X, and Y, at Cape Helles, the peninsula's southern tip. The Anzac troops were to land at an undefended cove further north, while the French staged a diversionary landing on the Asiatic shore.

On the morning of 25 April, Robeck's warships appeared off Gallipoli. As they bombarded the shore, the troops

18,000 The number of Allied soldiers who came ashore on the first day of the Gallipoli landings, 25 April 1915.

12,000 The number of Anzac troops who landed at Gallipoli the same day.

disembarked into rowing boats, towed to shore in lines behind steam pinnaces (small naval boats). At W Beach on Cape Helles, the Lancashire Fusiliers suffered more than 50 per cent casualties, coming under rifle and machine-gun fire as they approached the shore and then finding their way blocked by barbed wire. At nearby V Beach, Turkish machine-guns killed hundreds of British soldiers coming ashore on gangplanks from the troopship SS *River Clyde*. Despite the losses, all the beaches were taken.

Death trap

Australian and New Zealand soldiers move among the dead and wounded on the beach at Anzac Cove. The landing site turned into a trap from which the troops could never break out.

Unfortunately, the Anzac troops had come ashore in the wrong place. They found themselves crowded into a small curve of beach enclosed by ridges and ravines – later known as Anzac Cove. There were no Turkish forces, but reaching the top of Sari Bair Ridge 3 km (2 miles) inland was a daunting physical challenge. As Anzac troops clawed their way towards the summit,

a Turkish counterattack was under way. The Turkish army and its chief German adviser, General Otto Liman von Sanders, had known an attack was coming but not where the landings would be made.

As soon as the naval bombardment began on 25 April, General Mustafa Kemal marched his Turkish 19th Division towards the sound of the

guns. He reached Sari Bair Ridge in time to fire down on Anzac troops caught in mid-climb. After a week's fighting failed to drive the Australians and New Zealanders back into the sea, Kemal ordered his men to dig trenches. The rest of the Cape Helles landings suffered the same fate, bogging down in early May in front of Krithia, just a few miles inland.

»

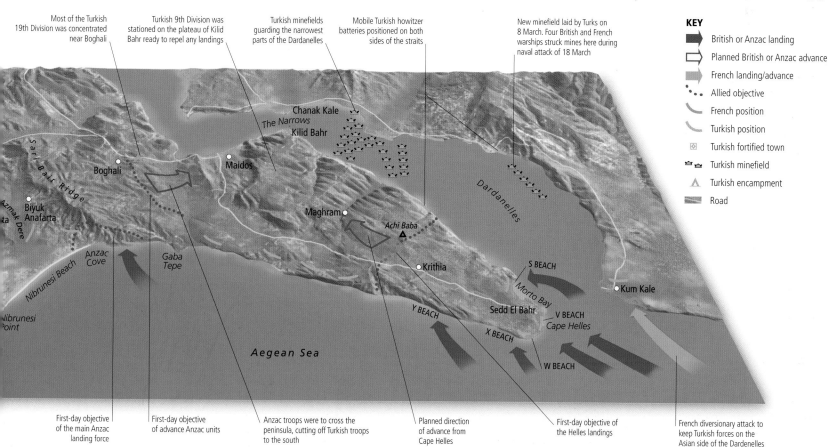

Most of the Turkish 19th Division was concentrated near Boghali

Turkish 9th Division was stationed on the plateau of Kilid Bahr ready to repel any landings

Turkish minefields guarding the narrowest parts of the Dardanelles

Mobile Turkish howitzer batteries positioned on both sides of the straits

New minefield laid by Turks on 8 March. Four British and French warships struck mines here during naval attack of 18 March

KEY

→ British or Anzac landing

⇨ Planned British or Anzac advance

⇛ French landing/advance

•••➤ Allied objective

╮ French position

╰ Turkish position

⊡ Turkish fortified town

⛴ Turkish minefield

△ Turkish encampment

▬ Road

Chanak Kale
The Narrows
Kilid Bahr
Maidos
Boghali
Sari Bair Ridge
Biyuk Anafarta
Azmak Dere
Maghram
Achi Baba
Dardanelles
Anzac Cove
Gaba Tepe
Nibrunesi Beach
Nibrunesi Point
Krithia
S BEACH
Morto Bay
Sedd El Bahr
V BEACH
Cape Helles
Kum Kale
Y BEACH
X BEACH
W BEACH
Aegean Sea

First-day objective of the main Anzac landing force

First-day objective of advance Anzac units

Anzac troops were to cross the peninsula, cutting off Turkish troops to the south

Planned direction of advance from Cape Helles

First-day objective of the Helles landings

French diversionary attack to keep Turkish forces on the Asian side of the Dardanelles

TURKISH GENERAL (1881–1938)

MUSTAFA KEMAL ATATÜRK

An officer in Turkey's wars in Libya and the Balkans before World War I, Mustafa Kemal was a divisional commander at Gallipoli, where his performance made him a national hero. After the war, he led a Turkish national revival, driving the Greek out of Anatolia in 1921–22 and replacing the Ottoman Empire with a Turkish Republic, with himself as president. From 1934, he was known as "Atatürk" – father of the Turks. He introduced many reforms including the emancipation of women, banning traditional Islamic dress, and replacing Arabic script with the Western alphabet.

An assault at Achi Baba in mid-July was a costly failure. Meanwhile, the ground forces lost the back-up support of naval guns as the warships were withdrawn in the face of attacks by German U-boats.

The failure of the Gallipoli landings was a factor influencing a change in British government in May 1915. Churchill, the person most publicly identified with the Dardanelles Campaign, lost control of the Admiralty.

While France continually pushed for all resources to be focused on the Western Front, Britain was not

Anzac push to capture Sari Bair Ridge and various diversionary attacks to keep other Turkish forces occupied.

The landings at Suvla Bay took place on 6 August 1915. Some 20,000 men came ashore easily against only light opposition, but inert leadership from the elderly commander of the Suvla force, General Frederick Stopford, left the soldiers waiting on the beaches while Kemal organized a swift and vigorous counterattack.

⟫ Spring mutated into an unbearably hot summer without significant movement. Trenches and bunkers swarmed with flies feasting on unburied corpses, and dysentery decimated the ranks. Anzac troops carrying food, water, and ammunition up from the beach to men perched on the rocky slopes passed the wounded and dead being carried down in the opposite direction.

On 19 May, Kemal launched a mass attack at Anzac Cove, attempting to swamp the Anzac positions with sheer numbers. It ended in 13,000 of his men

being killed or wounded. The heaps of corpses in No Man's Land were so unbearable that a temporary truce was negotiated so that the dead on both sides could be buried.

Renewed offensives

In June and July, the British who were entrenched in the north of Cape Helles, now supported by the French on their right flank, attempted new offensives. Reinforced by Gurkhas and newly arrived Territorials, the Allies succeeded in gaining a certain amount of ground to no decisive effect.

6 The number of Victoria Crosses awarded to the Lancashire Fusiliers in the contested landing at W Beach, Gallipoli, on 25 April 1915.

7 The number of Victoria Crosses awarded to Australians for their role in the Battle of Lone Pine, on 6–10 August 1915.

prepared to accept a humiliating defeat. Fresh divisions were found for General Hamilton, who was ordered to break the deadlock. A plan was devised for new landings at Suvla Bay, north of Anzac Cove, to coincide with a major

Close-quarter battles

Meanwhile, Anzac troops engaged in some of the fiercest fighting of the war. A mere diversionary attack by the Australians at Lone Pine developed into an epic close-quarter struggle when the attackers broke into the Turkish trench system. Fighting with grenades and bayonets in a warren of tunnels and bunkers, the Australians

Turkish rifle

The Turkish army ordered large numbers of 9.5 mm Mauser rifles and carbines in 1888 and some were still in use in World War I, alongside 7.65 mm Mausers. Most Turkish equipment was supplied by Germany.

eventually took the position, winning an astonishing seven Victoria Crosses.

In the main Sidi Bair offensive, New Zealanders captured the ridge of Chanuk Bair in two days of savage combat, only to be driven off again by artillery fire and a Turkish counterattack. Australian troops designated to attack another key objective, Hill 971, became lost in the maze of ridges and gullies and never found their target.

In a notorious incident on 7 August, at a ridge known as the Nek, soldiers of the Australian Light Horse, fighting as infantry, were thrown forward in repeated futile frontal assaults ordered by General Alexander Godley. They suffered more than 60 per cent casualties. By 10 August, stalemate had resumed. On 21 August, the British attempted to reignite the campaign with attacks against Scimitar Hill from Suvla Bay and Hill 60 from Anzac Cove, but the frontal charges against prepared Turkish positions, poorly supported by artillery, ended in failure.

Disease and hardship

There was no more serious fighting at Gallipoli, but the terrible losses continued. Disease took a heavy toll on troops in the trenches. They were poorly supplied with food and drink and had very limited medical support. The excessive heat of the Turkish summer was followed by deadly floods and blizzards in the autumn and winter months.

Complaints about the state of the troops and the quality of command, especially from Australia, led to Hamilton's dismissal in October. His

British artillery in action

A British 60-pounder heavy field gun bombards Turkish trenches at Cape Helles. The gun required a crew of ten men, who could fire two rounds per minute to a range of over 9,000 m (10,000 yd).

Kitchener at Gallipoli

British Minister for War Lord Kitchener visits the trenches at Gallipoli in November 1915 to view the situation at first hand. The evacuation of Allied forces began the following month.

successor, General Sir Charles Monro, took a swift look at the situation and recommended withdrawal. His view did not win easy acceptance in London, where bold spirits were pushing for a new attempt at a naval breakthrough in the Dardanelles. After visiting Gallipoli, Kitchener put an end to such fantasies and proposed evacuation of Suvla Bay and Anzac Cove.

Allied evacuation

On 7 December, the British cabinet ordered the evacuation of all troops from Gallipoli. This tricky operation was carried out with skill and efficiency. More than 100,000 troops were embarked from Suvla Bay and Anzac Cove between 10 and 20 December, followed by the remaining 35,000 from Cape Helles by 9 January 1916. This logistical feat was the most successful episode in the whole campaign.

> "Accept this **honourable desire** of ours and **make our bayonets sharper** so we may **destroy our enemy!**"
>
> HASSAN ETHEM, TURKISH SOLDIER, PRAYER, 1915

AFTER

More than 44,000 Allied troops died at Gallipoli. The Turkish death toll was much higher, with possibly as many as 90,000 killed in the successful defence of their country.

LASTING EFFECTS
The British and French suffered far more casualties at Gallipoli than the Australians and New Zealanders, but the campaign would always have a **special significance** in the history of the colonies and on their road to becoming **independent nations**. The campaign also had a marked emotional **significance for Turkey**, a country evolving from a multinational empire into a nation state. Militarily its effect was to allow Turkey to fight on for three more years. The **Allied failure** encouraged **Bulgaria to enter the war** on the side of the Central Powers in October 1915, sealing the **fate of Serbia 140–41 »**.

TURKISH ARMY UNIFORM

Battle of Lone Pine

On 6 August 1915, the First Australian Division made a diversionary attack at Lone Pine to support the Allied landings at Suvla Bay, Gallipoli. While the initial assault succeeded in capturing the Turkish trenches, the Australians soon faced waves of Turkish counterattacks. Lone Pine developed into a brutal, five-day, close-quarter battle ending in up to 3,000 Australian and 7,000 Turkish casualties.

"We reached the Turkish lines and found the first trench covered in with logs and branches… There was a partial check, some men fired in through the loopholes, others tried to pull the logs apart. Out runs our officer, old Dickie Seldon, waving a revolver, 'This won't do men! On! On! On!'

I slid down into the trench… The Turks ran round a corner and got into a large cave place… Captain Milson took command… and asked if we would follow him. We all said 'yes' so he threw a bomb and dashed across. A dozen Turks shot him and he fell dead… I was next and as I ran I threw my rifle into the possie and pulled the trigger. I suppose they had never got time to load… but no one followed and I was there alone with no bombs and only my rifle.

I felt a little dickie I can tell you… Whack! Like a sledgehammer on the head and down I went across Milson's body and several Turks, some of whom were only wounded, and groaned and squirmed from time to time. I bled pretty freely and then I got a crack on the shoulder from a shrapnel pellet, which hurt badly…

Soon I heard someone call behind me 'Hullo Australia' and I crawled down the trench and found Seldon with one eye shot out, but still going, leading a party, and I explained the position to him and he sent me away to a temporary dressing station while he went and fixed up the Turks… I got my head bandaged and a drink of rum… I picked up a rifle and… went on… to dig in the now captured trench."

HUGH ANDERSON, FIRST BRIGADE, AUSTRALIAN IMPERIAL FORCE, IN A LETTER TO HIS PARENTS

Anzac troops at Gallipoli
The Gallipoli Campaign of 1915, the first major engagement of Anzac troops in the war, was a series of fierce battles lasting more than eight months. It resulted in thousands of casualties on both sides.

200,000 Algerians, Moroccans, and Tunisians fought on the Western Front and at Gallipoli, along with more than 160,000 West African troops. The West Africans were engaged in some of the harshest fighting of the war, and about 30,000 died in the conflict.

> **TIRAILLEURS** A French term for lightly armed skirmishers or riflemen. It was applied indiscriminately to all locally recruited French colonial troops.

The French colonies also helped in the production of munitions. Some 50,000 Vietnamese and 13,000 Chinese from French Indochina worked in French munitions factories. Tens of thousands of Chinese labourers, recruited by the British and the French, were brought to perform support work on the Western Front.

The Indian Army

Britain could call on troops from its self-governing, white-ruled colonies – Canada, Australia, New Zealand, and South Africa – but India was a potentially much larger source of manpower. The regular army of India numbered around 155,000 soldiers at the beginning of the war. These were organized into divisions, each of which included a battalion of British troops alongside the Indian battalions.

Primarily intended for use on India's northern frontier or for suppressing internal revolts, the Indian Army was short of modern weapons and equipment, and its officers were not used to the demands of European warfare. The standard of its troops at the start of the war was high, but the quality was diluted by the rapid expansion in numbers.

An Indian expeditionary force of two infantry divisions and a cavalry division reached France in time to take part in the fighting in Flanders from October 1914. When the war descended into the stalemate of trench warfare, they proved a valuable addition to Britain's overstretched and depleted front-line forces, and they fought bravely at Neuve Chapelle, the Second Battle of Ypres, and Loos. The Germans especially feared the Gurkhas because of their skill at mounting silent raids across No Man's Land with their sharp-edged kukris (knives with a curved blade).

Transferred to Mesopotamia

By autumn 1915, the morale of Indian troops in France was in serious decline, mostly because of a loss of vital cohesion. Heavy casualties resulted

French colonial troops
A company of Tirailleurs Annamites – infantry from French Indochina – wait for action after joining the Allied forces at Salonika, Greece, late in the war. The diversity of troops underlined the global nature of the conflict.

in troops fighting in fragmented formations under unfamiliar officers. By December 1915, all Indian infantry were being transferred from the Western Front to Mesopotamia, where it was thought they would be more used to the terrain and hot climate.

In total, 1.25 million Indian soldiers contributed to the British war effort. More than 70,000 were killed in the service of the Empire.

The question of loyalty

A large proportion of the colonial troops employed by both France and Britain were Muslim. The entry of Turkey into the war in October 1914 raised the possibility of such troops being asked to fight fellow Muslims. In fact, Turkey's call for all Muslims to join in a jihad against the Allies had little effect. There were rare instances of soldiers refusing to fight – such as when the 15th Lancers in Basra would not march on Baghdad in February 1916 – but on the whole, Muslim soldiers fought the Turks without reservation, whether at Gallipoli, in Mesopotamia, or in Palestine.

For their personal honour, the honour of their regiments, and their meagre pay, they served the empires to the end.

> "**Gurkhas** had **crawled** far behind enemy lines… and dealt out **destruction** with their kukris before **being killed.**"
>
> CAPTAIN R.F.E. LAIDLAW, AT GULLY RAVINE, GALLIPOLI, JUNE 1915

KEY MOMENT

THE SINGAPORE MUTINY

Early in the war, Germany backed an attempt by an Indian nationalist group, the Ghadar Party, to promote an anti-British mutiny in the Indian Army. Ghadar agents achieved influence over the Muslim Indian Fifth Light Infantry garrisoned in Singapore. Falsely informed that they were to be sent to fight Muslim Turkey, the regiment mutinied on 15 February 1915. More than 40 British soldiers and European civilians were killed. German prisoners were offered arms, but they refused to join the mutineers. Marines and sailors from British, French, and Russian ships combined to suppress the mutiny. A court martial condemned 47 of the mutineers to death by firing squad. The executions took place in public at Outram Prison.

TIMELINE

1904 Commander-in-chief of the British Indian Army, Lord Kitchener, reorganizes the force to create a field army of 10 divisions.

1910 French General Charles Mangin publishes his book *La Force Noire* advocating the use of colonial troops to defend France in the event of a European war.

August 1914 French colonial troops from Africa are ferried to France at the outbreak of war and take part in the first battles on the Western Front.

1 September 1914 Indian troops land at Mombasa in British East Africa for a campaign against German East Africa; they suffer a defeat at the Battle of Tanga on 5 November.

26 September 1914 Indian Expeditionary Force A lands in France to join the British Expeditionary Force on the Western Front.

October 1914 Indian troops see action for the first time on the Western Front, at La Bassée.

5 November 1914 Indian Army Force D lands in Mesopotamia (Iraq) and goes on to occupy Basra on 3 November.

11 November 1914 Ottoman Sultan Mehmed V calls on all Muslim subjects of Britain and France to join a jihad against the colonial powers.

GURKHA KUKRI

February 1915 Indian infantry stage a mutiny against their British officers in Singapore. The mutiny is quickly suppressed.

March 1915 On the Western Front, two Indian divisions play a prominent part in the failed British offensive at Neuve Chapelle.

22 April 1915 French colonial troops are among the casualties in the first poison gas attack on the Western Front at Second Ypres. Some break rank in panic.

April 1915 British Indian troops and French colonial soldiers, the Tirailleurs Sénégalais, take part in the Gallipoli landings.

November 1915 The Indian Corps is withdrawn from the Western Front and transferred to Mesopotamia.

30 April 1916 Indian troops of the Sixth (Poona) Division surrender to the Turks at the siege of Kut al-Amara in Mesopotamia.

24 October 1916 During the Battle of Verdun, French colonial troops perform outstandingly in the retaking of Fort Douaumont.

March 1917–October 1918 A large contingent of Indian troops takes part in the successful British campaign against Turkey in Palestine.

June 1918 The British Cabinet approves a proposal by Secretary of State for India, Edwin Montagu, for an increased measure of representative government in India.

French colonial cavalry
The Spahis were Arab and Berber cavalry regiments, brought from French North Africa to fight in France at the start of the war. Their appearance attracted the photographer Jules Gervais-Courtellemont, who took this colour autochrome image in 1915.

Turkish–German cooperation
A unit of Bavarian artillery struggles forwards to aid the Turks in their campaign in Mesopotamia. Movement of troops and equipment was difficult, especially during seasonal floods along the Tigris and Euphrates rivers.

« BEFORE

The Ottoman sultan's call for a Muslim holy war against the British Empire in November 1914 was a direct challenge to Britain's position in India and the Middle East.

FAILURE TO STIR REVOLT
Turkish and German plans **to carry the war** through **Persia to Afghanistan** and Muslim areas of **northern India** came to nothing. **Egypt also failed to rise up** against British rule, even when the Turks

100 MILLION The estimated number of Muslims living under British rule in 1914. This was more than a third of the world's entire Muslim population at the time.

attacked the **Suez Canal « 75** in February 1915. The situation inside **Persia was precarious**, with Russia, Britain, and Germany vying to extend their influence there. In November 1914, an expeditionary force from British India **occupied Basra** in southern Mesopotamia to strengthen the British position in the oil-rich Persian Gulf.

Disaster in Mesopotamia

In 1915, British Indian forces advanced from Basra towards Baghdad in an overt display of imperial authority. But the prestige of the British Empire suffered a humiliating blow when British forces had to surrender to the Turks at Kut al-Amara in April 1916.

The operation in Mesopotamia was launched and controlled by the British Government of India in Calcutta. Initially only a few thousand troops of the Indian Army were landed at the mouth of the Shatt al-Arab waterway, in southern Mesopotamia, and their mission was limited. They were to establish a defensible position and prevent any Turkish interference with British-owned oilfields across the border in southern Persia (now Iran).

The need for a "forward defence" led to the occupation first of the port of Basra and then of Qurna, further north at the junction of the Tigris and Euphrates rivers. Unlike the British

authorities in Cairo, the Government of India felt no inclination to encourage an Arab revolt against the Turks. Local Arab irregulars thus sided with Turkish forces in a vigorous counterattack in April 1915. This was repulsed by entrenched Anglo-Indian troops at Shaiba outside Basra.

A newly appointed commander of the expeditionary force, the ambitious General Sir John Nixon, took this defensive victory as a springboard for the occupation of the whole of southern Mesopotamia as far north as Nasiriya and Amara, expanding the campaign well beyond its original goals. Given the Allies' setbacks against

the Turks in the Gallipoli Campaign, the conquest of Mesopotamia was seen as a way for Britain to reassert its prestige in the eyes of its Muslim subject peoples.

The Anglo-Indian advance
Despite doubts expressed by the War Office in London, Nixon was authorized by the Government of India to advance troops first to Kut al-Amara, reached in late September, and then onwards towards the historic Muslim city of Baghdad. While Nixon stayed in Basra, the troops on the ground were commanded by General Sir Charles Townshend, an officer with

"We drink river water... Except for the barren, naked plain there is nothing to see... our hope is in God alone."

ABDUL RAUF KHAN, 21ST COMBINED FIELD AMBULANCE, MESOPOTAMIA, LETTER, 7 MARCH 1916

an experience of colonial warfare in India, including holding the fort at Chitral against a rebel siege. However, Townshend was not confident in his mission. Every step towards Baghdad extended the overstretched supply line that linked him to the base at Basra. Moreover, men were decimated by disease and debilitated by the heat.

The Turkish forces

As Townshend's forces advanced up the Tigris, accompanied by river gunboats, Turkish forces prepared to defend Baghdad. Under the command of Ottoman General Khalil Pasha and German veteran Baron Colmar von der Goltz, the Turks dug into trenches at Ctesiphon south of Baghdad. The commander on the ground was Nur ud-Din Pasha.

Townshend attacked the Turkish position on 22 November. The front-line trench was taken and then held against Turkish counterattacks, but by 25 November Townshend had only 4,500 men fit enough to fight – less than half his original force. He decided to withdraw back down the Tigris to Kut al-Amara.

The Anglo-Indian force reached Kut in poor condition. They had been harassed en route by Arab tribesmen. The many sick and wounded lacked adequate medical care. Townshend had only a hazy notion of the state of his food supplies, but decided to sit tight and await relief rather than

Decorated water flask
A British soldier's water bottle is engraved with scenes from the Mesopotamian Campaign. Lack of clean drinking water was a major cause of illness for the troops operating in what is now Iraq.

continue the withdrawal to Basra. On 7 December, Nur ud-Din's forces arrived and, after failing to take Kut by assault, settled into trenches for a siege.

In Basra, the British reorganized. Nixon was dismissed and a new Tigris Corps was created to mount

a relief effort. Plagued by problems of transport and logistics – there were no proper roads or railways, and the river seemed always either too low or in flood – British relief forces pushed northwards from Basra. They were repeatedly repelled by determined Turkish troops, who were dug into defensive positions south of Kut.

Meanwhile, inside Kut conditions were quickly deteriorating. Disease and lack of food reduced the garrison to a pitiable condition. Mules and horses were slaughtered for meat. Morale collapsed and relations between the British officers and their Indian soldiers rapidly deteriorated. An attempt at breakout was out of the question; Townshend was unable even to mount harassing attacks against the Turkish siege trenches.

Forced to surrender

On 22 April, the last British relief expedition was brought to a halt 16 km (10 miles) from Kut. Four days later, Townshend opened negotiations with Khalil Pasha, proposing to pay for his force to be paroled. This improbable offer was refused and on 29 April Townshend surrendered. Some 10,000 British and Indian troops passed into Turkish hands. Their treatment was harsh, with about 4,000 dying in captivity. Townshend, meanwhile, was allowed to live in a comfortable house near Istanbul for the rest of the war.

Townshend at Kut al-Amara
An officer in the British Indian Army, General Sir Charles Townshend commanded the Sixth Indian Division in the Mesopotamian Campaign from April 1915 to the surrender at the siege of Kut a year later.

AFTER

Viewing the surrender at Kut as a blow to its prestige, Britain devoted much time and many resources to the capture of Mesopotamia.

RETAKING KUT
In summer 1916, London took over control of the Mesopotamian Campaign from the Indian Government. Basra's **port facilities were expanded, roads and railways built**, and **modern weaponry** supplied. Under General Sir Stanley Maude, **British forces retook Kut al-Amara** in February 1917 and **occupied Baghdad** in March. After Maude died of cholera in November, the British effort was scaled down. The British **occupied the oil town of Mosul** at the end of the war.

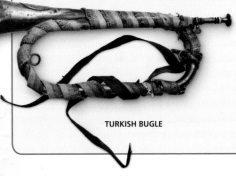

TURKISH BUGLE

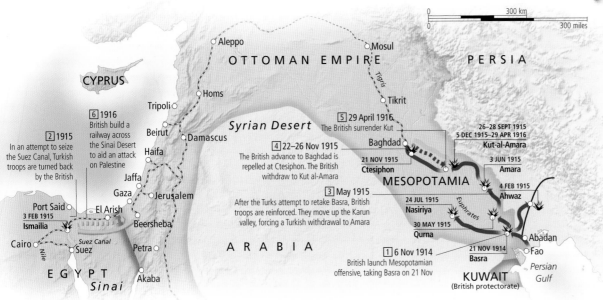

War in Egypt and Mesopotamia
British forces repelled a Turkish attack on Egypt at the Suez Canal, but in Mesopotamia a British advance was stopped by the Turks at Ctesiphon and then forced back to the garrison at Kut al-Amara.

KEY

British offensive	British retreat
Turkish offensive	Turkish retreat
Battle or siege	Oil pipeline
Major railway	

Map labels:

6 1916 British build a railway across the Sinai Desert to aid an attack on Palestine

2 1915 In an attempt to seize the Suez Canal, Turkish troops are turned back by the British

4 22–26 Nov 1915 The British advance to Baghdad is repelled at Ctesiphon. The British withdraw to Kut al-Amara

5 29 April 1916 The British surrender Kut

3 May 1915 After the Turks attempt to retake Basra, British troops are reinforced. They move up the Karun valley, forcing a Turkish withdrawal to Amara

1 6 Nov 1914 British launch Mesopotamian offensive, taking Basra on 21 Nov

26–28 SEPT 1915
5 DEC 1915–29 APR 1916
Kut-al-Amara

3 JUN 1915 Amara

4 FEB 1915 Ahwaz

24 JUL 1915 Nasiriya

30 MAY 1915 Qurna

21 NOV 1914 Basra

3 FEB 1915 Ismailia

21 NOV 1915 Ctesiphon

Places: Aleppo, Mosul, OTTOMAN EMPIRE, PERSIA, CYPRUS, Homs, Tripoli, Tikrit, Beirut, Damascus, Syrian Desert, Baghdad, Haifa, Jaffa, Gaza, Jerusalem, MESOPOTAMIA, Amara, Port Said, El Arish, Beersheba, Cairo, Suez, Petra, ARABIA, Abadan, Fao, EGYPT, Sinai, Akaba, KUWAIT (British protectorate), Persian Gulf, Suez Canal, Nile, Tigris, Euphrates, Karun

0 300 km
0 300 miles

« BEFORE

Britain's Royal Navy had experienced a mixed start to the war in 1914, with a number of successes offset by humiliating setbacks.

BRITISH ERRORS

In August 1914, Britain made the mistake of allowing the **German warships** SMS *Goeben* and SMS *Breslau* to sail to **Constantinople** **« 74–75**, helping to **bring Turkey into the war** on the German side. Britain also lost ships to German submarines and mines and suffered a **defeat in the Pacific at Coronel « 83** in November. For the British public, the worst incident came on 16 December when **German battlecruisers shelled** towns on the **east coast of England**.

NAVAL BLOCKADE

The British had recorded **victories** at **Heligoland Bight** in the North Sea, on 28 August 1914, and at the **Battle of the Falkland Islands « 83** in the South Atlantic, on 8 December. **Germany** remained **under British naval blockade** and its High Seas Fleet was unable to leave port for fear of **destruction** by the Royal Navy's Grand Fleet.

TURKISH SWORD BAYONET

The **Battle** of **Dogger Bank**

In January 1915, the stand-off between the British and German fleets in the North Sea flared into battle at Dogger Bank. Vice-Admiral Franz von Hipper's German battlecruisers were met by a British force under Vice-Admiral David Beatty and narrowly avoided a major defeat.

German naval strategy was built on the hope of eroding Britain's naval superiority through piecemeal destruction of warships, especially by mines and submarines. To avoid this, the Royal Navy did not attempt a "close blockade" of the German coast, which would have put British ships at risk, but used its control of the exits from the North Sea (around Scotland in the north and Dover and Dunkirk in the south) to maintain a "distant blockade" of Germany.

In principle, this strategy left the German surface fleet free to sortie into the North Sea at will. However, if German warships left port, the Royal Navy aimed to drive them back home or, preferably, destroy them. The British Admiralty had a secret weapon in this cat-and-mouse game. Naval intelligence under Admiral Reginald "Blinker" Hall had obtained German naval code books and set up listening posts to monitor the radio traffic of German ships. By 1915, the codebreakers in Hall's Room 40 at the Admiralty in London could warn of a sortie before the German ships had left port.

German aims

On 23 January 1915, Vice-Admiral Franz von Hipper, who had led a raid on English coastal towns in December, was ordered to take his fleet into the North Sea to attack British trawlers and patrol boats at Dogger Bank, a shallow area 100 km (62 miles) off England's east coast. Hipper had three battlecruisers – his flagship SMS *Seydlitz* leading *Moltke* and *Derfflinger* – plus destroyers and light cruisers.

German commander
Admiral Franz von Hipper, the commander of the battlecruisers of 1 Scouting Group, led the German squadron that fought the British at Dogger Bank.

Battlecruisers were the stars of naval warfare, with guns as heavy as those on battleships but with more speed. When Room 40 informed the Admiralty that Hipper was setting to sea, Vice-Admiral David Beatty was ordered to lead the Royal Navy's response. Leaving the Scottish port of Rosyth, he steamed south with five battlecruisers – his flagship HMS *Lion* leading *Tiger*, *Princess Royal*, *Indomitable*, and *New Zealand* – joining up with light cruisers and destroyers at Harwich.

Sinking of SMS *Blücher*
German sailors scramble to escape from the cruiser *Blücher* as it capsizes at the end of the battle. There were only 234 survivors out of a crew of more than 1,000 men.

Shortly after 7am on 24 January, the outlying ships of the opposing forces exchanged fire. Hipper quickly realized he had fallen into a trap and turned for home at full speed. Beatty led the chase in the fast-moving *Lion*, with his other battlecruisers trying to keep up. Leading the German fleet on board the *Seydlitz*, Hipper was hampered by the need to keep in touch with his slower ships, especially the out-of-date armoured cruiser *Blücher*.

Gaining on the Germans, the British battlecruisers opened fire shortly before 9am. The range was extreme – more than 18 km (11 miles) – and the ships were moving at maximum speed, so

hits were infrequent. At 9:43am, the *Lion* landed the first major blow, exploding *Seydlitz's* two aft turrets with an armour-penetrating shell. More than 160 men were killed, and a worse disaster was averted only through the heroism of a German sailor, Wilhelm Heidkamp, who flooded the magazines to protect them from fire. *Blücher* also took a battering and fell further behind the rest of the German force.

Missed opportunity

The British, however, failed to distribute their fire evenly between the German ships. The battlecruisers *Moltke* and *Derfflinger* were untouched and, as

Battlecruiser HMS *Lion*

The flagship at the Battle of Dogger Bank, HMS *Lion* was, like other battlecruisers, fast and heavily armed, but it proved vulnerable to well-directed German shells.

the range shortened, their shells hit the *Lion* with increasing frequency. By 10:45, Beatty's flagship was so battered it came to a stop. The battlecruiser *Tiger* was also badly damaged.

From the British point of view, the battle that had opened so promisingly degenerated into a mess. Beatty first ordered an unnecessary turn to avoid a nonexistent U-boat and then, using flag signals instead of radio, failed to convey his order for the pursuit to be resumed with all speed. Instead, Beatty's subordinates concentrated the fire of their four battlecruisers on the *Blücher*, which Hipper had resolved to abandon to its fate. The *Blücher* finally capsized and sank, while Hipper led his battlecruisers safely back to port.

The crippled *Lion* was towed back to Rosyth, where it received a hero's welcome. The battle had, after all, been a demonstration of British naval strength. But Beatty had fumbled an opportunity to inflict a crushing defeat on the German navy.

The British and German navies drew very different conclusions from their experience of the Battle of Dogger Bank.

SUBMARINE WARFARE

Kaiser Wilhelm II was appalled by the risk that had been taken with his precious warships and **banned further sorties**, not relenting until the following year. The commander of the German High Seas Fleet, Admiral Friedrich von Ingenohl, was replaced by Hugo von Pohl, who

THE IMPERIAL GERMAN NAVY FLAG

in February 1917 gave the order to adopt **unrestricted submarine warfare 220–21 »** against Allied shipping.

THE BATTLE OF JUTLAND

To counter **superior German gunnery,** the British concluded they must increase their rate of fire at the expense of safety procedures. This led to many deaths at the **Battle of Jutland 170–71 ».**

"The **ship was capsizing...** men **fell or ran** down her side **into the water...**"

PAYMASTER HUGH MILLER ON THE CRUISER HMS ARETHUSA, DESCRIBING THE SINKING OF THE BLÜCHER

BEFORE

After its defeat at the Battle of the Falklands, the German navy started using submarines to attack Allied shipping.

CHANGE OF STRATEGY

Germany's **submarines** were initially intended for use in coastal defence and to sink British warships. The German navy planned to use surface commerce raiders against **Allied merchant shipping**. However, after Germany's decisive defeat at the **Battle of the Falkland Islands** ❮❮ **83** in December 1914, its ability to threaten Allied commerce with surface vessels was curtailed.

NORTH SEA WAR ZONE

While trade to Britain was unimpeded, the Royal Navy maintained a **maritime blockade** of Germany. In November 1914,

U-BOAT LINE-THROWING GUN

the British declared the **North Sea a war zone**, which German ships would enter at their peril. German submarines began **attacks** against British merchant shipping. The first merchant ship destroyed by a German U-boat was the steamship SS *Glitra*, sunk off Norway on 20 October 1914.

The **Sinking** of the *Lusitania*

In February 1915, Germany launched a campaign of submarine attacks against Allied shipping off the British coastline. This led to the notorious sinking of the transatlantic liner *Lusitania* and set the Germans on course for a confrontation with the United States.

Germany began discussing the possibility of a systematic submarine campaign against merchant shipping in the late autumn of 1914. The U-boat fleet numbered only a few dozen boats, but they were proving capable of attacks on merchant ships in the North Sea. Submarine commanders were respecting accepted "prize rules", which meant they had to surface, stop a ship, and allow its crew and passengers to disembark before sinking it. If a more intensive campaign was to be mounted, U-boats would need permission to attack without warning, firing torpedoes while submerged. The risk of outraging neutral opinion in doing this, especially in the USA, was outweighed by the need for a more effective response to Britain's naval blockade.

Easy prey

On 4 February 1915, Germany announced that Allied merchant ships in waters around Britain and Ireland were liable to be sunk and it would be impossible "to avert the danger thereby threatened to crew and passengers".

About 20 U-boats were dispatched to seek suitable targets. With no convoy system in place, isolated merchant ships were easy prey. On 22 April, the German embassy in Washington, D.C. published a warning to passengers intending to cross the Atlantic on the British liner *Lusitania*, reminding them that ships entering the war zone around the British Isles were liable to be destroyed. Nevertheless, on 1 May, the liner left New York for Liverpool with almost 2,000 people on board. In the hold was a small amount of military cargo, chiefly rifle ammunition.

On the afternoon of 7 May, Captain Walther Schwieger, commanding the submarine *U-20*, sighted the *Lusitania* off the south coast of Ireland. The U-boat was too slow to mount a pursuit, especially when it was submerged to attack, but the liner turned into its path. Schwieger struck the *Lusitania* with a single torpedo in the centre of the ship. Desperate attempts to launch the ship's lifeboats were cut short when the liner sank only 18 minutes after being hit.

The death toll of 1,198 comprised 785 passengers and 413 crew. Almost 100 of the victims were children, and 128 were US citizens. Germany tried in

1.9 The average number of merchant ships being sunk by U-boats every day by August 1915.

Final voyage
The Cunard liner *Lusitania* leaves New York on what was to be its last voyage, on 1 May 1915. Launched in 1906, it was awarded the coveted Blue Riband the following year for the fastest crossing of the Atlantic.

by Zeppelins and the first use of poison gas created an image of Germany as a militarist aggressor. Nonetheless, President Wilson's Secretary of State in 1914, William Jennings Bryan, was determined to maintain US neutrality and non-involvement. He was outraged by the British naval blockade of Germany, which interfered with the USA's right of free trade. On the other hand, the British were courteous, listened politely to American concerns, paid compensation for confiscated goods, and did not kill Americans.

Germany had no means of blockading Britain except by using submarines. The U-boat sinking of the liner RMS *Lusitania* in May 1915, with heavy American loss of life, tipped the balance of US public opinion – and Wilson's personal stance – against Germany. The pacifistic Bryan was replaced by Robert Lansing as Secretary of State. Lansing adopted "benevolent neutrality" – still aiming to keep the USA out of the war if possible but backing the Allies.

Financial motives

The USA also had a strong economic interest in the Allied war effort. It had a third of the world's industrial capacity, as well as being a major producer of food and raw materials. The Central Powers and the Allies wanted to draw on these immense resources. German agents worked at purchasing vital goods and routing them through neutral countries to avoid the British naval blockade, but their efforts had limited success.

The British and French were able to place orders and ship goods at will. Initially this was funded by selling off

$2.3 BILLION The sum lent by US banks to the Allies by April 1917.

$27 MILLION The sum lent by US banks to Germany by the same date.

British assets in the USA, but from 1915 American banks were authorized to supply massive loans to finance trade with the Allies – money they knew they would never see again if the Allies lost the war.

Business boomed, with US exports rising to double their pre-war level by the end of 1915 and share prices on Wall Street going up by 80 per cent.

German agents in the USA mounted a campaign of sabotage, such as setting fire to ships and warehouses, to inhibit the supply of war material to the Allies. The British intelligence services made sure the US authorities were kept informed of these illegal activities. Franz von Papen, the military attaché at the German embassy in Washington, was expelled in December 1915 for promoting sabotage attacks.

To the rescue
American volunteers drove ambulances from the start of the war, helping British, Belgian, and French troops. This painting by Victor White shows the American Field Service aiding a wounded soldier at Cappy-sur-Somme.

Meanwhile, many individual American volunteers had been actively involved in the European war from its earliest stages. In 1914, the expatriate colony of Americans resident in Paris embraced the French cause. They set up the American Field Service, which became a valued source of medical support for Allied forces in the field. Those Americans with a taste for combat joined the French Foreign Legion, including the Harvard-educated poet Alan Seeger, who wrote one of the war's most famous poems, *I Have a Rendezvous with Death*, before being killed on the Western Front. American volunteers flew as pilots in French air units, forming the Lafayette Escadrille (Squadron) that fought in the skies over Verdun in 1916.

Tension builds

In 1915, pro- and anti-war argument raged. The Preparedness Movement, led by former US Chief of the General Staff General Leonard Wood and former President Teddy Roosevelt, argued that the USA needed to make ready for war by introducing universal military service. It argued that

In the US presidential elections of 1916, Wilson was re-elected as "the man who kept us out of the war". But this stance didn't last.

THE USA DECLARES WAR
Wilson's preferred role was as a mediator. He sent his envoy, "Colonel" Edward House, to European capitals to **seek a peace settlement**, but in vain. Meanwhile, evidence of hostile German intent mounted, including the **Zimmermann Telegram 212–13 »** of January 1917 encouraging Mexico to attack the USA. Congress declared war in April 1917 after Germany adopted **unrestricted submarine warfare**, which affected US shipping.

WAKE UP, AMERICA!
CIVILIZATION CALLS EVERY MAN WOMAN AND CHILD
MAYOR'S COMMITTEE 50 EAST 42nd ST

WARTIME PROPAGANDA POSTER

conscription would unite the nation's ethnically fragmented population. This stance was opposed by anti-war groups, notably socialists, women's groups, and church organizations.

The consequence of contradictory pressures was a compromise: the National Defense Act of December 1915. The army was to double in size, but there would be no conscription, and the National Guard was to be enlarged. The outcome was seen as a defeat for the Preparedness Movement and a victory for those who wanted to keep the USA out of the war.

FIGHTER PILOT (1894–1961)

EUGENE BULLARD

The world's first black fighter pilot, Eugene Bullard was born in Columbus, Georgia. He left the USA as a teenager and emigrated first to Britain and then to France. In 1914, he joined the French Foreign Legion and saw action as an infantryman on the Western Front, for which he was awarded the Croix de Guerre. In 1917, Bullard learned to fly and joined the Lafayette Escadrille Squadron, American volunteers serving in the French air service. He flew on combat missions between August and November 1917. His fellow American pilots joined the US Army after the USA entered the war, but Bullard was rejected on account of his colour.

" There is such a thing as a **nation** being **so right** it does not need to **convince others** by **force** that it is **right.**"

WOODROW WILSON, US PRESIDENT, SPEECH IN PHILADELPHIA, 10 MAY 1915

The Zeppelin Raids

In 1915, Germany mounted bombing raids using Zeppelin and Schütte-Lanz airships against Paris, London, and other cities. Although limited in effect, the night-time attacks of these giant aircraft made an indelible impression on the people who witnessed them.

Airship firebomb
This incendiary bomb was dropped by Zeppelin *LZ38* in the first airship raid on London on 31 May 1915. Too small to cause much damage, the bomb was released by hand out of the airship's gondola.

« BEFORE

Count Ferdinand von Zeppelin, a former German cavalry officer, developed his first airship, *LZ1*, in 1900. "Zeppelin" became a generic term for all lighter-than-air craft.

MILITARY POTENTIAL
The possibility of **airships attacking cities with bombs** was widely imagined before World War I – appearing, for example, in H.G. Wells's 1908 fantasy novel *The War in the Air* – and was discussed by senior German commanders.

Germany had acquired a dozen metal-framed **Zeppelin** and wooden-framed **Schütte-Lanz** rigid airships by the outbreak of the war. Other combatants used a range of rigid airships and non-rigid airships known as "blimps", but Germany was well ahead of them in this field.

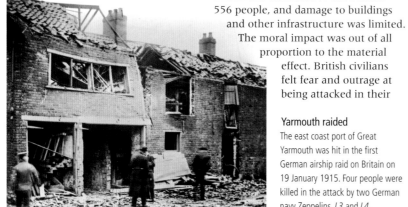

Yarmouth raided
The east coast port of Great Yarmouth was hit in the first German airship raid on Britain on 19 January 1915. Four people were killed in the attack by two German navy Zeppelins, *L3* and *L4*.

Deployed by the German army and navy from the start of the war, airships proved effective in a naval reconnaissance role, and the idea of also using them to bomb targets in Britain fascinated German military commanders. Kaiser Wilhelm had qualms about authorizing bombing raids on Britain, but was led by stages to lift restrictions on airship operations.

Mounting a bombing campaign was, however, no easy matter. The airships' huge bulk and slow speed – the largest were 200 m (650 ft) long and travelled at 80–95 kph (50–60 mph) – made them vulnerable to being shot down. To prevent this, attacks were made at night, but this posed a challenge to navigators, especially after Britain and France introduced blackouts. In addition, airships required favourable weather. Many missions were aborted because of poor weather or operating problems such as engine failure.

Bombing Britain

The campaign against Britain began with attacks on England's east coast towns from January 1915. London was bombed for the first time on 31 May and raids later spread to the Midlands and northeast England.

Captain Peter Strasser, head of the German navy's airship fleet, imagined Britain being overcome by "extensive destruction of cities, factory complexes, dockyards…". But Germany never had many airships – 16 took part in the largest raid of the war – and their bombload was modest. In total, 51 German airship raids on Britain are estimated to have killed 556 people, and damage to buildings and other infrastructure was limited. The moral impact was out of all proportion to the material effect. British civilians felt fear and outrage at being attacked in their homes. Politicians responded to public opinion by switching resources from the Western Front to home defence. Fighter aircraft were brought back from the front to intercept the raiders, and London was ringed with searchlights and anti-aircraft guns in an effort to repel the airships.

Air attacks were mounted, with some success, against Zeppelin sheds in Belgium and Germany. Through 1916, the airships faced more losses. In February, two were shot down by anti-aircraft fire over the French city of Nancy. In June, an airship returning from an abortive raid on Britain was destroyed over Belgium when a British pilot dropped bombs on its gas bag.

> **71** The number of people killed in the war's deadliest airship raid on London, on 31 October 1915. One bomb struck London's Lyceum theatre, killing or injuring 37 people.

Deflated and defeated

The development of incendiary rounds made it easier for aeroplanes to attack airships. On the night of 2 September, Lieutenant William Leefe Robinson, flying a BE2c biplane, shot down airship *SL11* within sight of London. By the year's end, five more airships had been shot down over Britain by ground fire or pursuit aircraft.

These were unsustainable losses for Germany. Refusing to abandon the campaign, the German navy lightened its airships to make them "height-climbers", operating at altitudes that aeroplanes could not reach. This made them invulnerable to enemy action but problematic for their crews, who were

Zeppelin look-out
The captain (left) looks out of the side of a gondola under the airship's gas bag, while a coxswain steers the craft. Operating an airship was a complex business, typically requiring at least 16 crew.

flying at over 4,900 m (16,000 ft) in unheated, unpressurized craft. Five "height-climbers" were lost on a single mission against Britain in October 1917. The airship bombing campaign had in effect been defeated.

AFTER »

Aeroplanes began to replace airships in bombing campaigns against Britain, though airships were still sometimes used to transport supplies.

REPLACED BY PLANES
Germany revitalized its bombing campaign against Britain and France in summer 1917 by using **Gotha aeroplanes** instead of airships **232–33 »**, inflicting more damage at lower cost. Occasional **airship raids on Britain** continued until August 1918, when German naval airship chief **Peter Strasser** was **killed** in an attack across the North Sea.

BANNED BY VERSAILLES
Germany was banned from possessing military airships after the war under the terms of the **Treaty of Versailles 338–39 »**, but in the 1920s it resumed its lead in commercial lighter-than-air flights. By World War II, all countries had abandoned airships as impractical.

Zeppelin downed by an aircraft
This painting, *Lieutenant Warneford's Great Exploit* by F. Gordon, depicts the first German airship to be destroyed by an Allied aircraft. Warneford, of the Royal Navy Air Service and flying a Morane-Saulnier monoplane, bombed the airship over Belgium.

Campaigns on the Eastern Front

In 1915, the overstretched Russian armies fought a series of disastrous battles, from the Baltic to the Carpathians. By contrast, the Austro-German Gorlice-Tarnow offensive was one of the most successful campaigns of the whole war.

In early 1915, the Russians and the Central Powers had more or less symmetrical plans for offensives. Russia aimed to strike against East Prussia in the north and through the Carpathian Mountains into Hungary in the south. Field Marshal Hindenburg and General Ludendorff planned a German offensive at the Masurian Lakes in East Prussia, to coincide with an Austro-Hungarian offensive in the Carpathians.

The Central Powers struck first. At the Second Battle of the Masurian Lakes, launched in a snowstorm on 7 February, Hindenburg and Ludendorff attempted to trap the Russian Tenth Army with a vast pincer movement. One Russian corps, finding itself encircled, surrendered en masse in the Augustow Forest, but the rest of the Tenth Army escaped, and the front restabilized.

On the Carpathian front, in March, Austria-Hungary was rocked by the fall of the fortress of Przemysl and its 120,000-strong garrison after a Russian siege lasting 133 days. Neither side made much progress in fighting in the

The Eastern Front in 1915

Between the Gorlice-Tarnow offensive on 2 May and the end of September 1915, the Russians suffered a series of severe reverses, obliging them to abandon Poland and Lithuania to German and Austro-Hungarian forces.

high Carpathian passes. Considering that Russian soldiers had been short of every form of equipment, from rifles, bullets, and shells to boots and overcoats, they had put up a creditable performance on both fronts.

The Gorlice-Tarnow offensive

Animosity between German Chief of the General Staff Erich von Falkenhayn and the Hindenburg–Ludendorff partnership shaped the next moves. Rejecting Hindenburg's and Ludendorff's pleas for an offensive in

BEFORE

The fighting on the Eastern Front in 1914 had produced no decisive result. The Russians suffered defeats against the Germans but won victories over Austria-Hungary.

FOCUS ON THE EAST

Field Marshal Paul von Hindenburg and his Chief of Staff Erich Ludendorff, in East Prussia, argued for maximum resources to **knock Russia out of the war**. German Chief of the General Staff Erich von Falkenhayn did not believe Russia could be easily defeated, but agreed to stand on the **defensive** on the **Western Front** and **transfer troops** to **the East**.

RUSSIAN GAINS AND LOSSES

By the start of 1915, Russia had pushed the Austro-Hungarians back to the Carpathian Mountains and was **besieging** the Galician fortress of **Przemysl ‹‹ 71**. The Russians had **defeated Turkish forces** at **Sarikamish ‹‹ 75** on the Caucasus front. They had, however, been forced to **pull back** behind Lodz in Russian Poland **‹‹ 70–71**.

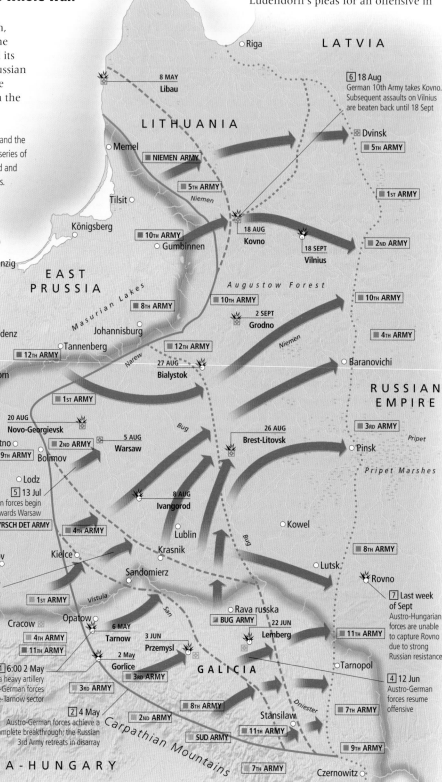

KEY

⊠ Major fort/fortified town
■ Austro-Hungarian army
■ German army
■ Russian army
➤ Austro-German movements
‿ Russian positions 1 May
⌐ Russian positions 1 Jun
⌐ Russian positions 13 Jul
⌐ Russian positions 15 Aug
⌐ Russian positions 30 Sept
24 SEPT Date of capture by Austro-Germans
❀ Major battle

8 MAY Libau

6 18 Aug German 10th Army takes Kovno. Subsequent assaults on Vilnius are beaten back until 18 Sept

○ Riga   LATVIA

LITHUANIA

○ Memel   ■ NIEMEN ARMY

☒ Dvinsk   ■ 5TH ARMY

○ Tilsit   Niemen   ■ 5TH ARMY   ■ 1ST ARMY

Königsberg   ■ 10TH ARMY   18 AUG Kovno   18 SEPT Vilnius   ■ 2ND ARMY

☒ Danzig   EAST PRUSSIA   Augustow Forest

■ 10TH ARMY   2 SEPT Grodno   ■ 10TH ARMY

■ 8TH ARMY   Johannisburg   Niemen   ■ 4TH ARMY

☒ Graudenz   Tannenberg   Masurian Lakes   ■ 12TH ARMY   ○ Baranovichi

Vistula   ■ 12TH ARMY   Narew   27 AUG Bialystok   RUSSIAN EMPIRE

☒ Thorn   ■ 1ST ARMY   Bug   26 AUG Brest-Litovsk   ■ 3RD ARMY   Pripet

20 AUG Novo-Georgievsk   ○ Pinsk   Pripet Marshes

Kutno ○   ■ 2ND ARMY   5 AUG Warsaw   8 AUG Ivangorod

■ 9TH ARMY   Bolimov

○ Lodz   5 13 Jul Austro-German forces begin advance towards Warsaw   ○ Kowel   ■ 8TH ARMY

■ WOYRSCH DET ARMY   ■ 4TH ARMY   Lublin   Bug   ○ Lutsk

Chenstokhov   Kielce ○   Krasnik   ❀ Rovno

Sandomierz   7 Last week of Sept Austro-Hungarian forces are unable to capture Rovno due to strong Russian resistance

3 15 May Despite Russian resistance, the retreat continues. By 1 Jun Austrians and Germans are established east of the San   ■ 1ST ARMY   Vistula   ○ Rava russka

Cracow ☒   Opatow ○   San   ■ BUG ARMY   22 JUN Lemberg   ■ 11TH ARMY   ○ Tarnopol

Chenstokhov   ■ 4TH ARMY   6 MAY Tarnow   3 JUN   ○ Tarnopol

■ 11TH ARMY   2 May Przemysl

1 6:00 2 May Following a heavy artillery bombardment, Austro-German forces attack in the Gorlice-Tarnow sector   Gorlice   ■ 3RD ARMY   GALICIA   Dniester   ■ 7TH ARMY

2 4 May Austro-German forces achieve a complete breakthrough; the Russian 3rd Army retreats in disarray   ■ 2ND ARMY   Carpathian Mountains   Stanislaw

■ 8TH ARMY   ■ SUD ARMY   ■ 11TH ARMY   ■ 9TH ARMY

AUSTRIA-HUNGARY   ■ 7TH ARMY   Czernowitz ○

4 12 Jun Austro-German forces resume offensive

0 ――― 100 km
0 ――― 100 miles

1 LEWIS GUN
(BRITISH)

2 LEWIS GUN DRUM
MAGAZINE (BRITISH)

4 SCHWARZLOSE M7/12
(AUSTRO-HUNGARIAN)

5 SCHWARZLOSE M7/12
AMMUNITION
(AUSTRO-HUNGARIAN)

6 VICKERS GUN (BRITISH)

8 MG 08/15 (GERMAN)

9 BROWNING M1918
AUTOMATIC RIFLE (US)

11 CHAUCHAT M1915 (FRENCH)

12 BROWNING
M1917 (US)

BEFORE

Although World War I started with Austria-Hungary's declaration of war against Serbia, by 1915 the Serbian front had become a backwater.

THE SERBIAN FRONT

After Serbia's successful resistance against **invasion by Austro-Hungarian forces ≪ 68–69** in the first months of the war, fighting subsided. Austria-Hungary did **not** have the resources to defeat Serbia while also fighting Russia and, from May 1915, Italy.

BULGARIA'S STANCE

Serbia's neutral neighbour **Bulgaria** had lost territory to Serbia, Greece, Turkey, and Romania in the **Second Balkan War** of 1913. It was courted both by the Allies and the Central Powers. Allied failure against **Turkey at Gallipoli ≪ 110–13** and the **Russian retreat from Poland ≪ 52–3** influenced Bulgaria's leaders to form an alliance with the **Central Powers**.

Serbia Crushed

The defeat of Serbia in the final months of 1915 completed a year of almost unrelieved military failure for the Allies. About a quarter of the Serbian population is thought to have died in the course of the war, mostly from hardship and disease.

In September 1915, negotiations between the Central Powers and Bulgaria were brought to a successful conclusion. In return for a promise of substantial territorial gains, the Bulgarians signed the Pless Convention on 6 September, agreeing to join in an invasion of Serbia within 35 days. Unimpressed by the performance of Austro-Hungarian forces, they stipulated that the invasion must include German troops and be under German command.

This was not to the liking of Austro-Hungarian Chief of Staff General Conrad von Hötzendorf, who was increasingly worried by German dominance, but it suited German Chief of the General Staff Erich von Falkenhayn. He wanted a swift defeat of Serbia that would bind Bulgaria into an alliance with the Central Powers and open up a direct line of communication between Germany and Turkey.

Invasion of Serbia

German and Austro-Hungarian forces under the command of General August von Mackensen launched the offensive on 6 October. Their main thrust was directed southwards

King Peter I of Serbia
Born in 1844, King Peter passed executive power to his son, Crown Prince Alexander, shortly before the start of the war. The king remained a focus for Serbian loyalty and stayed with the army through the retreat of 1915.

across the Danube. The river was in spate but the crossing was achieved with the support of heavy artillery and the guns of Austro-Hungarian gunboats. The Serbian forces were in poor shape. As well as being outnumbered and short of weapons and munitions, they had been decimated by a typhus epidemic. The capital, Belgrade, had already fallen by the time the Bulgarian army attacked across Serbia's eastern border on 11 October. Under its experienced

Serbia attacked
An illustration in the French magazine *Le Petit Journal* shows Serbia defending itself against Austria-Hungary's Emperor Franz Joseph and Kaiser Wilhelm II of Germany while being stabbed in the back by Bulgaria.

HONGRIE

DANUBE BELGRADE

SERBIE

NISCH

ROU

BULGARIE

SOFIA

Serbian Campaign, 1915

Attacked by Germany and Austria-Hungary from the north and Bulgaria from the east, the defeated Serbian forces withdrew into Albania. Allied troops who had landed at Salonika in Greece were unable to intervene.

KEY

- ■ Austro-Hungarian army
- ■ Bulgarian army
- ■ German army
- ■ Serbian army
- ⌐ Serbian position 6 Oct
- ➡ Austro-German offensives 6 Oct–23 Nov
- ➡ Bulgarian offensives 6 Oct–23 Nov
- ▮▮ Serbian retreat from 25 Nov
- ➡ Anglo-French landings
- ➡ French relief force
- ◉ Town captured by Central Powers, with date
- ---- Major railway

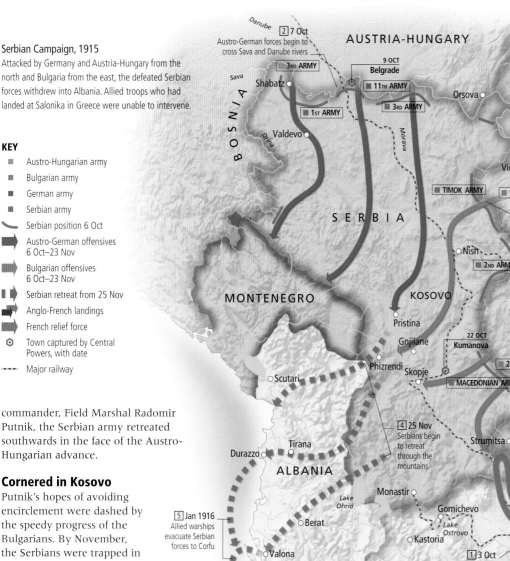

AFTER

There were outbreaks of revolt in Serbia against harsh rule by Austro-Hungarian and Bulgarian occupation forces, but the Balkan front remained largely inactive until 1918.

PARTIAL WITHDRAWAL

In autumn 1916, Allied forces from Salonika, including Serbian troops, advanced across the border from Greece and **forced the Bulgarians to withdraw** from part of southern Serbia. No further progress was made in 1917, as the Allies focused on persuading Greece to join the war, a goal achieved in June 1917. **Serbia was liberated** by an Allied offensive launched in September 1918. The **Corfu Declaration** of July 1917 foreshadowed the creation of the Serbian-led postwar state of Yugoslavia.

> "We **slowly creep** toward the sheer cliffs… **step by step** on the compacted **snow.**"

JOSIP JERAS, SERBIAN REFUGEE, DIARY ENTRY, DECEMBER 1915

---

commander, Field Marshal Radomir Putnik, the Serbian army retreated southwards in the face of the Austro-Hungarian advance.

Cornered in Kosovo

Putnik's hopes of avoiding encirclement were dashed by the speedy progress of the Bulgarians. By November, the Serbians were trapped in Kosovo, facing a choice between a fight to the death or a retreat across the mountains.

Serbia might have hoped for some assistance from the Allies, but none was forthcoming. Only three days before the launch of the Austro-German invasion, advanced parties of an Anglo-French force, known in France as the Army of the Orient, had landed at Salonika in neutral Greece, from where they were to proceed by rail to Serbia. But their arrival provoked a political crisis in Greece. The prime minister, Eleftherios Venizelos, who had invited the Allied troops, was dismissed by the country's pro-German King Constantine. The Allies suddenly found themselves unwelcome.

Under the command of General Maurice Sarrail, some 45,000 French troops advanced across Macedonia into southern Serbia. After brief clashes with the Bulgarians they withdrew again to Salonika.

Flight through the mountains

In the last week of November, Putnik ordered a general retreat across the mountains to the Adriatic. Some

Soldier's pipe

The underused Allied troops at Salonika had plenty of time on their hands. This pipe was carved by a British private in the Durham Light Infantry.

200,000 soldiers and civilians set off on this trek, including the Serbian government and the 71-year-old King Peter, carried in a sedan chair. The roads were deep in snow and temperatures were far below freezing. Thousands died of exposure. Although bad weather dissuaded enemy forces from mounting a pursuit, Albanian warlords attacked the Serbians passing through their territory.

The survivors reached the Adriatic coast after about three weeks. From there they were evacuated by Allied transport ships, chiefly to the Greek island of Corfu. But the island had no

adequate food or shelter for a sudden influx of 140,000 military and civilian refugees.

The Germans made no attempt to continue the Serbian Campaign towards Salonika, where the Army of the Orient was in a potentially perilous position. Falkenhayn decided to leave the Balkan front dormant while he turned his attention to an offensive against the French at Verdun.

Bulgaria was satisfied with its victory over the Serbs. Austria-Hungary, however, was not – Conrad disliked the fact that it had been

Serbians flee

The winter retreat of the Serbian army through the mountains into Albania was a nightmare of hardship. At least 50,000 Serbian soldiers and civilians died on the journey to the Adriatic coast.

achieved under German command. Relations between Austro-Hungarian and German leaders deteriorated and cooperation declined. Meanwhile, Corfu became the seat of a Serbian government-in-exile, complete with parliament. Much of the Serbian army joined the Allied forces in Salonika, waiting for the chance to wage a war of national liberation.

The Artois-Loos Offensive

BEFORE

At a conference held at Chantilly on 7 July 1915, the Allied countries agreed that they must take action together to put maximum pressure on the Central Powers.

OPPORTUNITY FOR THE ALLIES

With **Russia** suffering **severe setbacks in Poland ❮❮ 70–71**, and **Italy** engaged in **offensives on the Isonzo ❮❮ 106–07**, France and Britain realized they needed to mount a major **offensive** on the **Western Front**. However, they knew that **attacking the German trenches** was unlikely to achieve a breakthrough, as failures earlier in the year, both in **Artois and Champagne ❮❮ 142–43**, had confirmed. A window of opportunity arose when large numbers of German soldiers were **transferred to the east** for the **onslaught against Russia**, leaving their troops on the Western Front **heavily outnumbered** by the Allies.

In September 1915, the Allied offensives in Champagne and Artois resulted in over 300,000 Allied casualties, including large numbers of British volunteers. The failure of Britain's contribution to the offensives led to the sacking of its commander-in-chief.

French commander-in-chief General Joseph Joffre's long-held plan for cracking the German trench system was to mount major offensives in Artois and Champagne, on the northern and southern flanks of the salient occupied by the German army in France. Joffre and British commander-in-chief Field Marshal Sir John French had a clear idea how the campaign might be won. Heavy artillery bombardment would devastate German trenches, allowing infantry to occupy the enemy front line, after which reserves would be brought through to continue the offensive in depth.

Whether the commanders really expected to succeed is doubtful. Apart from the need to support Allies on other fronts, Joffre justified the offensives as essential to maintain morale. Otherwise, he said, "our troops will little by little lose their physical and moral qualities". British Minister for War Lord Kitchener told his commander-in-chief Sir John French, "We must do our utmost to help the French, even though by so doing, we suffer very heavy losses indeed."

The plan unfolds

The British, reinforced by the first volunteer troops of Kitchener's New Armies, held most of the Artois front with a single French army on their right. French forces were concentrated on the Champagne front, where they outnumbered the German defenders by three to one. Joffre assembled over 2,000 artillery pieces for the

Hard hat
Introduced in autumn 1915, the French Adrian helmet was the first steel helmet issued to troops of any country in World War I. Its light steel offered protection against shrapnel.

French troops at Artois
Zouaves (French light infantry) from North Africa in the Artois sector of the front. By this stage, they had abandoned their traditional uniforms, but had not yet been issued with steel helmets.

Meeting the troops

Pétain visits a group of French Territorials at soup time. He was unusual among World War I generals for his habit of talking with the ordinary troops on the ground.

Maintaining supplies was recognized as vital by Pétain, and he tackled the problem energetically. Sensing that morale would collapse if men were exposed for too long to the horrors of the artillery-saturated battlefield, he instituted an eight-day rotation of units at the front. His orders of the day were delivered plainly, without bombast. He spoke to the soldiers, handed out medals, and visited the wounded – a kind of direct contact scrupulously avoided by most of the other World War I generals.

Sidelined by Joffre

A national hero after the defence of Verdun, Pétain was less admired in France's ruling circles, where his approach was perceived as negative. To Joffre, his readiness to cede

of firmness and understanding in this, punishing ringleaders but making concessions on matters such as leave and food, which were very important to the troops. Above all, he let the men know there would be no more wastage of lives in futile, overly ambitious offensives. The French army was placed on a predominantly passive footing, waiting, Pétain said, for "the tanks and the Americans".

Morale and discipline were duly restored, as the French performance in the great battles of 1918 would show. Once again, however, Pétain was not judged to be the man for the top job.

In spring 1918, it was General Ferdinand Foch, the fiercest advocate of offensive warfare, who was made Allied Supreme Commander. Pétain was considered too defeatist and anti-British for the job, although he was still an effective commander-in-chief of the French forces.

After World War I

In the decades after the war, Pétain was actively engaged in shaping French military policy. Faced with spending cuts that weakened the French army, he embraced a defensive strategy and construction of the Maginot Line fortifications along the border with Germany.

At some point, his native pessimism and bitter experience of war tipped over into defeatism. Brought into government in World War II to stiffen resolve, he advocated an armistice in June 1940 during the German invasion of France. As head of the collaborationist Vichy regime, he saw himself as restoring order to France, purging it of the vices that had brought about its downfall. Instead, he became an accomplice in crimes against Jews and resistance fighters.

In 1945, aged 89, Pétain was convicted of treason and sentenced to life imprisonment by a French court. He died in prison six years later.

> ## "Upon the day when France had to **choose** between **ruin** and **reason,** Pétain was promoted."
>
> CHARLES DE GAULLE, ON PÉTAIN BECOMING COMMANDER-IN-CHIEF IN MAY 1917

ground and his reluctance to order counterattacks at Verdun were unacceptable. Unable to sack a man who had become the embodiment of French resistance, in April 1916 Joffre promoted him to command the Army Group controlling the Verdun sector, formally increasing his authority but in practice removing him from front-line responsibility.

Pétain suffered another rebuff when the optimistic General Robert Nivelle was promoted over his head to succeed Joffre as commander-in-chief in December. However, in May 1917, Pétain was appointed to replace Nivelle in order to deal with widespread mutinies following the failure of the Nivelle Offensive at Chemin des Dames. Pétain showed a mixture

Liberation of Alsace

Pétain visits an area of Alsace retaken from the Germans in October 1917. He became a focus for conservative patriotism in the postwar years, trusted by many because of his reputation as a humane general who cared about his men.

TIMELINE

- **1856** Born at Cauchy-à-la-Tour in the Pas de Calais region, northern France.
- **1876** Joins the army, later entering the Saint-Cyr Military Academy.
- **1911** Promoted to colonel. Commands the 33rd infantry regiment.
- **August–October 1914** Earns rapid promotion in the first phase of World War I, commanding a division at the First Battle of the Marne. He is made a corps commander in October.
- **May 1915** Leads his corps in the spring offensive in Artois, winning promotion to command of the Second Army in June.
- **September–October 1915** Leads the Second Army in the failed Champagne offensive.
- **February–March 1916** Mounts a defence of Verdun and prevents a German breakthrough.
- **April 1916** Relieved of control of Verdun by promotion to command of Army Group Centre.
- **May 1917** Appointed commander-in-chief as mutinies sweep the French army in the wake of the Nivelle Offensive. Restores order.
- **March 1918** In the German Spring Offensive, Pétain is subordinated to Ferdinand Foch.
- **November 1918** Given the honorary rank of Marshal of France.
- **February 1922** Appointed Inspector General of the Army, a post he holds until 1931.
- **September 1925** Commands the French forces sent to suppress the Riff Rebellion in Morocco.
- **February–November 1934** During a political crisis in France, accepts a government post as Minister of War.

COMPAGNONS DE FRANCE

FRENCH POSTER DURING THE VICHY REGIME

- **June 1940** Appointed prime minister. With France facing defeat by Germany, he agrees an armistice.
- **July 1940** Becomes head of state of the French government at Vichy.
- **August 1945** After the liberation of France, he is tried and sentenced to death for treason, later commuted to life imprisonment.
- **1951** Dies in prison on the Ile d'Yeu.

BEFORE

Initial German success at Verdun was halted when French commander Philippe Pétain took up the reins.

FRENCH AND GERMAN POSITIONS
The **German offensive at Verdun** **«** **154–55** in February 1916 was fought to a standstill in early March. **Pétain** depended on artillery fire to hold back the German infantry. The most effective gun positions were on the west bank of the Meuse and they were ready

259 The number of French infantry regiments (out of a total of 330) that fought at some point at Verdun, because of Pétain's system of troop rotation.

to repel German troops attempting to advance on the east bank. On 6 March, the **Germans launched a second offensive**, this time on the west bank.

SACRED CAUSE
The patriotic press in France turned the battle for Verdun into a sacred cause. The narrow French supply route to the battlefield, dubbed **La Voie Sacrée** (Sacred Way) by the press, carried 50,000 tonnes of ammunition and 90,000 men to the front every week.

> "I thought: if you **haven't seen Verdun** you **haven't seen anything** of **war.**"
>
> PRIVATE J. AYOUN, FRENCH SOLDIER, 1916

TECHNOLOGY

FLAMETHROWERS

The German army adopted flamethrowers in 1911. They ranged from large static devices to portable backpacks. When operated, pressurized gas forced a stream of ignited oil out of a tube. First used effectively by the Germans against the British at Hooge, Flanders, in July 1915, they became standard stormtrooper equipment. Although they had some drawbacks, including unwieldiness and a short range, they had impressive psychological effect and were useful in clearing trenches. The British, French, and Italians had their own versions.

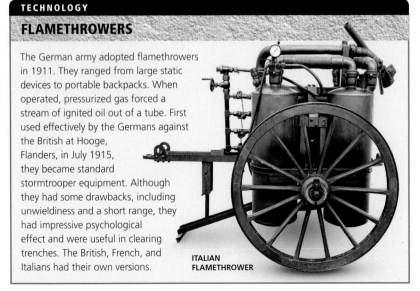

ITALIAN FLAMETHROWER

The French Fight Back at Verdun

From spring through to winter 1916, the German and French armies remained locked in combat at Verdun, expending hundreds of thousands of lives in a sustained battle. In the end, France could claim a defensive victory, but a huge price had been paid.

Battles on the Western Front defied the generals' efforts to impose a shape and sense of purpose on the fighting. German Chief of the General Staff Erich von Falkenhayn's decision to use a reserve corps to launch an offensive on the west bank of the Meuse in early March was logical: French guns were savaging his troops on the east bank.

But the new offensive immediately turned into a stalemated struggle for control of a ridge stretching between two key French positions, Le Mort Homme and Côte 304. Unable to take the crest of the ridge, the attempted German advance bogged down. Falkenhayn tried again on 9 April, launching simultaneous attacks both east and west of the river using massive artillery support. The German guns exhausted 17 trainloads of shells.

This onslaught sorely tried French morale, prompting General Pétain to end his order that day with the phrase *"On les aura!"* – "We shall have them!". Whether encouraged or not by this optimism, the French held firm.

Battle of the generals

In May, the Germans took Côte 304 and Le Mort Homme after an artillery bombardment that in places reduced the height of the ridge by 7 m (23 ft).

View of the battlefield
German soldiers use periscopes at an observation post on Côte 304, a ridge on the west bank of the Meuse wrested from the French in April–May 1916.

Yet this only brought them up against the next French defensive line at the Bois Bourrus. Falkenhayn was urged by Crown Prince Wilhelm, commander of the German Fifth Army at Verdun, to call off the battle, but the German Chief of Staff had become too closely identified with Verdun to admit it had been a failure. Meanwhile, on the French side, Pétain's cautious posture was frustrating commander-in-chief General Joseph Joffre.

The saving of Verdun in February 1916 had made Pétain a national hero, but Joffre removed him from control on the battlefield by promoting him to the command of the Army Group overseeing Verdun. On 19 April, General Robert Nivelle, who shared Joffre's belief in attack, took over front-line responsibility, with General Charles Mangin in command of a division. The French infantry was soon being thrown forwards in the wasteful manner Pétain had avoided.

The fight for the forts

On 22 May, Mangin led a brave attempt to retake Fort Douaumont. Its failure, at the cost of many lives,

had a seriously detrimental effect on French morale, and the troops nicknamed Mangin "the Butcher".

Ten days later, the Germans mounted a full-scale assault on Fort Vaux. Its heroic defence by Major Sylvain-Eugène Raynal and his small garrison was one of the minor epics of the war. German infantry broke into the building on 1 June, but the French held out in a maze of tunnels and corridors, communicating with the outside world by pigeon. They resisted poison gas and flamethrowers, but eventually succumbed to thirst, surrendering on 7 June with their water supply exhausted.

Battle raged in the air as well as on the ground. It was over Verdun that combat between fighter aircraft was invented, with ace pilots such as the Germans Max Immelmann and Oswald Boelcke and the French elite of the *Cigognes* (Storks) squadron contesting command of the air.

Turning point

On the whole, the aerial battle was won by the French, but on the ground the Germans held the upper hand into early July. On 23 June, they captured Fleury, within 5 km (3 miles) of Verdun, provoking Nivelle to end his order of the day with the phrase: *"Ils ne passeront pas!"* ("They shall not

162,440 The estimated number of French soldiers killed at Verdun.

143,000 The estimated number of German dead at Verdun.

pass!"). On 11 July, using diphosgene gas for the first time, the Germans attempted to storm Fort Souville. This was a desperate moment for the French troops who successfully repulsed the attack. By then, however, the tide had already turned in favour of the French, because of events elsewhere.

Falkenhayn had been forced to transfer troops to the Eastern Front in response to the crisis caused by the Russian Brusilov offensive in June. The launch of the British-led Somme

On les aura !

2ᴱ EMPRUNT
DE
LA DÉFENSE NATIONALE

Souscrivez

DEVAMBEZ IMP PARIS

offensive on 1 July made continuing the concentration of German forces at Verdun impossible. Falkenhayn's great offensive had failed and he paid the price, losing his job as Chief of the General Staff on 27 August.

French success
On the French side, Nivelle was now the rising star. With Mangin, he retook Fort Douaumont on 24 October in a lightning attack that combined artillery and infantry. Fort Vaux was recaptured nine days later. By the time the battle ended in December, the French had returned roughly to their position before it began. For this, some 300,000 French and German soldiers had died.

Boosting French morale
This war bond poster designed by French illustrator Jules-Abel Faivre combines a classic image of the French infantryman with General Pétain's famous morale-boosting order of the day for 10 April 1916: *"On les aura!"* ("We shall have them!").

 AFTER

The enormous number of French and German casualties at Verdun strained morale and resources on both sides.

CHANGES AT THE TOP
His reputation sky-high after his successes in the later stages of the battle, **Nivelle replaced Joffre** as French commander-in-chief in December 1916. The over-ambitious offensive he launched the following spring led to **widespread mutinies in the French army 224–25 »**. The Germans did not launch another Western Front offensive until March 1918. **Verdun** was remembered by the **French** as **their greatest sacrifice** of the war. Remains of French and German soldiers fill the **Douaumont Ossuary**, a memorial completed on the Verdun battlefield in 1932.

DOUAUMONT OSSUARY

" Certainly, **humanity has gone mad!** It must be mad to do what it's doing. **Such slaughter!** Such scenes of **horror and carnage!**"

LIEUTENANT ALFRED JOUBAIRE, DIARY ENTRY AT VERDUN, 22 MAY 1916

Fort Douaumont today
One in a ring of fortresses around Verdun, Fort Douaumont was much fought over during the 1916 Battle of Verdun. Captured by the Germans in February, it was retaken by the French in October.

BEFORE

The outbreak of World War I occurred at a critical moment in Irish history, as Britain prepared to grant the country Home Rule.

RELIGIOUS DIVIDE
In 1914, the British parliament had passed a bill giving Ireland an **elected assembly with limited powers**. Welcomed by most Irish Catholics, it was opposed by Ulster Protestants, who armed a militia, the **Ulster Volunteer Force** (UVF), to resist it. The Catholics responded by forming the **Irish Volunteers**. When Britain entered World War I, a political truce was agreed with Ireland. **Home Rule** was enacted but deferred until the end of the war. The **UVF became the 36th (Ulster) Division** of the British Army. Many **Irish Catholics also joined the British Army**, with most forming part of the 16th (Irish) Division **《 33**.

IRISH NATIONALIST (1868-1916)

JAMES CONNOLLY

Born and raised in Edinburgh by Irish Catholic parents, James Connolly moved to Ireland as young married man, taking up the position of secretary for the Dublin Socialist Club in 1896. After a spell in the USA from 1903–06, he returned to Dublin, setting up the Citizen Army to protect trade unionists in 1913. He joined with the Irish nationalists in January 1916 and played a leading role in the Easter Rising. Gravely wounded in the fighting, he was condemned to death by a British military tribunal. On 12 May, he was taken from hospital in a military ambulance to the execution yard in Dublin's Kilmainham Jail. Unable to stand, he was tied to a chair so that he could be shot.

The Easter Rising

An armed rebellion against British rule in Ireland, the Easter Rising attracted little public support and was swiftly suppressed. The execution of the rebel leaders, however, outraged Irish Catholics and strengthened the Republican cause.

Rebels' gun
In 1914, before the outbreak of war, Germany had supplied the Catholic Irish Volunteers with Model 1871 Mauser rifles. Many of these were used by Irish rebels against British soldiers during the Easter Rising.

World War I divided opinion in Catholic Ireland. A majority of people supported John Redmond, the leader of the Irish Party in the Westminster parliament, who called for the Irish to back the British war effort in return for Home Rule, which granted limited independence. A minority rejected Redmond's stance, seeing the war as an opportunity to shake off British rule completely.

The Irish Volunteer militia reflected this split, with a minority of its members advocating that it reject Redmond's proposal and prepare for a future rebellion. As well as the anti-Redmond Volunteers, radical nationalist organizations included the secretive Irish Republican Brotherhood (IRB), with Patrick Pearse as its main spokesman, and the trade union-based Citizen Army, led by the socialist James Connolly. There was broad agreement among them that a rising should be attempted but disagreement about its aims. The IRB felt a "glorious failure" would serve the cause, but others, such as the Irish Volunteers' chief of staff Eoin MacNeill, wanted German support for a fight to defeat the British.

German backing
Roger Casement, a former British diplomat and a critic of colonialism, became the Irish nationalists' key link with the Germans. Casement failed to find recruits for a rebel brigade among Irish soldiers in German prisoner-of-war camps, nor would Germany send forces to invade Ireland. The Germans did, however, promise to ship arms to the Irish rebels.

In January 1916, IRB leaders and Connolly agreed to stage an uprising on Easter Sunday, 23 April. The IRB had taken over key positions in the Volunteers, but did not control the

116 The number of British soldiers killed in the course of the uprising.

318 The number of Irish rebels and civilians who died.

organization. Their plan depended on drawing the mass of Volunteers into the rebellion, since their own followers numbered only a few thousand, chiefly in Dublin. MacNeill was induced to issue the Volunteers with orders for a nationwide uprising.

In the event, all the plans went awry. The promised arms shipment from Germany arrived at the Kerry coast on

Men of the Easter Rising
This painting shows the 14 Irish rebels executed for their part in the Easter Rising in Dublin. A 15th Irish nationalist, Thomas Kent, was also executed in May 1916 for killing a policeman in Cork.

the steamer SMS *Aud* on 20 April but there were no Volunteers to unload it. Trapped by the Royal Navy, the *Aud* was scuttled to avoid capture. Casement landed in Ireland from a German submarine and was instantly arrested (the British hanged him as a traitor the following August). Faced with a potential fiasco, MacNeill revoked the order for an uprising. Pearse, Connolly, and their colleagues, however, decided to go ahead.

The uprising
On Easter Monday, a day later than planned, about 1,600 armed rebels seized control of key buildings in Dublin. Standing on the steps of the General Post Office, which the rebels had taken as their headquarters, Pearse read out a proclamation on behalf of "the Provisional Government of the Irish Republic".

Dubliners reacted with initial bemusement, followed by a wave of looting as police withdrew from the streets. In the rest of Ireland, there were isolated uprisings, but most Volunteers followed MacNeill's order to stay at home. The British response was delayed by a lack of troops on the spot. Few of the soldiers garrisoning Dublin had ammunition for their rifles.

On 26 April, troop reinforcements arrived from England. Soldiers of the Sherwood Foresters, marching into the

"In the name of **God** and of the dead generations from which she receives her **old tradition** of **nationhood,** Ireland… strikes for her freedom."

PATRICK PEARSE, PROCLAMATION OF THE PROVISIONAL GOVERNMENT OF THE IRISH REPUBLIC, 24 APRIL 1916

After the fighting
Dubliners walk through the ruins of the city's General Post Office after the suppression of the Easter Rising. Used as the rebel headquarters, the building was destroyed by British artillery fire.

city from the port of Kingstown, came under fire from rebels at Mount Street Bridge on the Grand Canal. Ordered to make repeated frontal assaults across the bridge, the British soldiers suffered 240 casualties.

Failure and the firing squad

Further British losses occurred when rebel positions were attacked by infantry, but mostly the British relied on artillery, shelling buildings held by the rebels until they became untenable. Driven from the burning General Post Office building on 29 April, Pearse ordered a surrender. The fighting ceased the following day.

As the rebels had conspired with Britain's enemies in time of war, harsh retribution was inevitable. Martial law was imposed under General Sir John Maxwell, and 15 Irish nationalists were executed in early May. Among those who faced the firing squad were Pearse and James Connolly. The executions outraged the Irish Catholics and won wider public support for republicanism than had ever existed before.

The British were not insensitive to the need for reconciliation. Almost 1,500 nationalists sent to internment camps following the uprising were released at the end of the year. Most death sentences were commuted, with those spared including the American-born future Irish leader Éamon de Valera. The alienation of Irish Catholic opinion would nonetheless prove fatal to the continuance of British rule in Ireland.

AFTER »

Political developments after World War I led to the formation of the Irish Free State in the south of Ireland, while parts of the north stayed British.

THE RISE OF SINN FEIN
Sinn Fein emerged as a unifying organization for Irish nationalists. In the general election held after the war, Sinn Fein achieved a **landslide victory** in Catholic areas and set up a parliament in Dublin. Sinn Fein's military arm, the **Irish Republican Army** (IRA), fought an independence war against Britain masterminded by Michael Collins. In 1922, the **Irish Free State** was founded, while Protestant-dominated Northern Ireland remained part of the UK.

FORGOTTEN ROLE
The contribution that many Irish Catholics had made to the war effort was forgotten. In Northern Ireland, the service of **Protestant soldiers at the Somme** was contrasted with **Catholic rebels** who had "stabbed Britain in the back". This prejudice still lingers on a century later.

MICHAEL COLLINS

Intelligence and Espionage

"The number of agents of the German Secret Police... working in our midst... are believed to be over five thousand."

WILLIAM LE QUEUX, "SPIES OF THE KAISER", 1909

Before World War I, tension between the European powers fuelled anxieties that foreign agents and traitors could undermine national security. States developed organizations dedicated to gathering foreign intelligence and protecting

military secrets. Much of the concern about espionage was exaggerated, but agents were undoubtedly employed to sketch foreign naval ports and other military installations, or to search wastepaper baskets for war plans. When war broke out, however, signals

intelligence – the interception of enemy messages – proved more fruitful. Although the experts of the French Deuxième Bureau were noted for their codebreaking skills, the most spectacular intelligence coups of the war were the work of the

British Naval Intelligence Division under the command of Admiral Reginald "Blinker" Hall. Captured German code books – notably those seized by the Russians from the cruiser SMS *Magdeburg* in the Baltic in late August 1914 – allowed Hall's codebreakers in Room 40, the British Navy's secret intelligence room, to read the German navy's radio traffic. The information gathered permitted the interception of the German High Seas Fleet at Jutland in 1916.

Of even greater importance was the decoding of diplomatic messages. Since Britain had cut the undersea cables linking Germany to the outside world, the Germans had no safe way of communicating with their embassies. In January 1917, a message from the German Foreign Minister, Arthur Zimmermann, to the embassy in Mexico was decoded by Room 40 and passed on to the American

Military communications
French soldiers man the switchboard at a military headquarters on the Western Front. The communications on which armies and navies depended were inherently insecure.

BUTTONS WITH CODED TEXT

HIDDEN CAMERA

INVISIBLE INK KIT

Spy kit

German agents employed a range of equipment to record and convey information. An invisible ink kit like this one was found among Mata Hari's possessions when she was arrested.

provided the Allies with valuable information on the movement of German troop trains. Typed encrypted reports were either smuggled across the border into the Netherlands or sent to France across German lines by carrier pigeon.

The Belgian resistance movement, much of which was operated by Catholic priests and nuns, also smuggled people out of the country, including Allied prisoners of war and Belgians of military age wanting to join the Belgian army fighting in Flanders. The executions of Edith Cavell and Philippe Baucq attracted world attention to these activities, but they

Mata Hari

Dutch exotic dancer Mata Hari was executed by firing squad by the French in October 1917 for being a German agent. France's wartime spy mania was then at its height.

were only two among hundreds of resisters killed by the German occupation forces.

In Russia, the belief that key figures in the tsarist court were German agents undermined confidence in the regime. After the revolution that overthrew the Tsar in March 1917, Germany actively supported anti-war revolutionaries, including the Bolshevik Vladimir Ilyich Lenin, who was provided with money and a train to bring him home from exile in Switzerland. After Lenin seized power the following November, Allied agents plotted against the Bolshevik regime. Their only achievement, however, was to stimulate Bolshevik paranoia and secret police activity.

government. Its instructions to the German ambassador to lure Mexico into attacking the USA helped bring America into the war against Germany.

Secret agents

Attempts to run spies in enemy countries had limited success. The Netherlands and Switzerland, neutral countries on the edge of the conflict, became hotbeds of espionage activity where rival intelligence agencies operated freely. The advantage of employing "neutrals" as agents was that they were generally free to cross borders into enemy territory.

However, counter-intelligence organizations exercising surveillance over foreigners and reading letters and telegrams generally picked up such agents quite swiftly. A total of 235 Allied agents were convicted of espionage by the Germans, without any notable intelligence emerging from their activities. France had a full-blown

spy scandal in 1917 when evidence emerged of payments made by German agents to anti-war elements in the country, notably the left-wing journal *Le Bonnet Rouge*. Among those arrested and executed, the best remembered is the dancer Mata Hari, whose alleged

11 | **The number of people in Britain executed for spying for Germany in the course of World War I.**

use of exotic charms to extract secrets from French officers appealed to the public's taste for the sensational.

Resistance networks

The activity of resistance networks in German-occupied Belgium and northern France was of far more practical importance than the work of secret agents. Groups such as the White Lady network based in the Belgian city of Liège, for example,

1894 French officer Captain Alfred Dreyfus is arrested for allegedly passing secrets to Germany. After his sentence to life imprisonment, his case becomes a dividing point in French politics.

CONTEMPORARY PORTRAYAL OF ALFRED DREYFUS

1906 After the political triumph of his supporters, Dreyfus is fully exonerated and reinstated in the army.

1907 The French Deuxième Bureau, first created in 1871, is reactivated to gather military intelligence abroad.

1909 The British government creates a secret service bureau to gather intelligence abroad and counter foreign spies in Britain.

May 1913 Colonel Alfred Redel, former head of Austrian counter-intelligence, commits suicide after being exposed as a double-agent working for Russia.

October 1914 British Naval Intelligence establishes Room 40, devoted to the decoding of intercepted German naval radio messages.

6 November 1914 German agent Carl Lody is shot in the Tower of London.

12 October 1915 British nurse Edith Cavell and four Belgian resisters, including Philippe Baucq, are executed by a German firing squad.

January 1917 British Room 40 cryptographers reveal German plans to induce Mexico to wage war against the USA.

June 1917 The Espionage Act is passed in the USA, suppressing opposition to the war.

July 1917 French anti-war magazine *Le Bonnet Rouge*, allegedly funded by German agents, is suppressed.

15 October 1917 Dancer Mata Hari is executed for espionage at Vincennes in France.

November 1917 Louis Malvy, a former minister in the French government, is arrested over alleged contacts with Germany.

17 April 1918 Paul Bolo, a German agent in France, is executed by firing squad.

RESISTANCE WORKER (1865–1915)

EDITH CAVELL

A British nurse working in Belgium before the war, Edith Cavell stayed there under the German occupation. A high-minded humanitarian, she became involved with a resistance network run by an architect called Philippe Baucq, helping wounded Allied soldiers or prisoners of war escape to Britain via the Netherlands. When the network was betrayed to the Germans, Cavell was arrested, tried, and shot. Cavell's execution was a propaganda gift to the Allies, causing outrage in Britain and the USA. Her reported last words included the famous phrase: "Patriotism is not enough."

Lancers on parade
Polish Uhlan lancers serving in the Austro-Hungarian army parade in Warsaw on the founding of the Polish Regency Council in October 1917. Regency Poland was a client state of the Central Powers.

« BEFORE

In 1914, Russia and Austria-Hungary were multinational empires. Their large Slavic populations had long-nourished hopes of independence.

DIVISION OF POLAND

Poland had been partitioned between Russia, Austria, and Prussia in the 18th century. Most Poles came under Russian rule, with a large population in Austrian-ruled Galicia. Substantial numbers also dwelt in Silesia and East Prussia, in Germany. There were **major uprisings** in Russian Poland in 1830 and 1863, suppressed by tsarist forces. The **struggle for Polish independence** was recognized as a just cause by liberal opinion across Europe.

AUSTRO-HUNGARIAN PACT

In 1867, the **Austrian Empire**, ruled by ethnic Germans, made a **power-sharing deal** with its **Hungarian population** to resist the nationalist aspirations of its Slav peoples – Czechs and Slovaks, Poles and Ruthenians, Serbs, Croats, and Slovenes. By 1914, Slav groups were a disruptive element in Austro-Hungarian politics.

Slav Nationalism

World War I gave the subject Slavs a chance to fight for independence. But which side they should take in the war was not always clear. Soldiers from oppressed Slav peoples in various European countries served both the Allies and the Central Powers.

The assassination of Archduke Franz Ferdinand by Bosnian Serbs wishing to shake off Austro-Hungarian rule triggered World War I. Yet the nationalist aspirations of Serbs and other Slav peoples became a side issue once the major powers went to war. Instead of rising up against their ruling empires, the impulse of the subject Slavs was to support them in the conflict. This enthusiasm rapidly waned, however, and mounting Slav disaffection was accompanied by the efforts of nationalist leaders to exploit the opportunity offered by the war.

The Polish position

Poland stood out as a country with a long-established claim to nationhood, but also as the principal battleground between Russia and the Central Powers. The leading Polish nationalists were split over their attitude to the war. The anti-Russian Josef Pilsudski sided with Austria-Hungary, while followers of the more pragmatic Roman Dmowski favoured Russia, on the grounds that it offered protection against German domination and was allied to the democratic Western powers.

At the start of World War I, Pilsudski led a personal militia from Galicia into Russian Poland, where he was surprised not to be greeted as a liberator. He was soon integrated into the Austro-Hungarian army, leading a brigade of the Polish Legions that he had helped to found. The Polish Legions proved their fighting quality in the costly combat on the Eastern Front, notably at the Battle of Kostiuchnowka in July 1916.

Polish Adrian helmet
Soldiers in the Polish Army in France wore the French Adrian helmet with its distinctive emblem. This force entered the fighting on the Western Front halfway through 1918.

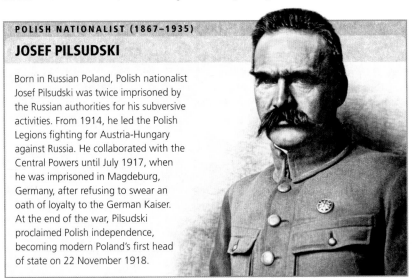

> # "Only the **sword** now carries any **weight** in the balance for the **destiny of a nation.**"
>
> JOSEF PILSUDSKI, 1914

At the end of World War I, assured of Allied support, Slav nationalists declared new independent states.

POSTER (1918) FOR POLAND'S INDEPENDENCE

future of Poland, but in November 1916 Germany declared its intention to found an independent Polish state. This gradually came into existence through 1917 – it was proclaimed a kingdom and governed, in the absence of a king, by a Regency Council – but its lack of genuine independence was clearly apparent.

In July 1917, Pilsudski was arrested by the Germans after urging the Polish Legions to reject an oath swearing loyalty to Germany.

Meanwhile, the revolution in Russia in March 1917 and the espousal of Polish independence as a war aim by the Allies ended any hope of the Central Powers winning Polish support. On the Western Front, a Polish Legion, recognized by the French as the "Polish Army", was formed from Polish emigrants to the USA and Canada. It fought in the epic battles of 1918.

Czechs and Slovaks

The idea that Czechs and Slovaks, Slav minorities in Austria and Hungary respectively, might make common cause had been mooted before World War I. It took solid shape in 1916 when Czech nationalists Edvard Benes and Tomas Masaryk and Slovak nationalist Milan Stefanik created the Czechoslovak National Council in Paris.

These leaders worked tirelessly to attract Allied support for their cause. Benes and Masaryk, who were both academics, established contact with Allied leaders, while Stefanik sought to create Czechoslovak Legions, primarily from prisoners of war or deserters from the Austro-Hungarian army. The Czechoslovak Legion in Russia distinguished itself in the Kerensky Offensive of summer 1917, fighting at the Battle of Zborov. It was later drawn into the Russian Civil War. Czechs and Slovaks also fought with the Allies in France and Italy.

Czech soldiers

The Czech and Slovak volunteers who joined the French Foreign Legion served on the Western Front from 1915. They later formed an autonomous Czechoslovak Legion fighting alongside the French army.

NEW NATIONS

In Poland, **independence** was declared on 11 November 1918. The Poles fought a major war against the Soviet Union before frontiers were finalized in 1922. **Czechoslovakia** became independent on 18 October 1918, with Tomas Masaryk its first president. On 1 December 1918, South Slavs joined with Serbia to form the **Kingdom of Serbs, Croats and Slovenes**, later renamed Yugoslavia.

Croats, Serbs, and Slovenes

While some South Slavs in Austria-Hungary – Croats, Serbs, and Slovenes – fought in the Austro-Hungarian army, others identified with an already independent combatant country, Serbia. In 1916, after the conquest of Serbia by the Central Powers, the Serbian parliament in exile in Corfu called for the creation of a kingdom of South Slavs. After the war, the new states came into being as the Kingdom of Serbs, Croats and Slovenes, the union of the three peoples cemented by Allied pressure.

On the whole, Polish popular opinion was initially more in favour of Russia, with Poles in Galicia often aiding advancing Russian forces, but the oppressive behaviour of these forces soon swung attitudes the other way. In fact, Polish civilians suffered at the hands of all the combatants. Before the Central Powers conquered most of Russian Poland in 1915, the country was devastated and partially depopulated by the "scorched earth" policy deployed by the retreating Russian soldiers. It was then ruthlessly exploited by Germany and Austria-Hungary as a source of food and forced labour.

There were sharp disagreements between the German and Austro-Hungarian governments over the

POLISH NATIONALIST (1867–1935)

JOSEF PILSUDSKI

Born in Russian Poland, Polish nationalist Josef Pilsudski was twice imprisoned by the Russian authorities for his subversive activities. From 1914, he led the Polish Legions fighting for Austria-Hungary against Russia. He collaborated with the Central Powers until July 1917, when he was imprisoned in Magdeburg, Germany, after refusing to swear an oath of loyalty to the German Kaiser. At the end of the war, Pilsudski proclaimed Polish independence, becoming modern Poland's first head of state on 22 November 1918.

BEFORE

Germany was desperate to break the naval blockade imposed by Britain's Royal Navy, which controlled the sea routes through the North Sea and the English Channel.

NORTH SEA SORTIES

For a year after the British success at the **Battle of Dogger Bank ≪ 124–25** in January 1915, the German High Seas Fleet stayed in port. In January 1916, however, the fleet received a new commander-in-chief, Vice-Admiral **Reinhard Scheer**.

An aggressive commander, Scheer ordered sorties into the North Sea in March and in April and **bombarded the English east coast towns** of Lowestoft and Great Yarmouth. Scheer's aim was to lure the Royal Navy into combat on his own terms and sink enough of its warships to undermine Britain's long-held naval superiority.

Battle of Jutland from the air

An artist's impression shows ships steaming in line, the formation that optimized chances for firing on the enemy. Much of the battle was fought at long range, with some guns hitting targets 16 km (10 miles) away.

The **Battle** of **Jutland**

The only full-scale encounter between the German and British fleets in World War I took place in the North Sea at the end of May 1916. A staggering 250 warships, including some of the world's largest battleships, fought a dramatic running battle, but with no decisive result.

On 30 May 1916, Admiral Sir John Jellicoe, commander of the Royal Navy's Grand Fleet, was informed by the Admiralty that the German High Seas Fleet was preparing to go to sea the following day. The information, from signals intelligence and the Admiralty's Room 40 cryptographers, was short on detail but sufficient for action.

The Battlecruiser Fleet, based in the Firth of Forth in Scotland, and commanded by Vice-Admiral Sir David Beatty, was dispatched towards the waters off Denmark's Jutland peninsula in the expected path of the German sortie. There, it was to be joined by the overwhelming might of Jellicoe's

Grand Fleet steaming from Scapa Flow in the Orkneys. If Beatty encountered the German High Seas Fleet, he was to lead it to Jellicoe, who would destroy it with his far superior weight of guns.

On 31 May, the German fleet steamed northwards with its battlecruisers, commanded by Vice-Admiral Franz von Hipper, in the lead, and Admiral Scheer's main fleet following.

Mighty confrontation

Hipper's forces comprised 99 warships, including 16 modern battleships and five battlecruisers. The British had 151 warships at sea, including 28 battleships and nine battlecruisers. Scheer's position was precarious. Bad

Award for heroism

This Victoria Cross was awarded to Jack Cornwell, a 16-year-old Boy Seaman. He was mortally wounded while serving aboard HMS *Chester*, but even so remained standing at his post.

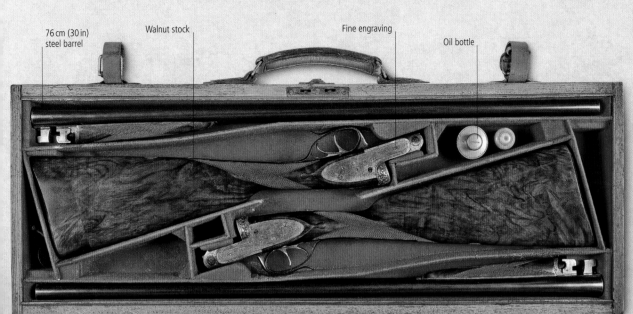

76 cm (30 in) steel barrel   Walnut stock   Fine engraving   Oil bottle

Haig's shotguns
A pair of 12-bore shotguns owned by Haig and made by J. Purdey & Sons was auctioned for £15,000 in 2011. The case is impressed with the initials "D.H.", and the brass escutcheon is engraved "7th Hussars".

He encouraged improvements in coordination between artillery and infantry, pressed for maximum use of aircraft, and was enthusiastic about the deployment of tanks. At the same time, he firmly believed in the importance of cavalry in modern warfare and in the need for cavalrymen to fight in the traditional manner, with sabre and lance.

High stakes
As commander of the largest army Britain had ever put into the field, Haig will always be judged by his offensives at the Somme in 1916 and Passchendaele (Third Ypres) in 1917. Fought at huge cost in lives, they failed to achieve major breakthroughs. Haig was sustained through these epic conflicts by his staunch belief in his eventual success. His optimism remained unshakeable – he wrote in his diary after the first day of the Somme that the casualties "could not be considered severe".

Always glimpsing success just around the corner, Haig continued the battles long after they had irremediably failed, driving men forward in renewed attacks for diminishing returns. On the other hand, no alternative to fighting in this way was available, if fighting was to take place at all.

Battles with Lloyd George
Haig's relations with David Lloyd George, British prime minister from December 1916, were based on mutual distrust. Lloyd George wanted an end to what appeared to be senseless slaughter. Yet he not only failed to offer an alternative to the continuing fighting on the Western Front but also failed to find any general prepared to take Haig's place.

The last man standing
In the crisis of spring 1918, when German offensives threatened to win

> ## "To **throw away men's lives** when there is no reasonable chance of advantage **is criminal.**"
>
> B.H. LIDDELL HART, "THE REAL WAR, 1914–18"

the war, Haig cooperated resolutely with his Allies, accepting subordination to General Ferdinand Foch. His order of the day on 11 April, calling for a fight "to the last man", showed surprising eloquence for a notably reserved commander.

Watching over the Legion
Earl Haig visits the British Legion factory making remembrance poppies at Richmond, Surrey, in 1926. After the war, Haig devoted time and energy to upholding the interests of ex-servicemen.

But Haig was not considered to have the popular touch. As a commander, he neither spoke to the men directly nor visited the wounded – apparently their terrible injuries upset him too much.

Both his private comments during the war, however, and his founding of the Haig Fund and British Legion to support ex-servicemen afterwards, suggest respect and concern for the ordinary soldier. His offensives cost many lives. Whether this sacrifice contributed proportionately to the Allies' eventual victory remains a matter for debate.

TIMELINE

- **1861** Born in Edinburgh to a family of famous whisky distillers.
- **1884–85** Attends the Royal Military College at Sandhurst and becomes a cavalry officer.
- **1898** Commands a squadron of cavalry in the Anglo-Egyptian army that defeats Mahdist rebels at Omdurman in Sudan.
- **1899–1902** Serves as a staff officer and commander of cavalry in the Boer War in South Africa.
- **1905** Marries Dorothy Vivian, a lady-in-waiting to Queen Alexandra.
- **1906** Appointed Director of Military Training at the War Office.
- **August 1914** Given command of I Corps, one of the two corps of the British Expeditionary Force (BEF).
- **October–December 1914** After leading I Corps at the First Battle of Ypres, Haig is given command of the new First Army in December.
- **March 1915** Commands the First Army at the Battle of Neuve Chapelle.
- **September–October 1915** Commands the British offensive at Loos. Blames its failure on Field Marshal Sir John French.
- **December 1915** Replaces French as commander-in-chief of the BEF.
- **July–November 1916** Directs the offensive at the Somme, which costs 420,000 British and Commonwealth casualties.
- **July–November 1917** Oversees the British offensive at Passchendaele (Third Ypres), in which British and Commonwealth casualties total around 260,000.
- **April 1918** Faced with a German breakthrough on the Western Front, Haig urges his men to fight with their "backs to the wall".

STATUE OF EARL HAIG

- **August–November 1918** Presides over British successes in the Hundred Days offensives.
- **1919** Raised to the British peerage as Earl Haig.
- **1921** Founds the Haig Fund for ex-servicemen and helps establish the British Legion ex-servicemen's organization.
- **1928** Dies of natural causes and is accorded a state funeral.

BEFORE «

As the point where French and British sectors of the Western Front met, the Somme was considered a good place to launch an Anglo-French offensive.

JOINT ACTION

A major offensive at the Somme was first proposed in December 1915. Plans were altered after the Germans attacked the French at **Verdun** « **154–55** in February 1916. Instead of an Anglo-French operation, it became a British offensive with French support. General **Sir Douglas Haig** « **178–79** wanted to delay the offensive until August, but the French insisted it go ahead sooner, to relieve the pressure on Verdun.

The **Somme Offensive**

The first day of the Somme Offensive, 1 July 1916, saw the heaviest loss of life in a single day's fighting in British military history. This was only the beginning of a sustained slaughter that eventually caused over a million casualties.

The German defences on the stretch of front chosen for the Allied Somme Offensive were among the strongest on the whole Western Front. The German front line consisted of a complex of trenches and fortified strongpoints with deep dugouts to shelter troops from artillery fire. A good distance behind this, there was a second defensive line, and in places a third behind that. The British plan to overcome these formidable defences relied upon a prolonged and heavy preliminary bombardment.

The plan and its execution

While the British engineers dug under the German lines to lay mines, and cut their barbed wire, the artillery was expected to demolish the German trenches and stun or kill the defenders. It would be the job of the infantry to move across from the British trenches and occupy the devastated defences.

British commander-in-chief General Sir Douglas Haig then envisaged cavalry breaking through into open country, over the German line. General Sir Henry Rawlinson, commanding the British Fourth Army, which had the

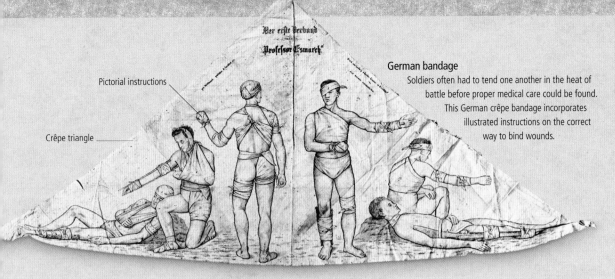

German bandage
Soldiers often had to tend one another in the heat of battle before proper medical care could be found. This German crêpe bandage incorporates illustrated instructions on the correct way to bind wounds.

Pictorial instructions

Crêpe triangle

Der erste Verband
Professor Esmarch

received during it. Providing timely tetanus jabs, for example, reduced the rate of tetanus infection among British wounded from around a third in 1914 to almost zero by the war's end.

World War I weaponry caused wounds that were appalling in both number and severity. Field surgeons, operating for up to 16 hours a day during a major offensive, resorted freely to amputation of limbs as the best hope for many of the wounded.

The use of anaesthetics was long-established and, by the later stages of the war, procedures to limit post-operative infection were as effective as could be achieved in the absence of antibiotics, which were not available

500,000 The estimated number of amputations performed during the course of World War I.

until World War II. A major innovation was the widespread use of blood transfusion, a life-saving procedure that became a practical proposition through the use of anti-coagulants and refrigeration, allowing blood to be

stored instead of transferred person-to-person. The prevalence of facial wounds saw progress in plastic surgery. Specialist hospitals were established for the reconstruction of faces. American surgeons in particular made advances in this field, although permanent disfigurement remained the fate of thousands.

Shell shock
Casualties suffered mental as well as physical trauma. Psychiatric medicine was becoming increasingly accepted in the early 20th century, and disturbed behaviour as a result of combat stress was recognized as a medical problem. The German army was broadly up to date with this modern thinking, but to many British and French army commanders "shell-shock" seemed a sign of weakness. It is not true that men suffering mental collapse were routinely executed as cowards, although there

were probably a few cases of this. As the war went on, all combatants established psychiatric wards and hospitals. The US army had 263

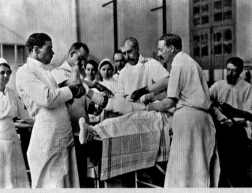

Wartime surgery
By 1914, operations had a reasonable success rate. During the last stages of the war, more than nine out of ten wounded men survived.

military psychiatrists in France in 1918. Therapy ranged from analysis of in-depth mental problems to crude electric-shock treatment.

Tending the wounded
Nurses were among the heroes of the conflict. Established bodies of military nurses were too small to cope with the scale of the war so there was a demand for volunteers such as the British Voluntary Aid Detachment (VAD) nurses or the 3,000 women who became Nursing Sisters in the Canadian Army.

Often from sheltered backgrounds, they coped astonishingly well with the task of tending severely wounded men. Women such as British VAD nurse Vera Brittain and American Ellen La Motte wrote some of the most eloquent testimonies of the war.

Red Cross symbol

Horsedrawn ambulance
At the start of the war, all ambulances were horse-drawn, but large numbers of motor ambulances were introduced later on. The Red Cross symbol was universally recognized, but did not stop ambulances coming under fire.

TIMELINE

1854 British nurse Florence Nightingale's interventions to improve sanitation and medical facilities in the Crimean War lead to major developments in military hospitals and nursing.

1854–56 French military surgeons widen the use of chloroform as an anaesthetic during the Crimean War.

1862 During the American Civil War, Dr Jonathan Letterman, surgeon-general of the Army of the Potomac, pioneers the use of a field ambulance service to evacuate casualties.

1864 The Red Cross is established, inspired by the Swiss businessman Henri Dunant.

1870–71 During the Franco-Prussian War, German military surgeons employ antiseptics, sharply reducing post-operative death rates.

1899–1902 In the Boer War in South Africa, British troops suffer 13,000 deaths from disease due to poor hygiene and failure to boil drinking water. This compares with 8,000 deaths in combat.

1904–05 At war with Russia, Japan greatly reduces losses to disease through use of antitoxins and good hygiene. Russia becomes the first country to recognize battle stress as a medical problem to be treated by psychiatry.

1909 In Britain, the Voluntary Aid Detachment (VAD) nursing organization is established.

1911 The US Army introduces compulsory typhoid vaccination for all recruits.

1914 The use of sodium citrate is shown to prevent coagulation (clotting) in blood transfusions. It is widely used during the war.

1915 The Gallipoli operation is a medical disaster for the British Army, which fails to maintain good hygiene, supply clean water, or evacuate the wounded efficiently by sea.

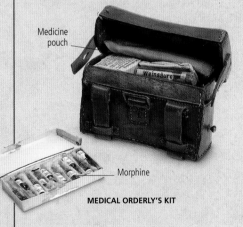

Medicine pouch

Weinsäure

Morphine

MEDICAL ORDERLY'S KIT

1916 The British Medical Corps records treating 2.65 million sick and wounded men during the course of the year.

1917 William Rivers pioneers shell-shock treatment.

1918 The US Army's medical service grows to a staff of 295,000, from 5,000 in June 1917.

1943 Mass production of penicillin provides the first effective antibiotics for use in World War II.

Dogfights and Aces

Air combat developed as an offshoot of trench warfare and had the same high death rates as the war on the ground. But the myth of ace fighter pilots as "knights of the air" engaged in chivalrous combat fulfilled a popular need for heroes in a grim industrialized war.

Fold-up collar

Goggles with tinted glass

Long flying coat

Sheepskin-lined flying boots

Rubber soles for secure grip

British pilot's clothing
Flying in an open cockpit, a World War I airman needed warm, head-to-toe clothing. This also offered a degree of protection if the aircraft caught fire, the most feared hazard of aerial combat.

BEFORE

The rival armies entered World War I with about 500 aircraft between them. The planes were flimsy and not armed for aerial combat.

RECONNAISSANCE ROLE
Aircraft had been used in war by the Italians in **Libya in 1911** and by the **Balkan states in the wars of 1912–13**. They had proved capable of attacking ground targets with grenades or small bombs, but the major European armies were interested in their potential for **reconnaissance ‹‹ 144–45**.

THE FIRST SHOT
At the start of the war, pilots had a supporting role. Their job was to **ferry observers**, who outranked them, on reconnaissance missions. On their own initiative, some observers carried pistols or carbines to **shoot at any enemy aircraft** they encountered. This proved ineffectual, but on 5 October 1914 a French observer **shot down a German aircraft** using a Hotchkiss machine-gun.

Most armies used aircraft during World War I. In trench warfare from 1915, generals found them invaluable for observing enemy lines and liaising with artillery.

Fighter aircraft developed later in order to shoot down enemy reconnaissance and bomber planes. But mounting a machine-gun on a propeller-driven plane was not easy. One solution, exemplified by the British Vickers "Gunbus", was to place the propeller behind the pilot while an observer with a machine-gun sat in a balcony in the nose of the aircraft.

Solo fighter planes
Single-seat aircraft with a front propeller performed much better. The introduction of the interrupter gear – allowing bullets to pass through a spinning propeller – enabled the German Fokker Eindecker monoplane to dominate the skies over France in the winter of 1915–16.

The Allies responded with their own solo fighters. The French Nieuport 11 "Bébé" biplane, introduced in early 1916, had a machine-gun mounted on its upper wing to fire over the

TECHNOLOGY
INTERRUPTER GEAR

The first man to fire a machine-gun through the arc of his spinning propeller was French pilot Roland Garros in April 1915. Garros had metal plates fitted to the propeller blades to deflect any bullets that struck them.

Anthony Fokker, a Dutch aircraft designer working for the Germans, trumped this by fitting his Eindecker monoplane with an interrupter gear. This device, which had been patented before World War I, synchronized the fire of the machine-gun with the rotation of the propeller, so the bullets passed through the arc without hitting the blades. This allowed the pilot simply to aim his aircraft at the target and fire, in effect making the solo fighter pilot possible.

Flying helmet with face mask

propeller. It was operated by the pilot pulling a chord. The Allies developed their own interrupter gear, using both wing-mounted guns and guns firing through the propeller. Once both sides had fighter aircraft, pilots fought one another as well as destroying reconnaissance craft.

Initially lone hunters, they were later grouped into squadrons. By summer 1915, German pilot Oswald Boelcke had formulated basic principles of air combat, such as to attack out of the sun and to open fire only at close range. He taught them to other pilots, including the top German fighter pilot Manfred von Richthofen, popularly known as the Red Baron.

Air aces

Air combat proved to be an activity at which a few individuals excelled, achieving multiple "kills" while their colleagues scored few or none. The German and French armies established a system for allotting "ace" status to pilots who shot down a certain number of enemy aircraft. The British army resisted a formal "ace" system, but the press celebrated the most successful fighter pilots. Men such as Charles Nungesser in France, Albert Ball in Britain, Billy Bishop in Canada, and Eddie Rickenbacker in the USA were glamorized as "knights of the air".

Deadly dogfights

From 1916 onwards, a struggle for air supremacy accompanied the great battles on the ground. As well as duelling with other aircraft in "dogfights", pilots were instructed to attack ground troops and observation balloons, activities that exposed them to ground fire. Squadrons suffered flying accidents and mechanical failure as well as actual combat. Airmen had no parachutes until the Germans began to issue them in 1918.

The strain on elite fighter squadrons such as the French Cigognes ("Storks") and Richthofen's Jagdgeschwader 1 (the "Flying Circus") was immense. The pilots were mostly young and few lived long – when British ace Albert Ball died in 1917 he was just 20 years old. During the Battle of Arras in spring 1917, the life expectancy of newly trained British pilots was two weeks.

Neither side was able to establish permanent air supremacy, for the advantage changed hands as new aircraft were introduced. The British and French won the production battle, however, manufacturing almost three times as many aircraft as Germany did in 1917.

Father of air combat
One of Germany's first air aces, Oswald Boelcke (centre) formalized the principles of aerial combat and founded the first elite fighter squadron. He was killed in action in October 1916.

French fighter ace
Rejected as too frail to serve in the infantry, French fighter pilot Captain Georges Guynemer became a national hero as a pilot in the elite Cigognes squadrons. He was killed in action in September 1917, aged 22.

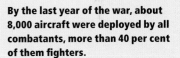
AFTER

By the last year of the war, about 8,000 aircraft were deployed by all combatants, more than 40 per cent of them fighters.

FIGHTING ANOTHER DAY
About 15,000 airmen were killed in the war. Some fighter pilots who survived went on to have notable postwar careers, including **Hermann Goering**, a member of Manfred von Richthofen's "Flying Circus". He became a leading figure in Adolf Hitler's Nazi regime.

In April 1918, Britain was the first country to create an independent air force, placing its army and navy aircraft under the control of the **Royal Air Force**. Germany was forbidden an air force under the **Treaty of Versailles 338–39 »**, but Hitler re-established it as the Luftwaffe in 1935.

Sheepskin gauntlets

Warm wool lining

Map case

Dogfight in France
Aerial combat over the Western Front was typically fought by biplanes with fixed undercarriages. In this painting by English painter William Wyllie, an aircraft has burst into flames, a fate feared by pilots.

Lloyd George was instinctively aligned with the anti-war tradition of the Liberal Party. However, during the Agadir crisis of 1911, when a visit by the German Kaiser to the Moroccan port was perceived as provocative by France and Britain, Lloyd George made a prominent speech advocating war if it was necessary to preserve Britain's vital interests and prestige.

Driving force

The German invasion of Belgium in August 1914 overcame any hesitations Lloyd George had about supporting the declaration of war. He established himself as the leading figure in a drive to mobilize the economy and, in May 1915, was the natural choice to head a new Ministry of Munitions. He bullied and bribed businessmen into turning factories over to war production, achieving an impressive increase of output. As an acknowledged radical,

Master orator

Lloyd George addresses a crowd at the unveiling of a war memorial in London in October 1927. He was a powerful orator, described by many as exercising an almost hypnotic grip upon his audience.

he was able to win acceptance from trade unions for "dilution" – the use of unskilled workers and women to do jobs previously restricted to skilled male workers.

Unlike old-fashioned Liberals such as Prime Minister Herbert Asquith, Lloyd George had no scruples about government interference in business or violation of individual freedoms. In December 1916, he won the support of the Conservative and Labour parties to replace Asquith as prime minister, splitting the Liberal Party.

He set about establishing a small war cabinet and expanded government control of national life in order to boost the war effort. Many areas of the economy, such as coal mining and merchant shipping, were taken over by the state for the duration of the war. New ministries were created to direct food production and labour.

Relations with the generals

Lloyd George was not always so successful in imposing his will on the generals conducting the war. Instinctively anti-militarist, he distrusted generals, while they regarded him as militarily ignorant. He sought an alternative to the slaughter on the Western Front, advocating a diversion of resources to Salonika or Italy. This was opposed by General Sir William Robertson, the Chief of the Imperial General Staff, and Field Marshal Douglas Haig commanding British forces in France. Lloyd George tried to undermine the generals, eventually ridding himself of Robertson in February 1918, but Haig proved immovable.

In his war memoirs, published in 1933, Lloyd George presents himself as the man consistently humane and right while the military leaders were brutal and foolish. But some of his claims – for example, to have been solely responsible for the introduction of the convoy system at sea in April 1917 – are now widely contested. He

has been blamed for withholding troops from the Western Front in early 1918, as part of his private war with Haig, leaving the British Army vulnerable to the German Spring Offensive.

Postwar career

Lloyd George won the postwar general election of 1918 partly by promising to make Germany pay reparations and to prosecute German war criminals, including the Kaiser. At the Paris Peace Conference in 1919, however, he tried to steer a course between French Prime Minister Georges Clemenceau's desire to permanently disable Germany and the idealism of US President Woodrow Wilson.

In domestic affairs he aspired to continue his pre-war radical reforms – he had set up a Ministry for Reconstruction as early as 1917 – but as the leader of a predominantly Conservative coalition had little scope for action. He returned to leadership of the Liberal Party from 1924, but that

Commemorative jug

An earthenware jug celebrating Lloyd George's wartime premiership bears text in Welsh as well as English. Lloyd George is the only Welshman to have held the post of British prime minister.

once great movement never recovered from the split he had engineered in 1916. In the run-up to World War II, Lloyd George admired Hitler's forceful leadership and favoured seeking peace in 1940. As a result, he had become an isolated figure in British public life by the time he died in 1945.

Juggling his allies

A wartime caricature presents Lloyd George as a circus strongman juggling his French, Russian, and Italian allies. His skill at diplomacy was never equal to his grasp of domestic policy issues.

> "I never believed in **costly frontal attacks** either in **war or politics,** if there were **a way round.**"
>
> DAVID LLOYD GEORGE, "WAR MEMOIRS", 1934

TIMELINE

- **January 1863** David George is born of Welsh parents in Manchester, England.
- **1884** Becomes a solicitor. Marries Margaret Owen, a farmer's daughter, four years later.
- **1890** Enters parliament as Liberal Member of Parliament for Carnarvon in North Wales.
- **1899–1902** Is a critic of British involvement in the Boer War in South Africa.
- **1906** Enters government for the first time as president of the Board of Trade.
- **1908** Becomes Chancellor of the Exchequer, a post he holds until 1915. He introduces old age pensions and unemployment insurance.
- **August 1914** Supports a British declaration of war in support of Belgium, preventing a major split in the cabinet.
- **May 1915** Appointed Minister of Munitions after the "shell scandal" and achieves a rapid expansion of war production.
- **June 1916** On the death of Lord Kitchener, Lloyd George becomes Minister for War.
- **December 1916** Becomes prime minister at the head of a coalition government, establishing a five-man war cabinet.
- **April 1917** Backs the adoption of a convoy system to counter German U-boats.
- **July 1917** Reluctantly acquiesces in General Douglas Haig's offensive at Passchendaele.
- **January 1918** Makes a firm statement of Britain's commitment to democracy and national self-determination as war aims.
- **December 1918** Wins a landslide victory in a general election at the end of the war.
- **1919** Represents Britain at the Paris Peace Conference.
- **1922** His coalition with the Conservatives collapses and he falls from power.
- **1936** Visits Germany and meets with Nazi dictator Adolf Hitler.
- **1940** Refuses the offer of a place in Winston Churchill's wartime government.
- **1943** A widower from 1941, he marries Frances Stevenson, his mistress since 1913.
- **1945** Dies shortly after being elevated to the peerage as Earl Lloyd-George of Dwyfor.

LLOYD GEORGE AND FRANCES STEVENSON AT THEIR WEDDING, 1943

Germany's New Order

From August 1916, the German war effort came under the control of the Third Supreme Command, spearheaded by Field Marshal Paul von Hindenburg and General Erich Ludendorff. Together, they began laying the foundations for a German-dominated Europe.

Chief of the General Staff Paul von Hindenburg and Quartermaster-General Erich Ludendorff exercised joint power over Germany's Third Supreme Command (Hindenburg being the third German Chief of the General Staff to lead the war). They controlled German military strategy and also dictated economic and diplomatic policies. Kaiser Wilhelm II was barely consulted on policy, and the

Chancellor, who headed the civilian government, depended on the approval of the Supreme Command. German military and business leaders worked closely together, pursuing the same nationalist and expansionist agenda.

The war machine
The policies of the Third Supreme Command grew partly out of an immediate need to cope with the war

were not controlled and manufacturers connected with the military regime made fortunes.

Inevitably, priority lay with meeting the immediate needs of the war effort. Conquered territories were plundered of food and raw materials.

Employing the labour of conquered peoples was also seen as essential, with the German workforce depleted by the demand for soldiers. From 1914, the work of prisoners of war, chiefly Russians, was invaluable to the German war effort. The Third Supreme Commander pressed to maximize the supply of workers from conquered territories. Thousands of Poles were deported to Germany and put to work. When the policy was applied in occupied Belgium in the autumn of 1916, protests organized by trade unions and by the influential Belgian spokesman Cardinal Mercier led to the deportations being halted in 1917.

German nationalism
The Supreme Command also reflected a broader vision of the future of Europe and Germany's place within it, articulated by German nationalists. They argued that Slavs were inherently inferior to Germans and that Germany had a historic "civilizing mission" in the east. In his influential book *Mitteleuropa* (Central Europe), published in 1915, the politician Friedrich Naumann envisaged Germany permanently dominating a swathe of Europe from the Baltic to the Black Sea.

Forced labour
Russian soldiers captured by the Germans work under armed guard. The labour of millions of such prisoners of war was essential to the war economies of the Central Powers.

Supreme commanders
German Chief of the General Staff Hindenburg is followed by his Quartermaster-General Ludendorff. As joint leaders of the Third Supreme Command they installed a virtual military dictatorship in Germany.

Some areas were to be emptied of their existing population and colonized by German settlers, others were to be placed under puppet governments and economically exploited. This vision was endorsed by Austria's German rulers – who intended to take control of the Balkan Slavs and of northern Italy – as well as by Germany itself, whose main interests lay in Poland, Ukraine, and the Baltic states. The Hungarians would exercise control over Croatian Slavs.

Conquered territories
Attempts were made to implement aspects of the "Mitteleuropa plan". In 1914–15, for example, victories

BEFORE

Germany entered World War I without clear war aims, but its leaders were soon tempted by the idea of creating a German-dominated Europe.

EXPANSIONIST PLANS
In September 1914, the German Chancellor drafted a plan for the **annexation** of Belgium, the Netherlands, and northern France and the **economic exploitation** of states in Central Europe. Though not officially adopted, this programme represented government thinking. The **battles of 1914–16** left Germany and Austria-Hungary in temporary control of parts of France, Belgium, the Balkans, and Eastern Europe.

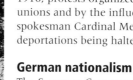

BELGIAN MILITARY PIN

situation, including shortages of labour, raw materials, and food. To maximize war production, the Third Supreme Command sought total state direction of the German economy, controlling the allocation of raw materials and taking powers to order workers into war industries. One of the ways in which it raised money for the war effort was to invite people to pin money and pledges to invest in war bonds on wooden statues of Hindenburg erected in German towns and cities.

Substantial increases in production were achieved, although organization of the war economy fell short of the level of efficiency to which it aspired. For example, in 1917 output of rifles and machine-guns hugely exceeded the army's requirements but production of steel, a vital war material, fell. Profits for business

Krupp arms factory
Most German artillery was manufactured by the steel manufacturer Krupp. The owners of such businesses worked in close collaboration with the military leadership to maximize production.

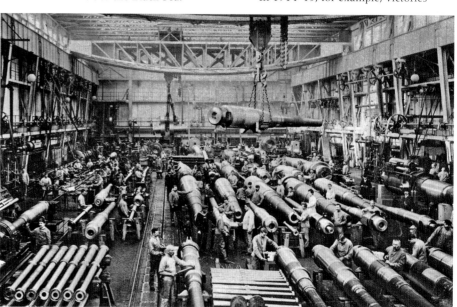

1917

ЗАЕМЪ СВОБОДЫ

ВОЙНА до ПОБѢДЫ

Russia's provisional government, taking power after the fall of the Tsar in March 1917, calls for Russia to continue the war "until victory". By the year's end, the Bolsheviks have seized power and concluded an armistice.

The Canadian Corps capture Vimy Ridge from the Germans in a famous assault in the Battle of Arras in April 1917. Overall, however, the Battle of Arras was a failure for the Allies.

The USA enters the war after President Woodrow Wilson gains approval from Congress. The USA formally declares war on Germany on 6 April 1917.

CANADA

UNITED STATES
OF AMERICA

MEXICO

ATLANTIC
OCEAN

PACIFIC
OCEAN

BRITISH HONDURAS
CUBA
DOMINICAN REPUBLIC
VIRGIN ISLANDS
HAITI
LEEWARD ISLANDS
GUATEMALA
HONDURAS
WINDWARD ISLANDS
BARBADOS
EL SALVADOR
NICARAGUA
COSTA RICA
TRINIDAD AND TOBAGO
CANAL ZONE
PANAMA
VENEZUELA
BRITISH GUIANA
DUTCH GUIANA
COLOMBIA
FRENCH GUIANA
ECUADOR

Hawaiian
Islands

Christmas
Island

Mariana
Islands

Marshall
Islands

GUAM

GERMAN PACIFIC TERRITORIES

Caroline
Islands

Gilbert
Islands

Cook
Islands

French Polynesia

JAPANESE
EMPIRE

PHILIPPINE
ISLANDS

FRENCH
INDOCHINA

BRITISH
NTH BORNEO

BRUNEI
SARAWAK

MALAYA

DUTCH EAST INDIES

Bismarck
Archipelago

KAISER
WILHELMSLAND

PAPUA

Nauru

Solomon
Islands

Ellice
Islands

New
Hebrides

Fiji

Tonga

German Samoa
(Western)

PORTUGUESE
TIMOR

AUSTRALIA

New
Caledonia

NEW ZEALAND

PERU

BRAZIL

BOLIVIA

PARAGUAY

CHILE

URUGUAY

ARGENTINA

FALKLAND
ISLANDS

French colonial troops employed in the war include these Tirailleurs Annamites, infantry from French Indochina. The colonies are an important source of manpower for Britain and France. Germany has no comparable resource.

THE WORLD IN DECEMBER 1917

The Central Powers

Central Powers conquests to Dec 1917

Allied states

Allied conquests to Dec 1917

Neutral states

Frontiers Jul 1914

army mutinied. Discipline was restored by a new commander-in-chief, General Philippe Pétain, and the appointment of Georges Clemenceau as prime minister stopped defeatism among French civilians. The British army took over the main burden on the Western Front. Operations such as the capture of Vimy Ridge in April and Messines Ridge in June showed a fresh tactical sophistication, but British troops suffered disillusion in terrible fighting at Passchendaele in the autumn.

Overall, outside Russia commitment to continuing the war held firm. In Italy, the shock of a major defeat at Caporetto strengthened rather than weakened national solidarity. On both sides, however, voices were raised in favour of reaching a compromise peace, notably in a resolution voted by the German Reichstag in July. But the collapse of Russia only confirmed the German military leadership in its unswerving pursuit of victory.

TIMELINE 1917

Unrestricted submarine warfare ▪ Revolution in Russia ▪ **The USA enters the war** ▪ French army mutinies ▪ **Slaughter at Passchendaele** ▪ Italian defeat at Caporetto ▪ **British take Jerusalem** ▪ Armistice on the Eastern Front

JANUARY	FEBRUARY	MARCH	APRIL	MAY	JUNE
9 JANUARY German military and political leaders agree to resume unrestricted submarine warfare.		**1 MARCH** The Zimmermann telegram is publicized in the US press, outraging public opinion.	**3 APRIL** Bolshevik leader Vladimir Ilyich Lenin returns to Russia. **6 APRIL** The USA declares war on Germany.		**4 JUNE** General Brusilov is appointed Russian army commander-in-chief.

⌃ German submariner's badge

⌄ French 1893 Lebel rifle

⌄ Lenin in Petrograd

16 JANUARY German Foreign Secretary Arthur Zimmermann sends a telegram promising Mexico US territory in return for an alliance. It is intercepted by the British.	**1 FEBRUARY** Germany resumes unrestricted submarine warfare, causing the USA to break off diplomatic relations.	**8 MARCH** Revolution begins in Russia as protesters take to the streets of Petrograd. **11 MARCH** British forces capture Baghdad.			**7 JUNE** At Ypres, the British blow up German positions on Messines Ridge, as a prelude to a successful offensive. **11 JUNE** King Constantine of Greece abdicates under pressure from the Allies.

⌄ German anti-war propaganda

	21 FEBRUARY On the Western Front, the Germans begin Operation Alberich, a tactical withdrawal to the Hindenburg Line defences. **24 FEBRUARY** British forces retake Kut in Mesopotamia.	**15 MARCH** Tsar Nicholas II abdicates as revolution grips Russia. A Provisional Government takes power.		**15 MAY** Pétain replaces Nivelle as French commander-in-chief. He ends mutinies in the French army.	**13 JUNE** German Gotha bombers raid London in daylight, killing 162 people.

⌄ Detonator

	26 FEBRUARY President Wilson asks Congress for permission to arm US merchant ships.	**26 MARCH** British Empire forces fail to break through Turkish defences in the First Battle of Gaza in Palestine. **31 MARCH** German U-boats sink almost a million tons of merchant shipping in two months.	**9 APRIL** British launch offensive at Arras. Canadians take Vimy Ridge. **16 APRIL** Start of the Nivelle Offensive. Its failure leads to mutinies in the French army.	**16 MAY** Battle of Arras ends with small gains for the British. **19 MAY** General Pershing is appointed to command the American Expeditionary Force.	

EXPLODER

20 JANUARY The Romanian front stabilizes at the Sereth river. **22 JANUARY** US President Wilson makes a speech calling for peace without victors or vanquished.					**25 JUNE** First troops of the American Expeditionary Force arrive in Europe. **29 JUNE** Greece declares war on the Central Powers.

« Canadian soldiers at Vimy Ridge

Enormous **masses of ammunition,** such as the human mind had never imagined… were **hurled on the bodies of men** scattered in **mud-filled shellholes."**

GERMAN GENERAL ERICH LUDENDORFF, DESCRIBING PASSCHENDAELE, AUTUMN 1917

JULY	AUGUST	SEPTEMBER	OCTOBER	NOVEMBER	DECEMBER
JULY The Kerensky Offensive, the last Russian offensive of the war, begins. It ends in disastrous failure.	**1 AUGUST** General Kornilov takes over from Brusilov as Russian commander-in-chief. **6 AUGUST** Central Powers launch successful offensive against Romanians in Moldavia.	**3 SEPTEMBER** Germans commanded by General Hutier capture Riga from the Russians in an attack that uses new "infiltration tactics".		**6 NOVEMBER** Turkish forces abandon Gaza, allowing the British to advance into Palestine. **7 NOVEMBER** The Bolsheviks seize power in Petrograd, setting up a government of people's commissars.	**4 DECEMBER** Battle of Cambrai ends with most of the early British gains lost. **7 DECEMBER** The USA declares war on Austria-Hungary.

9 SEPTEMBER
General Kornilov is accused of attempting a coup and dismissed as Russian commander-in-chief. Kerensky arms workers' militias, the Red Guard.

9 NOVEMBER
Italian Chief of Staff General Luigi Cadorna is replaced by General Diaz. The Allies form a Supreme War Council to coordinate strategy.

❯❯ Appealing for tank crews

TREAT 'EM ROUGH!

JOIN THE TANKS
United States Tank Corps.

⌃ Austro-Hungarian troops

⌃ Mata Hari

5 JULY
Arab irregulars capture the Red Sea port of Aqaba from the Turks.

10 AUGUST
British Ypres offensive is renewed towards the Gheluvelt plateau, but little progress is made. A further attack on 16 August also fails.

14 AUGUST
China declares war on the Central Powers.

16 SEPTEMBER
Colonel T.E. Lawrence leads an Arab attack on the Hejaz railway in Arabia.

20 SEPTEMBER
At Ypres, British, Australian, and New Zealand forces attack with some success at the Menin Road.

12 OCTOBER
At Ypres, Australian troops lead a failed attempt to take Passchendaele Ridge.

15 OCTOBER
In France, exotic dancer Mata Hari is shot as a German spy.

10 NOVEMBER
The third Battle of Ypres ends with Passchendaele in British hands.

15 NOVEMBER
Georges Clemenceau is appointed French prime minister.

16–19 JULY
Popular disturbances in Petrograd, the July Days, are suppressed. Lenin flees to Finland to avoid arrest.

17 JULY
British royal family changes its name from Saxe-Coburg and Gotha to Windsor.

19 JULY
German Reichstag votes for a Peace Resolution.

31 JULY
The British launch a major offensive in Flanders, beginning the Third Battle of Ypres.

26 SEPTEMBER
British Ypres offensive continues with a successful attack at Polygon Wood.

24 OCTOBER
An Austro-German breakthrough at Caporetto drives the Italian army into chaotic retreat.

26 OCTOBER
Canadian troops spearhead the final assault on Passchendaele Ridge.

30 OCTOBER
Vittorio Orlando becomes Italian prime minister.

31 OCTOBER
The British attack Turkish defences at Gaza and Beersheba in Palestine.

⌃ General Luigi Cadorna

20 NOVEMBER
A British offensive at Cambrai using massed tanks achieves a short-lived breakthrough.

26 NOVEMBER
The Russian Bolshevik government asks for an armistice.

8 DECEMBER
French and British troops arrive in Italy to help stabilize a defensive line at the Piave river.

9 DECEMBER
Romania signs an armistice with the Central Powers.

11 DECEMBER
General Allenby leads the formal entry of British forces into the holy city of Jerusalem.

15 DECEMBER
Bolshevik Russia and Germany sign an armistice at Brest-Litovsk.

« US recruitment office

« BEFORE

At the start of the war, Russia's social and political problems were briefly forgotten, but divisions reopened as military disasters and economic hardship unfolded.

STRING OF DEFEATS
Russia suffered a series of military setbacks from its **defeat at Tannenberg « 64–65** in August 1914 to the **Great Retreat from Poland « 70–71** in summer 1915. Although the **Brusilov Offensive « 174–75** in summer 1916 was initially a major victory, it did not bring an end to the war any closer.

ROLE OF RASPUTIN
Distrust of Russia's rulers centred on alleged treachery at court. With **Tsar Nicholas II away at the front** commanding the Russian army, suspicions fell on his German-born wife, **Alexandra**, and her associate, the mystic **Rasputin**. In December 1916, Rasputin was murdered by noblemen trying to restore the reputation of the monarchy.

CARTOON OF NICHOLAS II, RASPUTIN, AND ALEXANDRA

The **Tsar Overthrown**

In March 1917, Russia's tsarist regime was toppled – partly for its failure to cope with the demands of modern warfare. The Provisional Government that took its place struggled to reinvigorate the Russian war effort while also holding off pressure for more radical change.

By early 1917, popular hostility towards the tsarist regime was widespread. In the army and navy, morale was poor and there were several mutinies. In the factories, workers staged strikes as wages fell behind the rapidly rising prices. In the countryside, peasants hoarded food and coveted the estates of landowners.

Educated Russians also resented the regime. Middle-class politicians in the Duma (the Russian parliament) despaired of the incompetence of the tsarist administration, which made fighting an effective war impossible.

The people revolt
The Russian capital, Petrograd (St Petersburg), was especially hard hit by shortages of food and fuel. Its population had expanded rapidly during the war and keeping the urban masses supplied was beyond the capacity of the railway system, which was crippled by a lack of coal. On 8 March 1917 (23 February according to the Julian calendar, then in use in Russia), demonstrators celebrating International Women's Day

were joined on the streets of the capital by striking factory workers. Protests focused on the shortage of bread.

By 11 March, the city's factories were at a standstill and demonstrators numbered hundreds of thousands. When soldiers garrisoning Petrograd were ordered to suppress the protests, most refused and joined the revolt.

Tsar Nicholas II, who had left Petrograd for military headquarters just before the uprising, attempted to return to the capital. But on

15 March, on the advice of his senior generals and ministers, he abdicated in favour of his brother, Grand Duke Michael. The Grand Duke, however, declined to take the throne until a new constitution was agreed.

In effect, Russia's monarchy was at an end. Nicholas sought exile in Britain, but King George V was advised that the former tsar's presence might provoke unrest among the British working class, and so refused to receive him. Nicholas thus remained under house arrest, with his family, at the Alexander Palace at Tsarskoe Selo.

In the absence of a tsar, a group of politicians from

Revolution in Petrograd
Russian workers and soldiers demonstrate in front of St Isaac's Cathedral in Petrograd (St Petersburg). The popular uprising led to the downfall of the tsarist regime in March 1917.

ZA NASZE I
WASZE SWOBODE

22 January 1917, he spoke in favour of "peace without victory". But the German resumption of unrestricted submarine warfare that month, in which merchant ships were sunk without warning, forced his hand.

Marching into Europe

Although Wilson was initially reluctant to enter the war, he was thorough and absolute in its pursuit once the decision was taken. His speech to Congress on 2 April 1917, requesting approval for a declaration of war, represented his intention to fight for the purest motives. America was going to march into Europe and remake the continent in accordance with principles of democracy and justice that would end war forever. Justified by such ends, he introduced compulsory military service, and banned criticism of the war.

Wilson never agreed a joint policy with the Allies. The USA would fight its own war for aims that the president expressed in the Fourteen Points

Stars and Stripes Forever

A poster dating from the peak period of Wilson's popularity during the war depicts him as the natural successor of America's greatest presidents, George Washington and Abraham Lincoln.

that he declared in front of Congress in January 1918. Widely publicized by American propagandists, Wilson's principles, stressing justice for all, including minorities, gave hope to millions of people worldwide who were desperate for peace and freedom.

Wilson's idealism and even-handed tone concealed his commitment to overthrowing German militarism, which he blamed for causing the war. His apparent fairness encouraged the German leadership to believe they might be able to avoid punitive peace terms in their negotiations with Wilson in October 1917. But when the Germans asked him for an armistice based on the Fourteen Points, Wilson instead joined forces with the British and French in imposing crushing armistice terms on Germany.

Hero's welcome

When Wilson visited Europe in December 1918 he was cheered, adored, and idolized. A great weight of expectation lay upon him, but he was not in any position to dictate his own

> " **... unless justice** be **done** to others it will **not be done** to **us.**"
>
> WOODROW WILSON, FOURTEEN POINTS
> SPEECH, 8 JANUARY 1918

peace terms. Forced to compromise with the interests of the other victors at the Paris Peace Conference, he settled for establishing the League of Nations as a future mechanism for maintaining peace. Returning to the USA, he toured the country delivering speeches to sell the idea of the League.

At that crucial moment, Wilson's health collapsed. Crippled by a stroke, he struggled to complete his term of office. Whether as a fit man he could have persuaded Congress to sign up for the League of Nations and the peace treaty will never be known, but in the event it accepted neither. Wilson's health never recovered and he died in 1924.

Visit to France

Wilson's motorcade passes through the streets of Paris on his first visit to Europe in December 1918. He was greeted as a saviour by the populations of the victorious Allied countries.

TIMELINE

December 1856 Born in Staunton, Virginia, the son of a minister in the Presbyterian Church. His family moves to Augusta, Georgia, in the following year.

1879 Graduates from Princeton University, New Jersey.

1883 Studies for a doctorate in history and political science at Johns Hopkins University, Maryland, taking his PhD in 1886.

1885 Marries Ellen Louise Axson, daughter of a Presbyterian minister.

1890 Becomes professor of jurisprudence and political science at Princeton.

1902 Appointed president of Princeton, a post that he holds until 1910.

November 1910 Elected Democratic governor of New Jersey with a reformist agenda.

November 1912 Elected as 28th President of the USA with 41.8 per cent of the popular vote, aided by a split in the Republican vote.

August 1914 His wife dies in the same week as the outbreak of war in Europe. Declares the USA strictly neutral.

May 1915 Protests strongly to Germany over the U-boat sinking of the liner RMS *Lusitania*.

December 1915 Marries his second wife, Edith Bolling Galt. Expands US armed forces through the National Defense Act.

April 1916 Threatens to break off diplomatic relations with Germany after the U-boat sinking of the British passenger ferry SS *Sussex*.

November 1916 Wins a second term of office in a close-fought presidential election.

December 1916 Sends a Peace Note to the combatants in Europe, inviting them to state their war aims.

2 April 1917 Asks Congress for approval of a declaration of war on Germany.

January 1918 Issues the Fourteen Points, intended as a programme for a just peace.

October 1918 Refuses German peace advances based on acceptance of continued rule of the Kaiser and military leadership.

December 1918 Visits France and Britain after the Armistice, receiving a hero's welcome.

June 1919 Attends the Paris Peace Conference, in which his principles are compromised by European political realities.

September–October 1919 Campaigns in the USA for acceptance of the League of Nations, but his health breaks down and he suffers a stroke.

December 1920 Awarded the Nobel Peace Prize for 1919.

1924 Dies on 3 February at his townhouse in Washington, DC.

WILSON'S IMAGE ON THE $100,000 BANKNOTE

Organizing America for War

When the USA entered the war on 6 April 1917, it was unprepared for a major conflict. To create a mass army and organize resources for the war effort, radical measures were needed, involving an unprecedented expansion of government and the sacrifice of basic freedoms.

« **BEFORE**

The USA remained neutral at the start of World War I, but pressure to enter the war built through 1915.

NATIONAL DEFENSE ACT
From 1915, President Woodrow Wilson came under pressure from the **Preparedness Movement «** 130–31, which wanted **conscription** introduced. Wilson compromised with the **National Defense Act** of June 1916, which expanded the US Army and the National Guard, a military reserve force, on a **voluntary basis**. However, by April 1917 there were only 120,000 Americans in the army and 180,000 National Guardsmen. This compared with European armies that numbered millions.

Industry was already **geared up for war**, fulfilling orders for armaments from the British and French. These orders were financed by **loans from American banks**.

The immediate task of the US government after its decision to go to war was to create a new national army. Its existing regular force was inadequate for the demands of a major European war.

President Woodrow Wilson had publicly stated his opposition to conscription as late as February 1917, and he remained briefly committed to the volunteer principle even after war was declared. Many of his Democrat supporters in the southern and western states regarded compulsory military service as an unacceptable offence against the liberty of the individual.

Introducing the draft

Volunteers were slow to come forward – just 97,000 had enlisted by the end of April 1917 – and so Wilson soon succumbed to the argument that conscription, as well as being fairer, would make it easier to balance the demands of the military against industry's need for skilled workers.

The Selective Service Act, passed on 18 May 1917, required all male American citizens aged 21 to 31 to register for the draft by 5 June (the age range later became 18 to 45). Local boards then had to decide who should be drafted. Federal or state officials and workers in designated industries were exempted, as were men whose family circumstances were deemed to require their presence at home. Only members of recognized pacifist religious group such as Quakers were exempted from the draft on grounds of conscience.

Liberty bonds
Investing in government bonds to raise money for the war was presented as a patriotic duty of all US citizens. This poster, with its diverse list of names, urges all ethnic groups to support the war.

ON THE JOB FOR VICTORY
UNITED STATES SHIPPING BOARD   EMERGENCY FLEET CORPORATION

Once inducted, draftees were fed into a training programme for which new army camps were established across the USA. Volunteers continued to join the regular army, as well as supplying sailors for the navy.

Racial segregation
Black Americans were drafted in disproportionately high numbers. All the American armed services were strictly segregated. Plans to field 16 black infantry combat divisions were scaled back after riots involving black soldiers in Houston, Texas, in August 1917, provoked racist fears about the consequences of arming African Americans. The majority of black draftees were assigned to supply units, involved in delivering and maintaining equipment, and limited to performing menial jobs as cooks or labourers. However, two black infantry divisions eventually saw combat in France.

Building ships for the war
A poster publicizes the vital role of shipbuilding in the American war effort. Under the US Shipping Board's Emergency Fleet Corporation, American shipyards vastly expanded output during the course of the war.

The Committee on Public Information, a government propaganda body headed by popular journalist George Creel was entrusted with selling the war to the American people. Creel enlisted the help of the media and sent public speakers across the nation to rouse patriotic sentiment. He also flooded the country with provocative propaganda posters.

Silencing dissent
Only a small number of Americans actively opposed the war or the draft, but the government took harsh measures against this minority. The Espionage Act of June 1917, reinforced by the Sedition Act in May 1918, gave

> **"Lead this people** into war and they'll **forget** there ever was such a thing as **tolerance. To fight** you must be **brutal and ruthless..."**
>
> PRESIDENT WOODROW WILSON, PRIVATE CONVERSATION, 1 APRIL 1917

Joining the army
Drafted men queue to be issued with their uniforms at Camp Travis in San Antonio, Texas. Almost 3 million Americans were drafted in World War I. Equipping and training this mass army was a formidable task.

the authorities sweeping powers to suppress dissent. The Socialist Party of America and the Industrial Workers of the World movement (popularly known as the "Wobblies") were targeted for harsh punishments. The Socialist Party's leader, Eugene Debs, for example, was sentenced to ten years in prison in 1918 for making speeches criticizing the draft.

Economic factors

Organizing the war effort also involved unprecedented federal intervention in the economy. The War Industries Board under

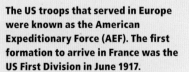

Bernard Baruch drove the production of munitions through cooperation with big business. Railways were taken under federal control and so were shipyards. Federal boards were set up to oversee production, and the consumption of food and fuel. Not all war industry developed smoothly – aircraft production failed to develop – but output was mostly impressive. The tonnage of ships completed multiplied fivefold between 1916 and 1918.

US Navy uniform for women
In 1917, the US Navy started enlisting women to perform support duties. Previously, the only women in the military services were nurses.

The government found it politically impossible to raise money for the war effort through extra taxes. Instead, it depended on patriotic appeals to invest in "liberty bonds". Some $21 billion was raised in this way.

Inevitably, the war had an impact on everyday life. There was little formal rationing, but patriotic Americans were urged to observe "meatless", "gasless", and "wheatless" days. Labour shortages drew more women into factory work and opened new job opportunities for African Americans, some 400,000 of whom migrated from the rural south to northern cities such as Chicago and New York between 1916 and 1918. For Americans of German origin, the war brought suspicion and occasional incidents of persecution.

AFTER ≫

The US troops that served in Europe were known as the American Expeditionary Force (AEF). The first formation to arrive in France was the US First Division in June 1917.

READY FOR BATTLE
Through 1917, First Division was joined by other formations, including the 42nd "Rainbow" Division of National Guardsmen. But it was not until spring 1918 that **General Jack Pershing 310–11 ≫**, commander of the AEF, felt he had sufficient troops to enter battle. By the war's end some **2.8 million American soldiers had been sent to France**. About 116,000 died on military service, half of them killed by the influenza epidemic of 1918–19. The Espionage Act was a permanent legacy of the war, remaining in use in the USA into the 21st century.

Peace Initiatives and War Aims

By 1917, the destructiveness of the war and the lack of any prospect of military victory had led to war weariness. Combatant states were under pressure to end the slaughter, and those determined to continue had to clarify their goals if they were to maintain popular support.

Pope Benedict XV

In 1916 and 1917, the pope launched a series of peace initiatives, arguing for an agreement placing "the moral force of right" above "the material force of arms". His initiatives were scorned by both sides.

<< **BEFORE**

Few people in the combatant countries had openly opposed the war in the early years of the conflict.

FORCES FOR PEACE
In Germany, **revolutionary socialists** Karl Liebknecht and Rosa Luxemburg were imprisoned for anti-war agitation in summer 1916. In Britain, notable pacifists included Scottish socialist **Keir Hardie** and philosopher **Bertrand Russell**. Anti-war **feminists** met at an International Congress of Women at the Hague in the Netherlands in 1915. At government level, Germany offered **peace negotiations** in December 1916, but these were tantamount to the Allies accepting a German victory.

In July 1917, British Army lieutenant Siegfried Sassoon issued a statement protesting against the war. He claimed it was "being deliberately prolonged by those who have the power to end it" and that the conflict had changed from "a war of defence and liberation" into "a war of aggression and conquest". Sassoon's personal protest – which had no practical effect – expressed an increasingly common feeling in all the countries involved in the conflict.

Evidence of mounting disaffection was widespread, from mutinies in the French army in May 1917 to industrial strikes in all combatant countries.

Anti-war forces
Opposition to the war had two main strands. Revolutionary socialists, such as the Russian Bolsheviks and the Spartacists, led by Rosa Luxemburg and Karl Liebknecht in Germany, saw the war as a capitalist swindle imposed on the international working class.

Moderate socialists and liberals, in contrast, were prepared to support the war as long as it was fought for national defence or idealistic goals, but not if it was for conquest. For many Germans, the overthrow of the tsarist regime in Russia in March 1917 ended the main threat to Germany and thus took away the justification for the war. In July 1917, Social Democrats and centre parties in the Reichstag, Germany's parliament, passed a resolution calling for "a peace of understanding and… reconciliation".

In the same month, an attempt by socialists to hold an international peace conference in Stockholm, Sweden, was sabotaged by the refusal of combatant countries, including France and Britain, to issue delegates with passports.

The seizure of power by revolutionary Bolsheviks in Russia in November 1917 gave the Bolshevik leader, Vladimir Ilyich Lenin, a platform for expounding the Bolsheviks' views on the war. He urged combatant countries to pursue a "just and democratic peace" without annexations or indemnities.

Peace broker
It was partly in order to seize back the moral high ground from Lenin that US President Woodrow Wilson launched his Fourteen Points peace programme in January 1918, in which he envisaged a postwar world based on the principles of democracy and national self-determination.

The British, French, and Italians had reservations about some of Wilson's points, but broadly endorsed the American aims. This did not, however, make peace negotiations any more likely. Ignoring the Reichstag, the German military leadership intended to dominate Europe, with virtual

British conscientious objectors
In May 1917, Britain's Independent Labour Party (ILP) mounted a demonstration in support of conscientious objectors held in Dartmoor prison. While the Labour Party backed the war, the minority ILP opposed it.

annexation of Belgium and control of Poland. The Allies had demands that went beyond evicting German troops from territory occupied during the war – France, for example, required the return of Alsace-Lorraine, annexed by Germany in the Franco-Prussian War.

Emperor Charles of Austria, however, was interested in peace. He viewed the war as a disaster that threatened the survival of his country. But his secret approach to the French government in March 1917 was fruitless, as he was incapable of a foreign policy independent of his German allies.

AFTER >>

The first peace negotiations of the war were held between Russia and the Central Powers at Brest-Litovsk, in December 1917. Their outcome was a brutal, imposed agreement.

BREST-LITOVSK TREATY
In March 1918, Russia, under duress, signed the **Brest-Litovsk Treaty 276–77 >>**, in which it lost territory containing about 30 per cent of its population. Germany also imposed a **harsh peace on Romania** in May. Exploitative and annexationist, these treaties were taken by the Allies as an example of the terms they could expect if they were defeated.

THE TABLES TURN
In October 1918, facing defeat, Germany sought an **armistice** on the basis of President Woodrow Wilson's **Fourteen Points 322–33 >>**. By then, anti-war feeling was rampant in Austria-Hungary and Germany. In Allied countries on the verge of victory, support for the war revived.

The dead vote for peace

An image from a 1917 German Social Democrat satirical magazine, *Der Wahre Jacob*, is captioned: "Those in favour of a negotiated peace, raise your hands." The scale of the deaths made it hard to accept that the war might have been fought in vain.

The **U-boat Onslaught**

A campaign of unrestricted submarine warfare launched against Allied merchant shipping from February 1917 almost won the war for Germany. The adoption of a convoy system by the Royal Navy cut Allied shipping losses, but the submarine menace was never overcome.

« BEFORE

The German submarine campaign against Allied merchant shipping in February 1915 was in response to the British naval blockade of Germany.

U-BOAT ATTACKS

Initially, Germany had only 20 U-boats, but they achieved considerable success. In May 1915, the submarine *U-20* **sank the liner RMS** *Lusitania* **« 126–27**, causing the deaths of 1,198 passengers and crew and provoking a protest from the US government. In May 1916, after US objections to an attack on the British passenger ferry **SS** *Sussex*, Germany suspended submarine warfare, but it resumed restricted operations in October.

SINKING OF THE *LUSITANIA*

On 22 December 1916, Admiral Henning von Holtzendorff, the German navy's Chief of Staff, sent a memorandum to Kaiser Wilhelm II arguing for unrestricted submarine warfare. The U-boat campaign had been a subject of intense debate among Germany's political and military leaders since early in the war, its negative impact on relations with neutral countries such as the USA balanced against its effectiveness as a weapon against Allied trade.

In late 1916, German U-boats were sinking a considerable number of merchant ships, but their operations were hampered by restrictions such as allowing crews to disembark first, to appease neutral states. Holtzendorff argued that such restrictions should be lifted and U-boats permitted to sink any ship bound for British ports without any warning. Since Britain was utterly dependent on food imports,

the British could be starved into submission in six months. At a meeting on 8 January 1917, the proposal for unrestricted submarine warfare was adopted by the German military leadership, although they knew it would almost certainly lead to war with the USA.

Forcing Britain to its knees

Germany had greatly expanded its submarine fleet since the start of the war and had 148 U-boats available

to begin the campaign in February 1917. The initial results were horrifyingly impressive. Holtzendorff had calculated that sinking 600,000 tons of merchant shipping a month would force Britain to its knees. Operating as lone hunters, the U-boats spread out across crowded shipping lanes and picked off any vessels that came into view. The most successful commanders were sinking several ships a day.

The British Admiralty's response, under First Sea Lord Admiral John Jellicoe, was to order the Royal Navy to hunt down the U-boats and destroy them. But this was impossible. The navy had developed hydrophones to

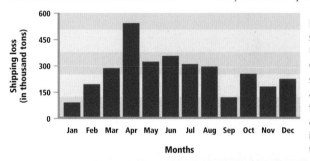

British merchant shipping losses to U-boats in 1917
German unrestricted submarine warfare increased attacks on merchant ships from February to April. The adoption of a convoy system in May reduced sinkings to a sustainable level.

> **"Submarine warfare** is… the **right way to end this war** victoriously…"
>
> ADMIRAL HENNING VON HOLTZENDORFF, MEMORANDUM, 22 DECEMBER 1916

listen for submarines underwater, and depth charges to destroy them once they were found, but submerged U-boats could rarely be located accurately enough to give any chance of a kill. Only nine U-boats were sunk from February through April 1917 – paltry losses that German shipyards could easily make up.

The convoy solution

While bizarre solutions such as training circus sea lions to detect U-boats were explored with enthusiasm, Jellicoe and the Admiralty staff resisted the introduction of a convoy system – merchant ships sailing together, protected by the Royal Navy – on the grounds that warships could not be spared as escorts.

In late April, with Britain facing disaster, Jellicoe approved a trial

German U-boat heroes
An illustration in a German wartime magazine presents a dramatic image of a heroic U-boat crew in action. Casualties were heavy, with half of all German submarines lost in the course of the war.

convoy. It proved successful, with 16 merchant ships reaching port without loss. Introduction of the convoy system was slow – about half of all merchant ships were travelling in convoys by the end of 1917 – but it saved Britain from defeat. U-boats found convoys more difficult to locate than the same number of vessels scattered across the sea and far more dangerous to approach and attack.

By the second half of 1917, monthly merchant shipping losses had fallen to an average of 400,000 tons and U-boat losses had risen to between five and ten a month. Use of convoys increased through 1918 as the number of escort vessels rose, including American destroyers.

Nets and mines

The Allies never overcame the German U-boat menace. Large-scale resources were devoted to creating and patrolling anti-submarine barriers across the Dover Straits and between Scotland and Norway. Comprising underwater nets and mines, these barriers presented an obstacle to U-boats, but with patience they could pass through safely. Increasing British use of air patrols, mostly with blimps (non-rigid airships), also made life more difficult for the German submarines, forcing them to submerge, which they could do for only short periods.

Yet in summer 1918, the U-boat campaign was still in full swing. In a notorious incident in June, a Canadian hospital ship, HMHS *Llandovery Castle*, was sunk by *U-86* and the survivors were fired on in their lifeboats. Long-range U-boats were deployed across the Atlantic, sinking ships in US coastal waters. As late as 10 October 1918, with the end of the war in sight, the mailboat RMS *Leinster* was torpedoed outside Dublin Bay, killing over 500 people.

In all, 5,000 Allied merchant ships were sunk by German U-boats during the war, set against 178 U-boats destroyed in combat.

Barrel

Gunsight

Breech

Gunner's seat

German U-boat gun
U-boats were typically armed with one or two deck guns for use on the surface. These guns, such as the 10.5 cm (4.1 in) shown here, were very effective with high rates of fire.

AFTER ≫

The U-boat campaign had many consequences. As well as drawing the USA into the war, it was a major preoccupation for Allied strategists.

ALLIED RESPONSE
The desire to attack U-boat bases on the coast of Flanders was a major motive for the British-led offensive at **Passchendaele (Third Ypres) 240–43 ≫** in July to November 1917. The U-boat bases were also targeted unsuccessfully from the sea by the Royal Navy in the **Zeebrugge Raid 292–93 ≫** in April 1918. The U-boat campaign had an impact on British food supplies, causing inflation to rise and some rationing in spring 1918, but there were never serious food shortages in Britain.

SUBMARINE BAN
After the war, Germany was **banned from possessing submarines** under the terms of the **Treaty of Versailles 338–39 ≫**. Over time, the Germans circumvented this restriction and Britain accepted the existence of a U-boat fleet in the 1935 Anglo-German Naval Agreement.

Underwater raider
A German U-boat rises to the surface during a patrol. The range of submarines increased during the course of the war – by 1918, they could cross the Atlantic to operate in American coastal waters.

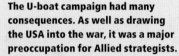

GERMAN GENERAL Born 1865 Died 1937

Erich Ludendorff

"Basically, **this war** comes down simply **to killing one another.**"

GENERAL ERICH LUDENDORFF, APRIL 1917

The son of an undistinguished Prussian landowner – lowly origins by the standards of the German officer corps – Erich Ludendorff made a brilliant career in the peacetime army through hard work and intelligence. He was appointed to a position on the General Staff, where he became an expert on war planning and mobilization.

Considered abrasive and arrogant by his fellow officers, he made no effort to ingratiate himself. He showed his indifference to conventional opinion by marrying a divorcee with four children. Although a consummate military professional, he also lacked the traditional soldier's respect for hierarchical authority. Shortly before the war, convinced that limits on

military spending were crippling the German army, he conspired with nationalist politicians to press for a change in policy. His outspoken criticisms outraged his superiors and he was sacked from the General Staff.

Man of action

When war broke out, Ludendorff was in command of an infantry brigade, a relatively lowly position. But his experience on the General Staff meant that he was also a leading expert on the Schlieffen Plan, Germany's initial war strategy. As such, he was immediately switched to a role on the staff of the Second Army, spearheading the invasion of Belgium. Entering combat for the first time at

Tough leader

Energetic and arrogant, General Ludendorff never troubled to make himself liked. He antagonized army colleagues and the Kaiser, but he was clear-sighted and determined.

Ludendorff Donation Fund
A postcard publicizes a charitable fund for servicemen disabled in the war. Set up in spring 1918, the fund borrowed Ludendorff's name for credibility, though he made little effort himself to aid crippled soldiers.

Captured Russian weapons
The Germans survey a collection of machine-guns seized from the Russians at the Battle of Riga in September 1917. This was the last military engagement before the final disintegration of the Russian army.

the offensive made some initial gains, with several kilometres of ground taken. The Germans, however, had already transferred divisions from the Western Front to meet the well-publicized attack.

The Russian advance stalled after two days. In many places, reserves refused orders to relieve the front-line troops. As the German and Austro-Hungarian counterattack got under way, Russian troops fled in a chaotic retreat that degenerated into mass desertion.

Spiralling crisis

Military disaster at the front was accompanied by political disturbances in Petrograd, known as the July Days. Demonstrators calling for the overthrow of the Provisional Government were suppressed by Kerensky with the aid of loyal military units. The Bolsheviks were blamed for the

protests, and their leader, Vladimir Ilyich Lenin, fled to Finland to avoid imprisonment. Tightening his grip on power, Kerensky became prime minister, while Brusilov, paying the price for the failed offensive, was replaced as commander-in-chief by General Lavr Kornilov.

Kornilov took command of Russia's disintegrating army. On 1 September, the German General Oskar von Hutier

launched an offensive at Riga, on the Baltic, using new infiltration tactics. The German forces easily defeated the demoralized Russians, taking Riga in just two days.

The battle at Riga was the last serious fighting on the Eastern Front. Hutier's forces began advancing on Petrograd, but quickly realized it was pointless. The Russian state and its army were falling apart.

The failure of the Kerensky Offensive helped send Russia into a political and social meltdown.

PRESSURE ON KERENSKY
After the Russian defeat at Riga, **Kerensky dismissed General Kornilov**, who was alleged to have been planning a military coup. To defend himself, Kerensky relied on the armed support of revolutionary workers and soldiers in Petrograd. He released Bolshevik leaders from prison, including **Leon Trotsky**.

THE ROAD TO CIVIL WAR
In November, the **Bolsheviks ousted Kerensky** and set up a **revolutionary government**. They sought an armistice with Germany and accepted a punitive **peace treaty** at **Brest-Litovsk 252–53 ≫** in March 1918. **Civil war** then broke out between the anti-Bolshevik White and the Bolshevik Red armies.

BOLSHEVIK BANNER

Advance in Galicia
Russian soldiers run past a church in the Galicia region, the main site of the Kerensky Offensive in July 1917. The Russian attacks quickly ran out of momentum and were repulsed by German and Austro-Hungarian troops.

The **Revolutionary Army**

When the Kerensky Offensive began to fail, Russian morale plummeted and the army started to disintegrate. Some troops refused to fight and soldiers' committees questioned whether officers should be obeyed.

"Since you could not fight bravely and beat the enemy for the old regime, under the threat of being shot, surely you will not now hesitate... to defend our freedom and exalt our great Revolution.

We will be ready then to sacrifice ourselves, to defend at whatever cost that which we have won, and, where it may be necessary, to hurl ourselves upon the enemy and crush him.

Then all hail to Mother Russia, and long may she live. And hail to our Provisional Government, and our War Minister, Kerensky, whose hope is in us. And I, comrade soldiers and officers, vouch for it to them that we will honourably, faithfully, and gallantly fulfil our duty. **"**

COMMANDER-IN-CHIEF ALEXEI BRUSILOV'S ADDRESS TO THE RUSSIAN ARMY BEFORE THE OPENING OF THE KERENSKY OFFENSIVE, 1 JULY 1917

"At 10 o'clock, July 19th, the 607th Mlynoff Regiment... left their trenches voluntarily and retired, with the result that the neighbouring units had to retire also. This gave the enemy the opportunity for developing his success.

Our failure is explained to a considerable degree by the fact that under the influence of the extremists (Bolsheviks) several detachments, having received the command to support the attacked detachments, held meetings and discussed the advisability of obeying the order, whereupon some of the regiments refused to obey the military command. The efforts of the commanders and committees to arouse the men to the fulfilment of the commands were fruitless.**"**

BRUSILOV'S OFFICIAL REPORT, 21 JULY 1917

Russian army disintegrates
A Russian soldier attacks a retreating comrade near Ternopil, Ukraine, in July 1917. In the face of the German counter-offensive, the Russian army began a rapid and chaotic retreat. Ternopil fell on 26 July, and Riga, in the north, was captured in early September.

Messines Ridge

The Battle of Messines Ridge in June 1917 is chiefly remembered for the massive explosions that destroyed German positions at the start of the British attack. It was an outstanding offensive success for the British Army, and a rare instance of German defenders suffering the heavier losses.

‹‹ BEFORE

The First and Second battles of Ypres in 1914 and 1915 left the British holding a salient, facing German troops entrenched on higher ground.

ALLIED FAILURES
From early 1916, British commander-in-chief **Field Marshal Douglas Haig ‹‹ 178–79** favoured an offensive at the **Ypres salient**, but the need to cooperate with the French led to operations at the **Somme ‹‹ 180–83** and **Arras ‹‹ 226–27**. The failure of the French **Nivelle Offensive ‹‹ 224–25** in spring 1917 and subsequent **mutinies** in the French army left the British to pursue their own plans. Haig envisaged a major offensive at Ypres, in preparation for which the British Second Army would seize Messines Ridge.

In early May 1917, British Second Army commander General Herbert Plumer, commander in the Ypres salient since 1915, was ordered to prepare an operation to take the low German-held ridge stretching from Messines to Wystchaete and a position known as Hill 60, 5 km (3 miles) southeast of Ypres. This would strengthen the British position south of Ypres as the prelude to a larger Flanders offensive further north. Plumer had proposed an attack on Messines as early as January 1916.

The underground war
By 1917, preparations were well advanced for destroying the German defences with buried explosives. The waterlogged ground in Flanders was on the whole unsuitable for tunnelling, but at Messines British Royal Engineers had found a usable layer of blue clay

Mining at Messines
Tunnellers at work under the Ypres salient. Excavation was hard and dangerous, and often done by candlelight in a slurry of mud. The tunnellers made as little noise as possible for fear of betraying their location to the enemy.

at a depth of 25–30 m (80–100 ft). Through 1916, around 30,000 British, Australian, Canadian, and New Zealand soldiers – a combination of military engineers and infantrymen who were miners in civilian life – had dug tunnels under the German-held ridge. At the end of each tunnel they hollowed out a chamber to hold explosives.

The work of tunnelling was arduous, despite the availability of portable oxygen tanks, electric light, and eventually mechanical diggers. The task was made more difficult by German counter-measures to locate and blow up the British tunnels. The British also listened for the Germans and mounted counterattacks, digging tunnels at lesser depth to intercept the German tunnellers. Occasionally, miners would break into an enemy tunnel, and hand-to-hand combat ensued. In August 1916, the German tunnellers had a major success in this underground war, when they broke into a British chamber and destroyed it.

More than 20 British tunnels remained undetected. The chambers were packed with explosives, much of

8,000 The estimated length in metres (26,000 ft) of the tunnels dug under Messines Ridge by British and Commonwealth engineers.

it in metal containers to protect against the wet conditions. Because tunnelling subsided towards the end of 1916, the Germans on Messines Ridge became complacent. By spring 1917, they had stopped worrying about mines.

Supply lines
General Plumer was a methodical commander with a reputation for being careful with his soldiers' lives. He had new light railways constructed behind the British lines to bring up ammunition and other supplies. Because thirst was a constant problem for troops in battle, pipelines were laid

On Messines Ridge
Gunner F.J. Mears, who served with the British artillery in France during the war, painted this picture of soldiers on Messines Ridge. The trees lining the road have been stripped bare by shellfire.

to ensure a supply of water at the front. An impressive concentration of artillery was assembled along a 16 km (10 mile) front, with 2,200 guns to support an infantry assault.

Defences organized in depth

The German defences presented a formidable challenge. By 1917, the German army had greatly refined its defensive tactics. Instead of facing a line of trenches, Allied soldiers were met with defences organized in depth. At Messines, this meant four systems of trenches, machine-gun emplacements, and concrete pillboxes, backed by further positions. The Germans accepted that an attack would break into these defences, but counterattack forces held at the rear were to come forward once the enemy onslaught lost momentum and drive the attackers back with heavy losses.

Messines Ridge was held by a corps of the German Fourth Army commanded by General Maximilian

von Laffert. He chose to maintain unusually large numbers of troops in his front two lines, a decision the Germans came to regret.

On 21 May, the British guns began a devastatingly effective preliminary bombardment that lasted for 17 days.

Plunger to activate

Explosives detonator

Most of the equipment used for digging mines and setting off explosive charges was identical to that employed by civilian miners and engineers. Nineteen charges were detonated almost simultaneously at Messines.

Electrical contact

Explosive box

Leather strap

The success of the Battle of Messines boosted British morale and encouraged Field Marshal Haig's plans for a full-scale offensive in Flanders.

PASSCHENDAELE
Haig launched the **Third Battle of Ypres 240–45 »**, known as the Battle of Passchendaele, on 31 July 1917. Continuing through to November, this turned into a vast attritional struggle without decisive result.

POSTWAR MESSINES
At least two of the buried **mines** at Messines remained **unexploded** after the end of the war. One of them erupted in 1955, fortunately killing only a cow. Since 1998, Messines has been the site of the **Irish Peace Tower**, commemorating Catholic and Protestant Irish soldiers who died in World War I.

THE IRISH PEACE TOWER AT MESSINES

Precisely targeted with the assistance of reconnaissance aircraft, British firepower destroyed a large part of the German artillery. German infantry positions were laid to waste. Front-line troops could not be relieved or supplied and ran short of food and water.

Walls of fire

The British attack was launched on 7 June. At 3:10am, just before dawn, the mines in 19 of the chambers under Messines Ridge were exploded by the engineers. The mines ranged from 7,700 kg (17,000 lb) to over 43,000 kg (95,000 lb) of explosives. Eyewitnesses

fire over their heads. The soldiers engaged in the assault were chiefly Australians and New Zealanders of the Anzac Corps, who captured Messines village, and Irish soldiers of the 16th Irish and 36th Ulster divisions. Formed in 1914 around the Catholic National Volunteers and the Protestant Ulster Volunteer Force respectively, militias that had been close to fighting one another in a civil war, the Irish forces advanced side by side, taking the village of Wystchaete.

Reserves were fed forward in the afternoon to capture further objectives and consolidate the gains. German

" Out of the **dark ridges** of Messines and Wystchaete… **gushed out and up…** volumes of **scarlet flame.** "

PHILIP GIBBS, WAR CORRESPONDENT, DESCRIBING THE EXPLOSIONS ON 7 JUNE 1917

described sheets of flame, clouds of smoke, and the ground shaking like an earthquake. The sound of the explosions was heard in London, over 160 km (100 miles) away.

As many as 10,000 German soldiers may have been killed in the eruption. Dazed survivors wandered towards the British lines to surrender. British troops advanced almost unopposed to occupy the German forward positions and prepared to assault the second line.

At 7am, after a considerable delay, the second stage of the assault opened. Troops advanced close behind a creeping artillery barrage, with massed machine-guns providing supporting

counterattacks were slow to materialize and were mishandled, with British artillery fire making it hard for the German troops to get forward.

Plumer's plan had been to seize and hold limited objectives, rather than achieve a total breakthrough. Fighting continued until 14 June, by which time the British were in possession of the ground they had sought to gain, dominating the Gheluvelt plateau.

The Germans had lost an estimated 25,000 men, including 7,000 taken prisoner, compared with British losses of 17,000 – a rare instance of the attritional balance favouring the side on the offensive.

Third Ypres

The Third Battle of Ypres, often known as Passchendaele, was a British-led offensive that became notorious for the suffering endured by the troops. Begun in pursuit of valid objectives, it degenerated into an attritional struggle fought by soldiers floundering in mud.

BEFORE

British commander-in-chief Field Marshal Douglas Haig had long wanted to mount a major offensive in Flanders. In summer 1917, he decided the time to attack had arrived.

PRESSURE MOUNTS
The **First and Second battles of Ypres ‹‹ 60–61, 102–03** in 1914 and 1915 had left the British dug into a salient around the ruined Belgian town. After the failure of the French **Nivelle Offensive ‹‹ 224–25** in spring 1917, Haig began planning a major operation at Ypres that would relieve pressure on the French and support offensives by Britain's Italian and Russian allies.

BADGE MARKING ALLIED COOPERATION

RECENT VICTORY
The success of new British tactics at the **Battle of Messines Ridge ‹‹ 238–39** in June 1917 encouraged Haig's offensive plans.

British plans for an offensive at the Ypres salient in summer 1917 were bold and strategically coherent. The declared aim was to capture ports in occupied Belgium that were being used as bases for German U-boat attacks on British merchant shipping.

Supported by the French, the British intended to break through the German defences in front of Ypres, and then join up with other British troops to make an amphibious landing on the Belgian coast behind the German lines. From the outset, however, British commander-in-chief Field Marshal Douglas Haig evaded commitment to the second part of the plan, arguing that an offensive at Ypres alone might crack the morale of the German army. Haig believed German resources were strained to breaking point, owing to its commitments on other fronts.

British Prime Minister David Lloyd George tried to oppose plans for an offensive at Ypres, but his suggestions for alternative uses of military resources, such as transferring troops to Italy, carried little weight. Backed by the Chief of the Imperial General Staff, General William Robertson, Haig was allowed to go ahead, although Lloyd George only grudgingly withdrew his veto.

4.25 MILLION The number of shells fired by British artillery in the two-week preliminary bombardment at Third Ypres.

---

2 10 Aug
After a two-week break in the fighting because of heavy rain, the British launch an attack against the Langemarck-Gheluvelt line. Langemarck is taken

3 22 Aug
On the right, British 5th Army makes little progress and is halted on the Menin Road

1 3:50am 31 July
Offensive is launched at dawn. Gains are made on Bixschoote, Pilkem and St Julien ridges to north of Ypres

(Map labels: Houthulst Forest, Poelcappelle, Passchendaele, Zonnebeke, Menin Road, Wervicq, Comines, Polygon Wood, Gheluvelt, 4TH ARMY, Langemarck, St Julien, Broenbeek, Shrewsbury Forest, Sanctuary Wood, 5TH ARMY, Steenbeek, 15 Aug, Pilkem, Zillebeke, Yser Canal, Bixschoote, 31 Jul, Yser Canal, Zillebeke Lake, Ypres, 1ST ARMY, Wytschaete, Messines, 2ND ARMY, Haanebeek)

0 — 5 km
0 — 3 miles

---

6 12 Oct
An assault is launched on Passchendaele. It is unsuccessful, as is a second assault on the 26th

7 6 Nov
Canadians launch a final offensive against Passchendaele and capture it the same day

2 26 Sept
5th Army advances towards Zonnebeke

4 4 Oct
2nd Army launches attack at Broodseinde and captures ridge

3 26 Sept
An attack secures half of Polygon Wood

The first phase
Launched on 31 July 1917, the Allied offensive, led by the British Fifth Army, made initial gains but lost momentum. A renewed attack in mid-August led to the capture of Langemarck. By 26 August, the operation had stalled.

The second phase
The offensive is resumed on 20 September. Despite more heavy rain, attacks continued through October at Broodseinde Ridge, Poelcappelle, and Passchendaele, which was taken on 6 November.

1 20 Sept
Renewed offensive launched against Gheluvelt plateau on the Menin Road

5 9 Oct
An attack in the Poelcappelle region is hampered by rain and mud. It results in virtually no gains

(Map labels: Houthulst Forest, 8 Nov, Passchendaele, 4TH ARMY, Broodseinde, Zonnebeke, Poelcappelle, Gheluvelt, Polygon Wood, Menin Road, Haanebeek, 5TH ARMY, Langemarck, St Julien, 20 Sept, Broenbeek, Shrewsbury Forest, Sanctuary Wood, Steenbeek, Pilkem, Zillebeke, Bixschoote, Zillebeke Lake, Yser Canal, Ypres, 2ND ARMY, 1ST ARMY, Wytschaete, Messines)

KEY
- ■ British army
- ■ French army
- ■ German army
- ➤ British advance
- ➤ French advance
- ⌐ British front line
- ⌐ French front line
- ▨ Road
- ▨ Railway

Battling the mud
British troops haul a gun through mud during the Third Battle of Ypres in September 1917. The appalling conditions under which men had to fight – the result of heavy rain and shelling – were the worst in the war.

> # "It looked as though some **appalling earthquake** had **torn the earth apart...** In the midst of this **men** just had to **hang on.**"

LIEUTENANT COLONEL SÜSSENBERGER, COMMANDING AN INFANTRY COMPANY AT THIRD YPRES

At the Ypres salient, the Germans held the higher ground and had spent almost three years organizing their defences in depth. Haig assigned the lead role in attacking this position to the British Fifth Army commanded by General Hubert Gough, a thrusting cavalry officer. Gough planned to advance 6,000 m (6,000 yd) on the first day, to reach the third line of German defences.

Hurricane of fire

In preparation for the assault, some 3,000 guns bombarded the German positions for a fortnight, firing four times the number of shells expended in preparation for the Somme Offensive the previous year. The damage inflicted on German positions was considerable. The bombardment rose to a climax in the early hours of 31 July. German General Hermann von Kuhl described the bombardment as "a hurricane of fire" in which "the whole earth of Flanders rocked".

Advancing behind a creeping barrage of artillery, the Allied infantry went "over the top" at dawn. They made considerable gains in places, with the British Guards Division, for example, progressing some 4,000 m (4,000 yd). Tanks aided the infantry, lumbering forward over reasonably dry ground. But in accordance with their doctrine

> **7,800** The number of British Fifth Army soldiers killed during the opening of the offensive at Third Ypres, between 31 July and 3 August 1917.

of "flexible defence", the Germans had held back their main strength for counterattacks, which soon began to have an impact on exhausted Allied troops. It also started to rain. Ground churned up by massed artillery fire turned to deep mud punctuated by water-filled shell craters. Wounded men from both sides crawled into these craters for shelter. As the water rose, the most seriously injured drowned.

By 3 August, the initial offensive had petered out far short of its objectives. The maximum advance in some sectors was just 500 m (500 yd). Haig reported to the British War Cabinet that the operation had so far been "highly satisfactory" and losses had been "slight" – in fact, there were around 35,000 Allied casualties in four days.

Crown Prince Rupprecht, the German Army Group commander at Ypres, also described himself as "very satisfied" with the results of the fighting, despite similar losses on the German side.

Renewed attack

After a two-week pause, the British resumed their offensive with attacks at Langemarck and the Gheluvelt plateau. To the south, the Canadian Corps assaulted a position known as Hill 70 outside the town of Lens. Their aim was to stop the Germans transferring troops to Ypres.

»

Fore sight

Barrel

Pan magazine

Cocking handle

Lewis gun
The British Army's standard light machine-gun, the Lewis gun was issued to every infantry section by 1917. In action, the barrel was enclosed in an aluminium tube for air-cooling.

Nach Passchendaele

German road sign
This road sign, "Towards Passchendaele", was erected by the German army. The village was the objective of the British offensive during the final stages of Third Ypres.

>> The Canadian operation went well. Hill 70 was taken and then held against large-scale German counterattacks. Gough's attacks, in contrast, were inadequate in planning and execution, achieving small gains for high losses. At the end of August, Haig sidelined Gough and his Fifth Army, and handed chief responsibility for the Ypres offensive to General Hubert Plumer and the Second Army, the victors at Messines Ridge in June.

Plumer had a clear strategy for the battle. There would be a series of rigorously prepared attacks, each designed to take a limited objective that would then be held against counterattacks. The strategy was called "bite and hold".

Plumer relaunched the offensive at the Menin Road on 20 September and followed up with successful attacks on

The wasteland
After the conclusion of the fighting at Passchendaele in November 1917, the landscape was a wasteland of mud and water-filled shell craters. For many people, Passchendaele symbolized the futility of war.

Polygon Wood on 26 September and Broodseinde Ridge on 4 October. Each attack was carried out in a limited sector with massive artillery support – guns firing both high explosive and gas shells. The infantry had plentiful Lewis guns and rifle grenades among its armoury. The ground was firm enough for tanks to move forward.

The advance was halted before the infantry outran their artillery support, so that German attempts at counterattacks ran into a curtain of shellfire. Overhead, Allied aircraft, defying German anti-aircraft guns, spotted targets for the artillery and machine-gunned German positions.

The Germans suffered notably heavy losses at Broodseinde, where German troops massed in the front line in preparation for an attack of their own were bombarded by British artillery. Large numbers of Germans were taken prisoner, reinforcing Haig's belief that German morale was approaching breaking point.

Waist-deep in mud

After 4 October, however, the weather changed. A return to heavy rain made the ground a sea of mud. Troops struggled to move forward along duckboards – wooden paths laid by engineers over the muddy morass. Where the duckboards ended, men could find themselves waist-deep in mud. Artillery could only be brought up along narrow plank roads, and engineers had to build platforms for the guns to stop them sinking.

In these appalling conditions, renewed attacks at Poelcappelle on 9 October and towards Passchendaele Ridge three days later were a failure. The Australians and New Zealanders suffered particularly heavy casualties. Their artillery support was inadequate because guns could not be manoeuvred into position. Many shells were simply absorbed into the deep mud without exploding. Floundering troops were cut down by flanking machine-gun fire from German concrete pillboxes.

For the New Zealand forces, 9 October was the costliest day of the entire war, with 2,700 casualties trapped in front of uncut barbed wire at Poelcappelle. The Australian Third Division, under General John Monash, experienced even heavier losses attacking at Passchendaele on 12 October.

The first attack on Passchendaele was a costly debacle for British and Commonwealth forces. Meanwhile, the Germans were under almost intolerable pressure. Crown Prince Rupprecht was seriously considering a full-scale withdrawal from positions in front of Ypres.

In reality, however, the British offensive had worn itself out. Germans reinforcements were arriving from the Eastern Front, where the Russian army had ceased to be a serious threat. The Germans also had increasing supplies of mustard gas shells. Above all, the terrible mud made a decisive Allied breakthrough unthinkable.

The last push

Although the British had abandoned plans for an amphibious landing behind German lines, Haig would not give up on his offensive. The morale of many units of the British Army had been badly shaken, so Haig turned to the Canadian Corps. He bullied and pleaded with its commander, General Arthur Currie, to lead a final push to take Passchendaele. Despite expressing coherent objections to the proposed operation, which he believed would be too costly

Identity tag
General John Monash was considered an outstanding Australian commander. He led a division at Third Ypres and later commanded all Australian forces on the Western Front.

to justify any advantage it might bring, Currie finally succumbed to pressure from Haig and accepted the task, with the promise of extra artillery.

The Canadian-led assault on Passchendaele proceeded methodically in three phases. On 26 October, a limited advance broke through key German defensive positions; further advances were made on 30 October; and on 6 November the ruins of Passchendaele fell to the Canadians. It cost 16,000 casualties to take the village. A final

assault on 10 November cleared the ridge of its remaining German presence and brought Third Ypres to a close.

The final count

There is no certainty about the casualty figures on either side in the battle, but it is probable that, between 31 July and 10 November, about 70,000 British and Commonwealth soldiers died at Third Ypres, with another 200,000 wounded or taken prisoner. German losses are even harder to establish, but they may have been broadly similar to Allied casualties.

The battle in the mud was severely demoralizing for soldiers on both sides, but perhaps especially for the British, many of whom learned a bitter distrust of their high command. The distinguished military historian John Keegan wrote: "On the Somme [Haig] had sent the flower of British youth to death or mutilation; at Passchendaele he had tipped the survivors into the slough of despond."

AFTER ≫

By the end of Third Ypres, the course of the war was being altered by events elsewhere.

MIXED FORTUNES
On the Western Front, the British achieved a shortlived breakthrough at **Cambrai 248–49 ≫** in November, ending Allied offensive operations for the winter. In March 1918, the German army launched the first of a series of offensives that, among other gains, **retook Passchendaele**.

DEVELOPMENTS IN ITALY AND RUSSIA
On the Italian front, German and Austrian forces achieved a **breakthrough at Caporetto 246–47 ≫** in the last week of October 1917. Haig was forced to transfer troops from the Western Front to Italy. In Russia, the **Bolsheviks 252–53 ≫** under Vladimir Ilyich Lenin seized power during the last days of Third Ypres. Lenin sought an **armistice with the Central Powers**.

ITALIAN FARINA HELMET

> "The **British army lost its** spirit of **optimism,** and there was a **sense of deadly depression** among the **officers and men…**"
>
> PHILIP GIBBS, WAR CORRESPONDENT, ON THE AFTERMATH OF THIRD YPRES

Recording Third Ypres
This image in chalk of action on the Ypres salient, entitled *Shellburst, Zillebeke*, was made by official British war artist Paul Nash in 1917. Nash recorded the bleak conditions in which the men had to fight.

‹‹ BEFORE

After Italy entered the war on the Allied side in May 1915, Italian and Austro-Hungarian forces were locked in a prolonged stalemate.

ALPINE WARFARE
The fighting took place in the area between Italy and Austria-Hungary, with active sectors in **Trentino** province to the north and at the **Isonzo river** to the east. Apart from an Austro-Hungarian attack at **Asiago in Trentino** in May 1916, the Italians took the offensive. Repeated Italian assaults in the Isonzo sector achieved no decisive result. In January 1917, after the **Ninth Battle of the Isonzo**, the Italians requested support from British and French forces, but none could be spared. Offensives continued through 1917, with the **Eleventh Battle of the Isonzo** in August.

RELIEF FOR GERMANY
Meanwhile, the collapse of the Russian army after the **Kerensky Offensive ‹‹ 234–235** reduced the number of German troops required on the Eastern Front.

Italian Disaster at Caporetto

The overwhelming victory of German and Austro-Hungarian forces at the Battle of Caporetto in October 1917 brought a sudden and spectacular end to more than two years of stalemate and attrition on the Italian front. It failed, however, to knock Italy out of the war.

The fighting on the Italian front was often conducted in terrible conditions. The Isonzo sector, on the modern border between Italy and Slovenia, consisted of barren limestone cliffs where soldiers survived in caves or makeshift shelters.

Repeated Italian offensives had brought high losses for both sides. The Eleventh Battle of the Isonzo, from August to September 1917, resulted in almost 150,000 Italian casualties and more than 100,000 Austro-Hungarian losses. Austrian Emperor Charles I and his senior commanders believed their forces on the Isonzo were close to breaking point and would not survive another defensive battle.

In line with the military thinking of the time, the Austro-Hungarians decided that the best solution was to take the offensive. The emperor asked the Germans to take over from Austro-Hungarian troops on the Eastern Front so that his forces could mount an attack on Italy. However, German military leaders doubted the competence of the Austro-Hungarian army and were keen to extend their own influence. They insisted on sending German troops to the Italian front and created a new combined German and Austro-Hungarian army, under German command.

German build-up
The Austro-German Fourteenth Army, commanded by General Otto von Below, was concentrated in a sector of the Isonzo front opposite the town of Caporetto (now Kobarid, Slovenia), where Italian positions were lightly held. German mountain troops were brought in, including the elite Bavarian Alpenkorps in which

"The farther we penetrated into the hostile zone of defence… the easier the fighting."

LIEUTENANT ERWIN ROMMEL, GERMAN COMPANY COMMANDER AT CAPORETTO

Army in retreat
Demoralized Italian soldiers withdraw towards the Piave river after the breakthrough of German and Austro-Hungarian forces at Caporetto. In some places, the Italian retreat degenerated into a disorderly rout.

> "The **tanks appeared** not one at a time but in **whole lines** kilometres in length!"

HEINZ GUDERIAN, GERMAN OFFICER, DESCRIBING THE BATTLE OF CAMBRAI, 20 NOVEMBER 1917

Leather
skull cap

Leather
visor

Chainmail
mouthpiece

hot and filled with engine fumes. The machine shook and the noise inside was deafening. Visibility was restricted and so was communication with the outside world. There were no radios in fighting tanks – the vehicles carried pigeons into battle for sending messages to the rear. The heavy tanks were so slow they sometimes had difficulty keeping pace with the troops advancing on foot.

Forging forwards

Tanks were in no sense wonder weapons that could win the war on their own, but they did play a part in ending the stalemate of trench warfare. They provided invaluable assistance to the infantry, clearing a path through layers of barbed wire and attacking strongpoints such as machine-gun posts. Deep mud, as at

British tank crew helmet and mask
When bullets struck a tank's armour, shards of metal sometimes flew off the inside of the hull, causing severe wounds. British tank crews were issued with helmets and face masks to protect against this hazard.

Third Ypres in autumn 1917, stopped the tanks, but they usually succeeded in forging a path across cratered ground and over trenches.

The British tank offensive, which briefly broke through at Cambrai in November 1917, demonstrated how effective tanks could be when used in conjunction with infantry and artillery. But it also showed that World War I tanks were not fast enough for the kind of mobile warfare that would occur in World War II.

Mk IV tank at Cambrai
A British Mk IV tank is manoeuvred over a trench at Cambrai in November 1917. Slow-moving and prone to mechanical failure, the armoured vehicles could only be effective as part of a combined arms operation with infantry and artillery.

TIMELINE

November 1904 American inventor Benjamin Holt demonstrates a working tracked tractor.

August 1914 French Colonel Jean Baptiste Estienne calls for the development of an all-terrain vehicle armed with a 75mm gun.

February 1915 The British government establishes the Landships Committee to investigate production of an armoured vehicle.

A CATERPILLAR TRACTOR

May 1915 In France, arms manufacturer Schneider begins development of an armoured vehicle based on a Holt tractor.

January 1916 Demonstration of the British Mk I tank, then known as Big Willie.

February 1916 The French army orders production of 400 Schneider CA1 tanks.

15 September 1916 Tanks are sent into combat for the first time by the British at Flers-Courcelette during the Somme Offensive.

16 April 1917 The French deploy Schneider CA1 tanks during the Nivelle Offensive.

May 1917 The British Mk IV heavy tank goes into production.

27 July 1917 The British Tank Corps is formed.

20 November 1917 British Mk IV tanks lead a shortlived breakthrough at Cambrai.

December 1917 The first British Whippet medium tanks are delivered to the Tank Corps.

21 March 1918 Germany's only operational World War I tank, the A7V, goes into combat.

24 April 1918 The first tank-on-tank combat occurs at Villers-Bretonneux, near Amiens.

31 May 1918 The French Renault FT light tank enters combat at the Fôret de Retz.

8 August 1918 The British Army employs about 600 tanks in the Amiens offensive.

12 September 1918 American tank units enter combat at the Battle of St Mihiel; they use French-supplied Renault FTs.

November 1918 The Anglo-American Mk VIII Liberty tank is about to enter service when the war ends.

FRENCH RENAULT FT LIGHT TANK

The Bolshevik Revolution

By autumn 1917, the Russian war effort had largely disintegrated. The revolutionary Bolshevik Party – soon to be renamed the Communist Party – seized power in Russia in November and immediately pursued an armistice with the Central Powers.

BEFORE

The overthrow of the tsarist regime in March 1917 failed to halt the disintegration of Russian society. After the failure of the Kerensky Offensive the army also collapsed.

THE PROVISIONAL GOVERNMENT

Set up in the wake of **Tsar Nicholas II's abdication «210–11**, the Provisional Government struggled to establish its authority. **Alexander Kerensky**, who emerged as the government's key figure, launched a **major military offensive «234–35** against the Central Powers in July 1917. Its failure ended in **mass desertion** and the effective **collapse of the Russian army**.

PETROGRAD'S JULY DAYS

In Petrograd (St Petersburg), the government was **challenged by the "soviets"** (workers' and soldiers' committees). Kerensky succeeded in **suppressing** the popular disturbances known as the July Days, and cracked down on the Bolshevik Party, which was blamed for stirring up unrest. Bolshevik leader **Vladimir Ilyich Lenin** fled to Finland to escape imprisonment. A **German victory at Riga** in September ended hopes of reviving the Russian war effort.

Russia's Provisional Government, led by Alexander Kerensky, was in a perilous situation in September 1917. The country was in a state of upheaval, with strikes in factories, peasants seizing land, and widespread looting. The newly appointed commander-in-chief of the Russian army, General Lavr Kornilov, demanded authorization to restore discipline by a series of tough measures, including the suppression of soldiers' committees and the disbanding of rebellious regiments. Kerensky agreed with the need to restore order but feared that Kornilov intended to seize power and institute military rule.

On 9 September, Kerensky accused Kornilov of planning a coup and dismissed him from his post. Kornilov responded by rebelling against the government. Fearing an advance on the capital by Kornilov's troops, the Petrograd soviet joined Kerensky in organizing a defence of the capital. Bolshevik leaders imprisoned after

Red Guard armband
Members of the Red Guard paramilitary units set up during the revolution wore red armbands. They fought in the early part of the Russian Civil War, but were eventually replaced by the Red Army.

the July Days, including Leon Trotsky, were released and arms were distributed to Petrograd factory workers, who formed Red Guard militias alongside pro-revolutionary soldiers and sailors. Kornilov was quickly arrested and the affair fizzled out, but the Red Guards kept their guns.

In the wake of the Kornilov affair, Trotsky was elected chairman of the Petrograd soviet, which was now dominated by the Bolsheviks. Lenin remained in hiding in Finland, to which he had fled after the July Days, but from there urged the overthrow of the Provisional Government. Meanwhile, Kerensky attempted to send the soldiers of the Petrograd garrison to the front. The soldiers mutinied.

The Bolsheviks seize power

With the Provisional Government defenceless, Lenin returned to Petrograd. A Military Revolutionary Committee dominated by Trotsky set about seizing power. On 6 November,

key points in the city, including the railway station, telephone exchange, and post office were taken over by revolutionary soldiers and Red Guards.

The Winter Palace, the seat of the Provisional Government, was defended by just a unit of female soldiers and Cossack cavalry. On the night of 7 November, the cruiser *Aurora*, in the hands of its sailors, fired a blank round across the Neva river to signal an attack on the Winter Palace. There was no resistance. Kerensky had already slipped out of the building and fled.

Barrel

RUSSIAN POLITICIAN (1870–1924)

VLADIMIR ILYICH LENIN

The leader of the Bolshevik Party, Vladimir Ilyich Lenin had been in exile for over a decade before the Germans facilitated his return to Russia in April 1917. A consistent opponent of the war, he proposed an immediate peace and socialist revolution.

After the Bolsheviks seized power in November, he rejected any concessions to democracy, dismissing an elected Constituent Assembly. Although he pressed for peace with the Central Powers regardless of the terms, he went on to lead Russia into a period of civil and foreign wars before the founding of the Soviet Union in 1922.

Mobile firepower
A machine-gun is mounted on a horse-drawn carriage for deployment on the streets of Petrograd by the Bolsheviks during the Russian Revolution. In the event, very little fighting took place in the capital.

Lenin proclaimed a Bolshevik government of People's Commissars, with himself as Chairman and Trotsky as Commissar for Foreign Affairs. On 8 November, addressing the All-Russian Congress of Soviets in Petrograd, he issued an appeal for an immediate end to the war. He called on the combatant powers to negotiate a peace "without annexations or indemnities". He also appealed to the working classes in Germany, Britain, and France to rise in revolution against their "imperialist governments".

Minority rule

Lenin's revolutionary government held sway in a limited area, with Petrograd and Moscow key bases. The Bolsheviks were in a minority even in the Congress of Soviets, and when a democratically elected Constituent Assembly met in January 1918 just 175 of its 703 deputies were

Women's Battalion of Death
Female volunteers formed combat units of the Russian army during 1917, adopting names such as "Battalion of Death" or "Shock Battalion". Several hundred of these women were assigned to defend the Winter Palace against the Bolsheviks.

Bolsheviks. Lenin closed it down after a day. The installation of a Russian government committed to ending the war was a disaster for the Allies. They not only lost their eastern ally but were also deeply embarrassed by the Bolsheviks' revelation of "secret treaties", found in Russian archives, showing the territorial gains that the Allies had hoped to achieve from the war. Germany, in contrast, was keen to respond to Russian peace feelers. The Central Powers agreed an armistice with the Bolsheviks on 16 December, ending the fighting on Germany's Eastern Front.

AFTER

The Bolshevik Revolution marked the beginning of a traumatic period in Russian history.

FROM WORLD WAR TO CIVIL WAR
Trotsky was entrusted with negotiating the **peace agreement** with the Central Powers. The punitive treaty dictated by Germany at **Brest-Litovsk 276–77 »** in March 1918 deprived Russia of a large part of its territory.

Immediately after the revolution, **civil war** broke out between the pro-Bolshevik Red and the anti-Bolshevik White armies in Russia, with **Allied forces intervening 300–301 »** on the side of the Whites.

ANTI-BOLSHEVISM POSTER

Box seat · Footboard · Shaft · Mounting step · Wooden wheel

> " The **government** considers it the **greatest** of **crimes against humanity** to continue this war."

BOLSHEVIK DECREE ON PEACE, 8 NOVEMBER 1917

German colonial troops
A field gun is manned by European and African soldiers of the East African Schutztruppe. Black troops, known as Askaris, formed the majority of fighting men on both sides.

BEFORE

The Allies occupied all of Germany's African colonies in the war, but met stiff resistance in German East Africa.

CROSS-BORDER RAIDS
German colonial forces under Lieutenant Colonel Paul von Lettow-Vorbeck launched cross-border raids into British colonies from German East Africa in September 1914. In November, a division from British India was defeated by Lettow-Vorbeck's forces at **Tanga** (in modern-day Tanzania) **≪ 76–77**.

REINFORCEMENTS ON BOTH SIDES
After the **conquest of German South West Africa** (Namibia) in July 1915, many South African troops joined the East African campaign. Meanwhile, sailors from the German cruiser SMS *Königsberg*, destroyed by the Royal Navy in East Africa's **Rufiji delta ≪ 76–77**, escaped capture to join Lettow-Vorbeck's forces.

ASKARI CAP

Guerrilla War in East Africa

The guerilla campaign mounted by German colonial troops in East Africa tied down substantial Allied forces at very little cost to Germany. Although just a sideshow in the context of the wider war, it was a catastrophe for the local African population.

German East Africa – mainland Tanzania, Rwanda, and Burundi – had an area of around 1 million sq km (386,000 sq miles). In 1914, its European population numbered barely 5,000. German rule was maintained by a defence force, the Schutztruppe, consisting of about 2,500 Askaris (black African troops) under the command of a few German officers. The colony was bordered by British, Belgian, and Portuguese colonies with an equally sparse white population.

When war broke out in Europe in 1914, the commander-in-chief of the Schutztruppe, Lieutenant-Colonel Paul von Lettow-Vorbeck, saw it as his duty to contribute to the wider German war

effort by engaging Germany's enemies wherever and whenever possible. This was to be the rationale for a campaign

> **40,000** The number of black African porters who died of hardship and disease in British service during the East African campaign.

that began in September 1914 and continued throughout the war.

In January 1915, Lettow-Vorbeck, pursuing this policy of aggression, had attacked the British Indian garrison at Jassin on the border between German East Africa and British East Africa, forcing the soldiers to surrender. This

had proved a hollow victory, however, since Lettow-Vorbeck lost several key officers in the attack and used up a large quantity of ammunition, which was in short supply. He was obliged to change his tactics, carrying out repeated cross-border raids, ambushing trains and destroying bridges, but avoiding battle. The Uganda railway, a key transport link in British East Africa, was a particularly vulnerable target.

The indomitable Schutztruppe
In 1916, the British embarked upon a major campaign to occupy German East Africa and defeat the Schutztruppe once and for all. South African General Jan Smuts was sent to lead the

Hunger on the Home Front

By the end of 1917, there was a marked deterioration in the living conditions of Germany's civilian populace. The drain on resources caused by war on multiple fronts and the Allied naval blockade was compounded by the harsh winter of 1916–17. Shortages of food, fuel, soap, and other items left those who could not pay for black market goods struggling to survive. Some estimates place the death toll due to malnutrition-related disease at more than 700,000 during the course of the war.

"Among the three hundred applicants for food there was not one who had had enough to eat in weeks. In the case of the younger women and the children, the skin was drawn hard to the bones and bloodless. Eyes had fallen deeper into the sockets. From the lips, all colour was gone, and the tufts of hair that fell over parchmented foreheads seemed dull and famished, a sign that the nervous vigour of the body was departing with the physical strength.**"**

GEORGE ABEL SCHREINER, US JOURNALIST, FROM "THE IRON RATION: THREE YEARS IN WARRING CENTRAL EUROPE"

"At long last, there's butter, flour, and chocolate in the house. But not much of it, only two small squares of chocolate each! It has been so long, it brings back memories of breakfasts before the war. We are having a hard time. It is very cold, which increases your appetite. My older brothers go to work in thick boots to keep their feet warm. But we have faith in France and God, and comfort ourselves with the thought that over in Germany they are almost as unhappy as we are. There is famine in Berlin, Dresden, and Bavaria. I hope they all die!**"**

AYVES CONGAR, FRENCH CIVILIAN, FROM "JOURNAL DE LA GUERRE 1914—1918"

Civilians crowd around a municipal kitchen cart on the streets of Berlin, in 1918
People in urban areas were most affected by acute food shortages and profiteering, leaving Germany's government unable to maintain morale on the home front.

Trench Warfare Transformed

In 1918, after three years of trench stalemate, a degree of mobility was restored to the fighting on the Western Front. The adoption of innovative tactics and new technology allowed armies to take the offensive with a good chance of success.

« BEFORE

The defensive firepower of machine-guns, rifles, and artillery could defeat massed infantry assaults, especially if the defenders were entrenched.

BREAKTHROUGH TACTICS
From 1915, commanders attempted to break through enemy trench lines using a prolonged **artillery bombardment** to prepare the way for an infantry advance. These tactics, used, for example, at the **Battle of the Somme « 180–85** in July 1916, achieved small gains at the cost of many lives.

DEFENCE IN DEPTH
The introduction of **poison gas « 104–05** in April 1915 and **tanks « 184–85** in September 1916 had no decisive impact. New offensive tactics, used in the **Russian Brusilov Offensive « 174–75** of June 1916, were matched by better defence, with trenches stretching far behind the front line.

World War I generals are often portrayed as unimaginative men who were forever marching their soldiers straight into the fire of enemy machine-guns. In reality, commanders on both sides in the war made constant efforts to improve the performance of their troops. Technological innovations were adopted with enthusiasm and new techniques were developed.

Transforming the battlefield
By 1918, artillery was a refined instrument of war. For set-piece offensives, gunners developed complex firing plans in coordination with infantry assaults. Different kinds of fuse and shell were allotted to various tasks, from cutting barbed wire to destroying enemy artillery batteries.

Assault troops in action
Stormtroopers advance through barbed wire during the German offensive on the Western Front in March 1918. Trained to maintain the momentum of their attack at all costs, these specialist assault troops proved capable of punching holes deep into Allied lines.

A brief but intense "hurricane" bombardment became the usual start to an attack, replacing the prolonged preliminary bombardments practised earlier in the war and restoring an element of surprise. The creeping barrage, introduced by the British and French in 1916, had been perfected so that attacking soldiers had the confidence to advance 50 m (50 yd) behind a protective curtain of shellfire. While this barrage crept forward, other guns would saturate the area behind the enemy front line with high-explosive and gas shells to pre-empt counterattacks.

Defensive artillery fire was effectively suppressed by the accurate shelling of enemy batteries. This was achieved through well-honed techniques for identifying their exact position, such as aerial reconnaissance, sound location, and "flash-spotting" – observing the flashes from the muzzles of the guns.

By 1918, infantry tactics had none of the crudity seen earlier in the war. Armed with light machine-guns,

Steel-welded cylinder

Operating lever

Portable flamethrower
The fuel tank of a German flamethrower was carried on a soldier's back while a comrade operated the firing tube. Flamethrowers were frequently used by stormtroopers as part of their shock assault equipment.

grenades, rifle grenades, and mortars, as well as rifles and bayonets, infantry sought to push forward at speed in small units. Official British infantry tactics from 1917 emphasized the platoon – around 40 soldiers – as the

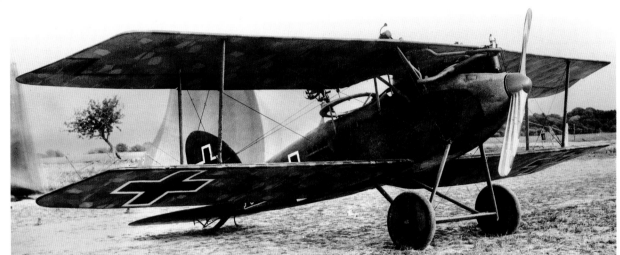

Attacks from the air
The highly manoeuvrable and robust Halberstadt CL.II was one of Germany's most successful ground-attack aircraft. This machine was captured by Australian forces at Flesselles, France, in June 1918.

defender could move in reserves to block a breakthrough more quickly than the attacker could exploit it.

Time to rethink
The Allies achieved a string of successes from August 1918 by abandoning the pursuit of a breakthrough and adopting a step-by-step approach – biting small chunks out of the German defences and then holding them against counterattacks, taking care to stay within range of supporting artillery. They consolidated a series of limited gains that progressively pushed the enemy line back towards Germany. The war was no longer static, but it was still hard, slow, and exhausting.

"We **crossed a battered tangle of wire** without difficulty and at a jump were over the front line."

ERNST JÜNGER, STORMTROOPER COMMANDER, IN HIS MEMOIR "STORM OF STEEL"

essential unit of combat, with one part of the unit pinning down the enemy defenders with suppressive fire while the other moved to attack.

Stormtrooper tactics
The Germans began developing specialist assault infantry from 1915. The success of an assault detachment under Captain Willy Rohr evolved into the creation of stormtrooper battalions as elite formations of shock troops. Stormtroopers were armed with light and heavy machine-guns, mortars, and flamethrowers, as well as light artillery pieces. Their role was to spearhead attacks, breaking through weak points and then penetrating in depth to capture enemy guns. German infantry would follow on to deal with strongpoints that had been bypassed.

These "infiltration tactics", usually preceded by a hurricane barrage of artillery, were employed successfully by General Oskar von Hutier's Eighth Army at Riga in September 1917. They are often referred to as Hutier tactics.

Combined attack
Aircraft were used increasingly in a ground-attack role in support of infantry. Advancing stormtroopers could expect close air support from Halberstadt aircraft or all-metal Junkers J4s. But the Allies made the best progress in combined air and land attacks. By the second half of 1918, they could field numerous tanks and

ground-attack aircraft, as well as artillery, in tight cooperation with infantry. Australian forces coined the term "peaceful penetration" to describe an assault in which the coordinated use of artillery, tanks, and aircraft as a shock force allowed infantry to occupy ground with relatively few casualties.

The Germans in particular still created defences in depth. They were prepared to sacrifice front-line troops to draw their enemy into a zone of concealed machine-gun nests and further trench lines, where they could then be engaged by counterattack troops.

Poor communication
Despite the progress made in tactics and technology, offensive operations on the Western Front in 1918 were still plagued with difficulties. Without effective mobile radios, communication was always a problem for troops on the offensive. The German stormtroopers could achieve a breakthrough in depth but they could not speed up Germany's creaky supply system, which mostly depended on horsedrawn carts, or the movement of heavy artillery across war-torn ground. It remained true that a

British postcard
A wartime comic postcard depicts, with a good deal of exaggeration, the fear inspired in German troops by British heavy tanks. The Byng Boys were popular music hall entertainers of the day.

Hood with face mask

Hand-painted linen

Sniper's mitten

Camouflage suit
Among wartime innovations was the development of the art of camouflage. This camouflage outfit was worn by a British sniper seeking to fire on German troops from a concealed position.

AFTER »

A lull in the fighting on the Western Front ended when the Germans launched the Michael Offensive on 21 March 1918.

THE SEARCH FOR VICTORY
Spearheaded by **stormtroopers 274–75 »**, the German army achieved **breakthrough offensives** from March through to June, but **not decisive victory**. From August 1918, aided by large numbers of American troops, the Allies began a new campaign of **offensives** that achieved an unbroken series of **military successes** lasting to the war's end in November.

After the war, the stormtrooper principle of shock attack in depth combined with the use of tanks and aircraft created the German "Blitzkrieg" tactics used in World War II.

Stormtrooper Equipment

The German stormtroopers *(Sturmtruppen)* were elite soldiers specially trained in trench infiltration tactics. As rapidly moving assault troops, they required their kit and weaponry to be quick to deploy, highly portable, and easily accessible inside the confined conditions of an enemy trench.

[1] **Gas mask** features a screw-fitted air filter and plastic goggles. [2] **M1917 Stahlhelm Helmet** The distinctive German helmet was introduced in 1916. The 1917 model saw improvements to the liner. [3] **Death's head badge** The *totenkopf* (death's head) symbol, originally used by cavalry in the Prussian army, was adopted by some stormtroopers during the offensives in 1918. [4] **Spoon and fork** Stormtroopers often had to eat quickly in lulls between fighting; they carried the necessary utensils. [5] **Battery-operated torch** It was important for assault troops to see into dug-outs and other dark spaces within trenches. [6] **Tunic** Many soldiers would cover their epaulettes with a strip of cloth, so the enemy could not identify their regiment. The top medal indicates the soldier has been wounded, the bottom one is an Iron Cross First Class. [7] **Bergmann MP18/I** Introduced in 1918, this was the first practical submachine-gun employed in combat. At least 5,000 were

used before the end of the war. [8] **Mauser KAR 98AZ** This carbine was preferred by stromtroopers over the Gewehr 98 rifle, as its shorter length made it more effective in trench warfare. [9] **Equipment belt** Items clipped to the belt included a water bottle, ammunition pouches, bayonet, axe, and bread bag. [10] **Books** A military pass, a *schiessbuch* ("shooting book" to record marksmanship training), a German-French dictionary, and a paybook. [11] **Stick grenade** The *stielhandgranate*, introduced by Germany in 1915, was called the "potato masher" by British troops. [12] **Assault pack** This backpack holds a shovel, used to entrench and as a weapon. It also contains a *zeltbahn*, a rain poncho that doubled as a tent. [13] **Puttee** These strips of cloth were wound around the leg, acting as support. [14] **Trousers** Three-quarter-length trousers with knee patches were worn by stormtroopers in 1918. [15] **Trench knife** Knives were used in hand-to-hand combat during assaults on trenches.

[1] GAS MASK

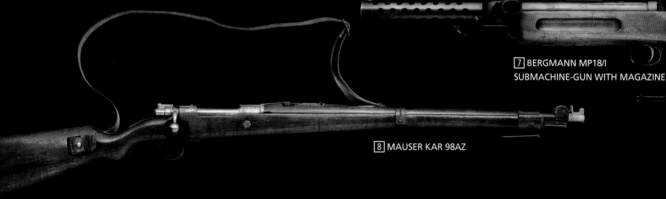

[7] BERGMANN MP18/I
SUBMACHINE-GUN WITH MAGAZINE

[8] MAUSER KAR 98AZ

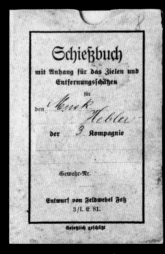

[10] BOOKS

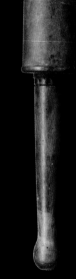

[11] STICK GRENADE

General Manuel Gomes da Costa. Portugal had entered the war in 1916 and a Portuguese Expeditionary Force had been deployed with British forces on the Western Front since summer 1917. Poorly led and suffering from low morale, the Portuguese troops were about to be relieved of front-line duties when the German offensive began. Stunned by a perfectly orchestrated German bombardment, the Portuguese faced German infantry in the morning fog. Despite individual acts of heroism, Gomes da Costa's troops put up little resistance. Some 7,000 Portuguese were taken prisoner and a similar number were killed or wounded.

Crisis for the British

The British 55th Division held its position to the south of the Portuguese, but to the north the British were forced to retreat, losing the town of Armentières on the second day of the battle. This was followed by further losses as the German Fourth Army launched the second phase of the offensive at the Ypres salient. Held by the British Second Army under General Herbert Plumer, this ground had become sacred to the British through the sheer scale of the sacrifice that had taken place there. Now Plumer was forced to abandon Messines Ridge and Passchendaele, withdrawing to a defensive line on the very outskirts of Ypres itself.

On 11 April, British commander-in-chief Field Marshal Douglas Haig's order of the day called for a fight in defence of "the safety of our homes

> ## "There is **no course...** but to **fight it out.** Every **position** must be **held...** there must be **no retirement.**"
>
> FIELD MARSHAL DOUGLAS HAIG, ORDER OF THE DAY, 11 APRIL 1918

and the freedom of mankind". Haig's rhetoric drew a mixed response from war-weary British soldiers, but it did express the enduring resolve of senior Allied commanders at a crucial moment of the war. Instead of falling apart, the Allies pulled together.

Foch takes charge

On 14 April, the British formally acknowledged French General Ferdinand Foch as Supreme Commander of the Allied Armies on the Western Front. Although Foch was slow to respond to appeals from Haig for reinforcements, rightly fearing an imminent German offensive against a French-held sector of the front, he eventually sent French troops to relieve exhausted British formations.

The Belgian army, on the British left, also stepped up its efforts.

By the third week in April, the Flanders offensive had degenerated into a series of local engagements in which stubborn defence by Allied troops slowed German progress to a crawl. Neither the French Channel port of Dunkerque nor the vital rail junction of Hazebrouck were seriously threatened. Further south, on 25 April, a German attack towards Amiens failed to take the city.

Still seeking the elusive decisive victory, Ludendorff gathered German strength for yet another major offensive, codenamed Blücher-Yorck, in May. Instead of reinforcing the effort in Flanders, he chose to attack at the Aisne river in northern France, held by the French Sixth Army. Some 6,000 guns and two million shells were

Prisoners of war

The Germans display Portuguese prisoners in Flanders in April 1918. The Portuguese were about to be relieved by British troops when they came under attack.

assembled for the initial bombardment, undetected by the Allies. The main weight of the attack was to fall upon the Chemin des Dames Ridge, captured by the French in May 1917. It was defended by British soldiers who had been transferred to this quiet sector from Flanders for a period of rest and recuperation. Crowded into forward positions in poorly organized trenches, the British were decimated by the German initial bombardment on the 27 May and then overrun by stormtroopers.

> | **50,000** | The number of Allied soldiers taken prisoner by the Germans in the Aisne Offensive between 27 and 30 May 1918. |

Allied troops retreated across the Aisne pursued by the Germans. A German advance of 15 km (9 miles) on the first day was maintained over the following week. By 3 June, the Germans had reached the Marne river. With Paris apparently under threat, France experienced the same sense of crisis that Britain had in April. Few people then recognized the truth – that the German offensives had failed to achieve any decisive objective.

Kladderadatsch

Nr. 15 — Berlin, den 14. April 1918

Preis 35 Pfennig einschl. Teuerungszuschlag.

LXXI. Jahrgang

Der liebenswürdige Hindenburg

Lord Haig: Stört es Sie, wenn ich währenddessen die Glückwunschdepesche lese, die Wilson an mich gesandt hat?"
Hindenburg: "O durchaus nicht!"
Haig liest: "Darf ich meiner glühenden Bewunderung für die Standfestigkeit und den Mut, mit dem Ihre Truppen dem deutschen Angriff Widerstand geleistet haben, und dem vollkommenen Vertrauen Ausdruck geben, mit dem alle Amerikaner erwarten, daß Sie einen sicheren Endsieg erringen werden."

Britain takes a beating
A cartoon published in a German magazine during the Lys Offensive in April 1918 shows Field Marshal Hindenburg thrashing British commander-in-chief Douglas Haig.

AFTER »

The Germans had hoped to win the war before US troops were engaged. By June 1918, time had run out.

THE TIDE TURNS
The **first Americans entered combat** under overall French command at the Aisne in late May 1918. The following month, US troops were prominently involved at **Belleau Wood**

| **650,000** | The number of American soldiers in France by the start of June 1918. |

284–85 » and the **Battle of Matz**. A final German offensive was defeated in July at the **Second Battle of the Marne 286–87 »**. Massive German losses since 21 March **demoralized German troops**, and there was an increasing sense that Germany had lost its strategic purpose. The tide was set to turn on the Western Front.

Hand-to-hand combat
French war artist Lucien Jonas made this image of
an American soldier grappling with the enemy in
Belleau Wood. The hand-to-hand fighting occurred
during the US assault on the wood on 6 June.

The **Battle** of **Belleau Wood**

At a crucial point in the war, with German forces advancing on Paris, American troops were thrown into combat for the first time. American marines and army infantry fought with outstanding courage against the Germans at Belleau Wood near the Marne river.

Half a million US soldiers had arrived in France by the start of May 1918. Although some divisions had spent time in trenches on quiet sectors of the front, none had entered battle.

The German breakthrough at the Aisne river on 27 May brought US forces into action for the first time, in support of the French. The next day, elements of the US First Division fought the Germans at Cantigny, 32 km (20 miles) southeast of Amiens.

As the Germans advanced to the Marne river, just 80 km (50 miles) from Paris, French commander-in-chief General Philippe Pétain called upon US assistance again. In response, commander of the American Expeditionary Force (AEF), General Jack Pershing, rushed the US Second and Third divisions to the Marne. Fighting alongside French colonial troops, the Third Division fought a successful holding action against the Germans at Château-Thierry on the Marne on 31 May.

In the first days of June, the Second Division dug in along the front to the left of the Third Division. The division, which included a brigade of marines under Brigadier General James Harbord, took up position opposite Belleau Wood, a few kilometres west of Château-Thierry. On 3–4 June, the Germans attacked in strength but were repelled by the French and Americans. German troops advancing out of Belleau Wood were cut down by marine rifle fire. During this engagement, the marines rejected advice from the French to conduct a tactical withdrawal. Marine Captain Lloyd Williams allegedly responded, "Retreat? Hell, we just got here."

Ferocious combat

The German failure on 4 June was a sign that the offensive launched at the Aisne eight days earlier was stalling. The French identified the moment as ripe for a counterattack and the Americans complied.

The counterattack was launched at dawn on 6 June, with the US Marines and Third Infantry Brigade attacking Belleau Wood and a nearby position known as Hill 142. Although the US troops had already demonstrated their fighting spirit, their shortage of combat experience was now evident. The attacks showed neither the tight cooperation between artillery and infantry nor the sophisticated infantry tactics that the British, French, and Germans had developed during the war. The Americans behaved as soldiers had in 1914, advancing in dense waves across open ground.

The wheatfields were soon thick with dead and wounded US troops, the marines suffering over 1,000 casualties on the day. The Americans nonetheless took Hill 142 and penetrated the German defences in Belleau Wood, engaging the enemy at close quarters.

Allied successes

The bloody battle for Belleau Wood and the nearby villages of Vaux and Bouresche continued for another 20 days, with desperate attacks and counterattacks by both sides. At times, there was hand-to-hand fighting. German troops learned a healthy respect for their US opponents, especially the marines.

Belleau Wood was in American hands on 26 June. By then, US troops had also helped the French repulse the Germans at the Battle of Matz (9–12 June), on the Matz river. The German advance towards Paris had been brought to a halt. With increasing numbers of US troops arriving in France – the size of the AEF passed a million men in July – any serious possibility of Germany winning the war had evaporated.

> **9,777** The total number of US casualties in the fighting from 6 to 26 June 1918, including 1,811 dead.

Camouflage helmet
American troops fighting in World War I wore the British Brodie helmet or its US-manufactured equivalent, the M1917.

BEFORE

German offensives in spring 1918 banked on US troops not being fully deployed. In fact, they were ready for action by May.

RECRUITMENT POSTER FOR THE US MARINES

THE AEF IS FORMED
The USA declared war on Germany in April 1917. However, the recruitment and training of an American Expeditionary Force (AEF) proceeded slowly. The AEF's commander, **General Jack Pershing**, wanted a US army to fight as an independent force and resisted pressure to provide units for the British and French armies. The crisis caused by the German **Michael Offensive ❰❰ 278–79** in March 1918 and **subsequent offensives in Flanders** and at the **Aisne ❰❰ 282–83** necessitated a change in US policy.

Witnessing Belleau Wood
The US war correspondent Floyd Gibbons lost an eye while trying to save a wounded soldier at Belleau Wood. The French awarded Gibbons the Croix de Guerre for valour in battle.

AFTER ❱❱

General Erich Ludendorff refused to accept that his offensive policy on the Western Front had failed.

GERMANY FLOUNDERS
In July, Ludendorff launched yet another ambitious offensive, precipitating the **Second Battle of the Marne 286–87 ❱❱**. The German attack failed and a French-led counter-offensive then turned the tables, forcing the Germans to withdraw from the ground they had won in late May. With limited manpower, Germany could not cope with huge troop losses, a situation made worse by the onset of a deadly **influenza epidemic**. An **Allied offensive at Amiens 304–05 ❱❱** in August proved a success. In September, General Pershing launched the first American-led operation at the St-Mihiel salient **306–07 ❱❱**, followed by the larger **Battle of Meuse-Argonne 308–09 ❱❱**.

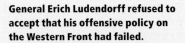

The **Second Battle** of the **Marne**

Fought in July 1918, the Second Battle of the Marne was a key turning point in the final phase of the war. A German offensive at Reims was halted and then trumped by a powerful French-led counter-offensive that seized the initiative for the Allies. The scene was set for an Allied drive to victory.

By summer 1918, the German high command was beginning to lose touch with the reality of the war. General Erich Ludendorff planned an offensive to encircle the city of Reims in Champagne, 30 km (18 miles) north of the Marne river. His aim was to draw the French into committing their reserves to a defence of the historic city, diverting troops away from Flanders where he then intended to strike a decisive blow. By then such grandiose plans were beyond the capacity of the

Courageous commander

General Henri Gouraud was widely praised for his leadership of the French Fourth Army during the opening defensive phase of the Second Battle of the Marne. Earlier in the war, Gouraud had lost an arm in the fighting at Gallipoli.

German army. It had been severely weakened by heavy losses in offensives since March and was showing increasing signs of declining morale.

On the Allied side, Supreme Commander of the Allied Armies General Ferdinand Foch, buoyed by the arrival of US troops in ever larger numbers, was also planning to take the offensive. Foch prepared an attack on the western side of the salient created

Renault FT tank

The most successful armoured vehicle of World War I, France's innovative Renault light tank had its main armament in a fully rotating turret. More than 3,500 FTs were manufactured during the war.

Gun

Entrance

Caterpillar tracks

Hatch through which the driver looks

« BEFORE

Between March and June 1918, the Germans achieved major advances on the Western Front.

THE SPRING OFFENSIVES
Following the **Michael Offensive** **«** 278–79, the Germans launched offensives in Flanders in April and at the **Aisne** **«** 282–83 in late May, but **failed to pursue a clear strategy**. German losses were heavy and their gains not decisive.

Meanwhile, the Allies made French General **Ferdinand Foch** their supreme commander. In June, US troops fought well at **Belleau Wood** **«** 284–85, halting the Germans at the Marne.

BRITISH BINOCULARS

1,143 The number of Allied aircraft used to support the offensive at the Second Battle of the Marne on 18 July 1918.

513 The number of Allied tanks assembled for the 18 July offensive.

by the German advance to the Marne river between May and June. The French Tenth Army was chosen to spearhead the operation, under the command of General Charles Mangin.

The Allies learned about the German offensive plans, chiefly through interrogation of enemy prisoners. The French commander-in-chief General Philippe Pétain wanted a maximum concentration of forces at Reims to

resist the German onslaught, but Foch refused to be deflected from pursuing his own offensive preparations.

Attack on Reims

The Germans attacked first. On 15 July, the First and Third armies struck to the east of Reims while the Seventh Army attacked to the west of the city. The defensive positions were held by the French Fourth Army under the command of General Henri Gouraud on the eastern side and the Sixth Army under General Jean Degoutte in the west. The French armies also had

under their command nine American and two Italian divisions.

The German attack to the east of Reims went badly from the start. Gouraud had prepared his defences in depth, leaving front positions only lightly held. His artillery carried out an effective bombardment of German troops as they assembled for the initial assault. When the Germans rushed forward, they easily overran the French front-line positions, but were brought to a halt in a fiercely defended battle zone to the rear. Gouraud infused the defence with his own ferocity of spirit, calling on his forces to "Kill them, kill them in abundance until they have had enough".

The Germans had had enough on 16 July, when the eastern attack was called off. To the west of Reims, however, it was a different story.

> " American comrades, **I am grateful** for the **blood you... spilled** on... **my country.** "
>
> FRENCH GENERAL CHARLES MANGIN, 7 AUGUST 1918

Rotating
turret

Tail

German stormtroopers established a bridgehead across the Marne. In the fierce fighting that followed, the US Third Infantry Division earned its nickname "the Rock of the Marne" for standing firm while other troops fell back.

Pétain wanted to transfer troops preparing for the Allied offensive to the defence of Reims, but Foch refused. Aided by the arrival of two British divisions, the Allied position west of Reims had stabilized by 17 July.

Return to the Marne

The German offensive had failed and it was time for the Allied offensive to begin. Foch's aim was to eliminate the large salient created by the German advance from the Aisne to the Marne in late May to early June. The attack was launched on 18 July from positions to the west of the Reims battlefields in the direction of Soissons. Impressive forces had been assembled for the operation, including over 1,000 aircraft and massed tanks, mostly the light Renault FTs. After a brief artillery bombardment, the Allied infantry went "over the top" at dawn, advancing behind a creeping

US troops on the move

Soldiers of the American Expeditionary Force (AEF) move up by truck towards Château-Thierry in preparation for the counterattack at the Marne on 18 July. American manpower altered the balance of forces in the war.

barrage accompanied by tanks. The majority of the troops were French, but the US First and Second divisions spearheaded the assault in the sector around Château-Thierry. Although German machine-gun and artillery fire inflicted heavy casualties, the tanks helped break through defensive positions and Allied aircraft bombed German troops.

Pushed back

The Germans were forced back, retreating some 10 km (6 miles) in the first two days of the offensive. By 22 July, the two US divisions had lost 11,000 men, either killed or wounded, but they had retaken Château-Thierry (lost to the Germans in June) and won the admiration of their French colleagues. The French were also impressed by the performance of African-American troops, assigned to separate formations in the segregated US Army. Regiments of the black 93rd Division performed outstandingly when seconded to French divisions, where they received more respectful treatment than they were used to under US command.

Harlem Hellfighters

The African-American 369th Regiment, known as the Harlem Hellfighters, was seconded to fight under French command at the Marne. The soldiers were issued with French rifles and Adrian helmets.

Through the last week of July, the Germans steadily gave ground and by 3 August had managed an orderly withdrawal across the Aisne river, returning to the positions they had held before their offensive in late May. Ludendorff had been forced to transfer troops south from Flanders to help hold the line against the French advance, ending any prospect of a renewed German offensive towards the Channel ports.

Although Ludendorff publicly disparaged the quality of US troops, in private the German leadership had to face the fact that their presence meant that military victory was no longer an option for Germany. The endgame of the war was about to begin.

AFTER ≫

The French-led offensive at the Marne was the first in a series of Allied attacks that continued to push the Germans back through 1918.

HONOURED GENERAL
The initial French reaction to the Second Battle of the Marne was **relief that Paris had been saved**. In recognition of his victory, Foch was granted the title of Marshal of France on 6 August 1918, the second French general accorded this honour during World War I. The first was General Joseph Joffre in 1916.

GRAND OFFENSIVE
The Allies resumed offensive operations with an important victory principally won by British and Commonwealth forces at **Amiens 304–05 ≫** on 8 August. From September, Foch orchestrated a simultaneous "Grand Offensive" by Allied armies on different sectors of the Western Front, including American-led operations at **St Mihiel** and **Meuse-Argonne 306–09 ≫** and British-led attacks on the **Hindenburg Line 312–13 ≫**.

Blinded by gas
In this painting entitled *Gassed*, by US artist John Singer Sargent, British infantry are led to a dressing station after a gas attack. Sargent witnessed the scene near Arras on 21 August 1918.

MARSHAL OF FRANCE Born 1851 Died 1929

Ferdinand Foch

"He is the **most courageous man** I have ever met."

BRITISH GENERAL SIR HENRY WILSON, 1920

The defeat of France by Germany in the Franco-Prussian War of 1870–71 was a formative experience for Ferdinand Foch. It not only gave him his first taste of the army as a volunteer, but also filled him with a lasting fear of German military power.

A love of military history led Foch to study the campaigns of the French Emperor Napoleon I (1769–1821).

Unshaken belief

Marshal Ferdinand Foch was the commander who led the Allies to victory on the Western Front in 1918. He was an aggressive commander, whose military thinking influenced many French officers.

earned him a reputation as an influential military theoretician. At France's War College, the École Supérieure de Guerre, a generation of French officers absorbed Foch's belief that a spirited attack would always overcome defensive firepower. It was a conviction that ultimately cost many Frenchmen their lives.

From desk to battlefield

At the outbreak of war, Foch was a 62-year-old general with no combat experience who had spent most of his career in desk jobs or lecture rooms. Leading XX Corps on the Lorraine front in August 1914, he attracted the favourable attention of French commander-in-chief General Joseph Joffre when he

LE MARÉCHAL FOCH

Front page news

Wearing the uniform of a Marshal of France, Foch was the natural choice for the front page of a French illustrated newspaper in August 1918, the month when the Allied armies turned the tide of the war.

As an officer in the artillery from 1873, Foch belonged to the section of the army most changed by technological progress, but his Napoleonic studies led him to believe troop morale to be the most crucial factor in warfare. He always favoured offence over defence. Commitment to the offensive suited his confident, energetic character, and he never abandoned it.

During the long peace in Europe between 1871 and 1914, Foch's clarity of mind and originality of thought

The Flying Circus
Albatros aircraft of Richthofen's Jagda 1 fighter wing line up at an airfield in France. Jagda 1 was known as the Flying Circus because of its aircrafts' bright colours. Richthofen himself became known as the Red Baron.

bombers, which were the German fighters' principal targets, these tactics allowed Richthofen to build up a high number of "kills" very quickly.

Flying ace
Richthofen became one of Germany's elite band of pilots on 23 November 1916 when he shot down one of Britain's most successful fighter aces, Major Lanoe Hawker. The British pilot, caught flying an inferior aircraft deep behind German lines, was pursued relentlessly by Richthofen's faster Albatros until the German was close enough to shoot him in the head.

In 1917, Richthofen was given command of his own squadron and then of Germany's first fighter wing, the four squadrons of Jagdgeschwader (Jagda) 1. He excelled as a commander, taking time to teach new pilots how to fight. The Flying Circus, as Jagda 1 came to be called, nurtured many ace

German hero
As well as being Germany's most celebrated pilot, Manfred von Richthofen was an outstanding leader of men. He was depicted by German wartime propaganda as a chivalrous "knight of the sky".

pilots, including Manfred's younger brother, Lothar. It was used as a trouble-shooting formation, sent to whichever sector of the Western Front was thought most crucial at the time.

Combat takes its toll
By spring 1917, with over 50 "kills" to his name, Richthofen was one of the most famous men in Germany. He was invited to meet the Kaiser, and urged to write his memoirs as a morale-boosting tale for the German public. Like all World War I fighter aces, however, he suffered from the nervous strain of combat and the frequent deaths of comrades. On 6 July 1917, he was shot in the head by a Lewis gunner in a British two-seater. Although almost blinded, he managed to land his aircraft safely. However, his health never fully recovered.

The injury occurred at a moment when Germany was losing its technical superiority to a new generation of Allied aircraft. Richthofen informed the German air staff of the "poor morale" of German fighter pilots

Buried by the enemy
The Australian Flying Corps gave Richthofen a military burial at Bertangles, near Amiens, on 22 April 1918. Some Allied fliers expressed respect for a fallen enemy, others were openly glad he was dead.

due to their "sorry machines". He used his prestige to push for the mass manufacture of the Fokker Dr.1 triplane, which would become his most famous mount, and then for development of the Fokker D7, which became the highest-performing fighter of the war.

By 1918, Richthofen was under pressure to withdraw from combat, since his death would be a heavy blow to German morale. But he refused, stating that it would be despicable to preserve his "valuable life for the nation" while "every poor fellow in the trenches… has to stick it out."

On 21 April, pursuing a potential victim over British lines with uncharacteristic recklessness, Richthofen was shot dead, either by Canadian pilot Roy Brown or by Australian machine-gunners on the ground. He was only 25 years old.

- **3 May 1892** Born into an aristocratic Prussian family near Breslau (now Wroclaw in Poland).
- **1903** Enters military cadet school at the age of 11.
- **1911** Graduates from the Royal Military Academy, joining an Uhlan light cavalry regiment with the rank of lieutenant in 1912.
- **May 1915** Transfers from the cavalry to the German air service, seeing action as an observer on reconnaissance missions.
- **October 1915** After meeting German ace Oswald Boelcke, he begins pilot training, qualifying in early 1916.
- **March 1916** Flies two-seater bomber aircraft at Verdun and on the Eastern Front.
- **August 1916** Becomes a fighter pilot, joining Oswald Boelcke's squadron Jagdstaffel (Jasta) 2 on the Western Front.
- **September 1916** Achieves his first "kills", shooting down two Allied aircraft.
- **October 1916** Witnesses the death of Boelcke in a collision during combat with British aircraft.
- **November 1916** Flying an Albatros D.1, he shoots down the British ace pilot Major Lance Hawker.
- **January 1917** Awarded the Pour le Mérite (Blue Max) for 16 "kills", Richthofen is appointed commander of a fighter squadron, Jasta 11, in northern France.
- **April 1917** Flying an Albatros D.3 fighter, he shoots down 21 Allied aircraft in a month during the Battle of Arras.
- **June 1917** Appointed commander of a flight wing of four squadrons, Jagdgeschwader (Jagda) 1, known as Richthofen's Flying Circus.
- **July 1917** Suffers a serious head wound in combat and has to undergo surgery.
- **August 1917** Returns to command of Jagda 1 during the Third Battle of Ypres, flying the Fokker Dr.1 triplane for the first time.
- **September 1917** Still suffering the effects of his wound, he takes convalescent leave to complete his memoirs, *Der rote Kampfflieger* (The Red Battle Flyer).
- **March–April 1918** Leading Jagda 1 in the German Spring Offensive, Richthofen raises his tally of "kills" to 80.
- **21 April 1918** Richthofen is killed either by ground or air fire while flying over the Somme. Hermann Goering takes over his squadron.

REPLICA OF THE FOKKER DR.1 TRIPLANE

"I approached… and **fired 50 bullets until** the **machine began to burn.**"
MANFRED VON RICHTHOFEN, DESCRIBING HIS LAST "KILL" ON 20 APRIL 1918

Allied Intervention in Russia

From spring 1918, the Allies intervened in Russia in a way that called into question their true motives towards the country. Initially aimed at advancing the war effort against Germany, their actions soon developed into a confused bid to overthrow the Bolshevik regime.

The collapse of Russia was a severe setback for the Allies, because it freed Germany from the need to fight a war on two fronts. The situation in Russia was also dangerously chaotic. The Bolsheviks controlled Petrograd and Moscow, but elsewhere former tsarist officers led "White" armies, a loose affiliation of anti-communist forces, in revolt against Bolshevik rule. Bolshevism was also contested by rival revolutionaries and ethnic groups.

« BEFORE

Revolutionary upheaval in Russia in 1917 created a confused situation for Russia's military allies, who were desperate to keep Russia in the war.

BOLSHEVIK REVOLUTION
Tsar Nicholas II was forced to **abdicate** **« 210–11** in March 1917. The Provisional Government that replaced the Tsar pledged to continue the war, and was provided with money and arms by Britain, France, and the USA. The failure of a **Russian summer offensive** was followed by the overthrow of the Provisional Government by **the Bolsheviks « 252–53** in November.

PEACE TREATY
The Bolsheviks agreed an **armistice** with the Central Powers in December 1917, but peace negotiations proceeded slowly. Allied hopes that the Bolsheviks could be persuaded to resume the war were dashed by the **Brest-Litovsk Peace Treaty « 276–77** in March 1918.

PROVISIONAL GOVERNMENT SOLDIER

As early as December 1917, the Allies agreed in principle to intervene in Russia to support any political force prepared to resume the war against Germany, and to protect military supplies stockpiled in Russian ports from falling into German hands. Action was slow to develop, however, partly because of mutual suspicion between the Allies. Japan was best placed to intervene, with troops available to land at the key Russian port of Vladivostok in eastern Russia, but fears of Japanese territorial ambitions made the other Allies hostile to an independent Japanese initiative.

The Czech Legion

By strange accident, the Allies found themselves with a substantial military force caught up in the chaos of post-revolutionary Russia. The Czech Legion was a body of Czech and

13,000 The number of American troops involved in military intervention in Russia.

40,000 The number of British troops sent to Arkhangelsk and Vladivostok.

Slovak soldiers recruited during 1916–17 from the Russian army and prisoners of war or deserters from the Austro-Hungarian army. They intended to fight for the Allies in the hope of being rewarded with national independence once the Central Powers had been defeated.

The Bolshevik government had agreed to allow the Czech Legion to cross Russia to Vladivostok, from where it could sail to France to join other Czechs and Slovaks fighting on the Western Front. Strung out along the Trans-Siberian Railway through

ВРАГ У ВОРОТ!!!

ВСЕ НА ЗАЩИТУ

Bolshevik propaganda
Proclaiming that "the enemy is at the gate", a Bolshevik poster calls on the people to fight in defence of the revolution. In 1918, the Bolshevik regime was under siege and seemed unlikely to survive.

May and June 1918, however, elements of the Legion came into conflict with Bolshevik authorities, who tried to disarm them and obstructed their progress. Local clashes developed into full-scale fighting. An organized and motivated force of some 50,000 men, the Czechs and Slovaks soon had control of a substantial area of Russia along the line of the Trans-Siberian Railway and at Vladivostok.

Also in June 1918, substantial numbers of Allied troops began to land in northern Russia. Large stockpiles of munitions, previously sent by Britain to aid their Russian allies, had accumulated at the ports of Murmansk and Arkhangelsk. These were vulnerable to attack by German forces active in Finland. To secure the munitions, a few thousand British and French troops landed at Murmansk and, in July, went on to occupy Arkhangelsk. A subsidiary objective of this operation was to provide an alternative route for the Czech Legion to leave Russia and sail for France.

The British, however, began to toy with an alternative plan for the revival of war on the Eastern Front. They proposed that the Allied forces at Arkhangelsk, the Czech Legion, and the White Army of Admiral Alexander Kolchak, based in Siberia, would join together to overthrow the Bolsheviks and reopen Russia's war with Germany.

KEY MOMENT

THE MURDER OF THE TSAR

From March 1917, former Tsar Nicholas II, his wife Alexandra, and their five children were placed under house arrest – first at a palace in Tsarskoe Selo near Petrograd and then at Tobolsk in Siberia. In April 1918, the Bolshevik authorities moved the family to a house in Ekaterinburg, a town between Tobolsk and Moscow, where they were subjected to petty harassment. By July, Ekaterinburg was under threat from the anti-Bolshevik forces of the Czech Legion. On 16 July, the Bolsheviks herded the entire family, along with their doctor and servants, into the basement of the house and shot them dead in a clumsily executed massacre. The bodies were buried in secret, the last remains not being discovered and identified until 2008.

> "The **strangling of Bolshevism** at its **birth** would have been an **untold blessing** to the human race."
>
> WINSTON CHURCHILL, SPEECH, 1949

Mixed motives

In summer 1918, Allied intervention in Russia gained momentum. President Woodrow Wilson sent US troops both to Arkhangelsk – a move known as the Polar Bear Expedition – and to Vladivostok. In August, 7,000 Japanese troops poured into Vladivostok, spreading out to occupy a substantial area of eastern Siberia.

The Allies were far from united in their strategy or objectives, however. Contingents of British, French colonial, and Italian troops landing at Vladivostok were ordered to head into central Russia to support a drive by the Czech Legion against the Bolsheviks. The Japanese concentrated on occupying territory in the east, which they hoped to hold on to after the war. The commander of the 8,000 US troops in Vladivostok, General William

Graves, refused to become involved in anti-Bolshevik adventures and concentrated on making the Trans-Siberian Railway fully operational. By autumn 1918, the Bolsheviks had turned their newly founded Red Army into an increasingly effective fighting force. Allied and White Russian troops advancing south from Arkhangelsk faced vigorous Bolshevik counterattacks.

On 11 November 1918, the day of the Armistice between the Central Powers and the Allies on the Western Front, British, Canadian, and US troops were fighting hard to repel a Red Army attack on the Dvina river at Tulgas.

Admiral Kolchak
Backed by foreign forces, Admiral Alexander Kolchak headed an anti-Bolshevik White government based at Omsk in Siberia. In 1920, he was captured by Bolshevik forces and executed.

The end of the war on the Western Front at least clarified the true purpose of Allied intervention in Russia all along – the straightforward support of the White armies seeking to overthrow the Bolsheviks. The French even expanded intervention to a new front by landing troops at Odessa in southern Ukraine to aid White Army forces in December 1918. Allied war-weariness would, however, soon call a halt to such ventures.

AFTER

Most Allied powers left Russia in early 1919, except for the USA and Japan, which stayed on in Vladivostok.

THE ALLIES DEPART
Under pressure both from the Bolshevik Red Army and war-weary public opinion at home, **Allied forces withdrew** from Murmansk and Arkhangelsk in the first half of 1919. The French left Odessa in April 1919 after a mutiny in their fleet. The **Czech Legion** negotiated an **armistice with the Bolsheviks** and returned to newly independent Czechoslovakia in early 1920. The **intervention at Vladivostok** lasted the longest, with most Allied troops, including the Americans, leaving in 1920. Japanese troops did not withdraw until 1922.

Allied troops in Vladivostok, 1918
French, British, US, and Japanese flags hang from a building in Vladivostok, on Russia's Pacific coast, during a march-past by Allied forces. Various foreign troops occupied the port between 1918 and 1922.

Writers at War

> " My **subject is war** and the pity of war. The **poetry** is in **the pity... All a poet can do** today is **warn.**"

WILFRED OWEN, BRITISH OFFICER AND WAR POET, 1918

The writings of poets and novelists who took part in World War I have shaped popular perception of the war, chiefly through underlining the suffering and waste of life it entailed. From the start of the war, however, many established writers were inspired by patriotism and lined up to serve their country.

In October 1914, for example, 93 leading German intellectuals signed a manifesto defending Germany's invasion of Belgium and declaring "the German army and the German people are one and the same". Novelist Thomas Mann, a future Nobel prize winner, was a prominent supporter of the German cause, asserting the superiority of Prussian militarism as opposed to "the pacifist ideal of civilization". In Britain, at a meeting organized by the government's propaganda bureau in September 1914, prominent authors, including Arthur Conan Doyle, Rudyard Kipling, and H.G. Wells, agreed to write essays and give public lectures in support of the war.

Fired by patriotism

Much of the writing published during the war was the work of individuals employing the time-worn clichés of honour and glory. But it would be wrong to see those who wrote in support of the war effort on both sides as insincere. Many were deeply moved by patriotism and the perceived justice of their country's cause, emotions that only deepened as the death toll mounted. Kipling suffered irreparable grief over the death of his son at the Battle of Loos in 1915, but it did not alter his commitment to Britain winning the war. Even citizens of the initially neutral USA were inspired by the conflict. The US novelist Edith Wharton, living in France when the war broke out, published essays expressing her admiration for the French, whom she described as nobly engaged in a struggle for survival.

Anti-war novel

Henri Barbusse's controversial 1916 novel, *Le Feu* (Under Fire) captured the horrors of trench warfare. It made a big impact in France and was published in English the following year.

Battle from the air

This oil painting by an unknown artist was based on an aerial photograph taken during the fighting at St Mihiel. Smoke and gas habitually obscured battlefields on the Western Front, hiding potential targets from artillery or air bombardment.

prepared defensive positions of the Hindenburg Line. Regarding the St Mihiel salient as indefensible, they began preparing a withdrawal as soon as the build-up of US troops in the sector became evident. This further weakened defences that stood no chance of resisting an attack of overwhelming force.

Battle commences

As well as half a million infantry, Pershing had 267 French Renault light tanks – the majority of them with American crews – under the command of Colonel George Patton. The French supplied 3,000 artillery pieces to support the offensive. In the air, General Billy Mitchell, the head of the US Army Air Service, commanded a force of around 1,400 aircraft that included squadrons from other Allied countries as well as American pilots in British- or French-supplied machines. Launched on 12 September, the operation was a precise and effective set-piece attack that took the Germans by surprise.

The battle opened with a four-hour artillery bombardment, followed by the advance of infantry and tanks behind a creeping barrage. American troops had to force a path through barbed wire entanglements, coming under intersecting fire from concealed machine-gun nests, and being threatened by buried mortar bombs strewn as booby traps across their line of advance. Some German soldiers were quick to surrender, but others fought on with great tenacity.

Advances from the south and west brought the salient under American control by 16 September.

The end game

Although they suffered 7,000 casualties, the doughboys had come through their baptism of fire well. Logistical support for the men in the field had not been so successful. Inadequate US staff work had led to huge traffic jams developing behind the lines. Many front-line troops went short of food and water because of serious failings in supplies.

In the euphoria of a first US victory, however, there was no inclination to analyse weaknesses. President Woodrow Wilson cabled his congratulations to Pershing, writing: "The boys have done what we expected of them, and done it the way we most admire."

Victorious American troops

Cheering US soldiers put up a sign dedicating their victory at the St Mihiel salient to President Woodrow Wilson. War-weary Europeans were impressed by the high morale and good physical condition of the men.

Even before the victory at the St Mihiel salient was complete, the USA was preparing for another, larger offensive at the Argonne forest.

PLAN OF ATTACK

The Meuse-Argonne Offensive **308–09 》** opened on 26 September 1918, as part of Foch's wider plan for concerted **Allied attacks** to breach the German Hindenburg Line defences **312–13 》**. The transfer of troops and equipment from the St Mihiel salient to a new front 97 km (60 miles) distant in ten days was a triumph of logistics. Masterminded by Colonel George Marshall, a future Chief of Staff, the offensive continued until the **Armistice** in November **322–23 》**, by which time the Americans were close to taking Sedan.

WILSON.U.S.A

BEFORE

The **Meuse-Argonne** Offensive

Although mostly forgotten today, the Meuse-Argonne Offensive was the largest battle in the US Army's history, involving 1.2 million troops and lasting 47 days. A brutal struggle against a capable enemy, it was the USA's biggest contribution to Germany's defeat on the Western Front.

In August 1918, the Allied armies began a relentless series of attacks. The onslaught, known as the Hundred Days Offensive, comprised a series of battles along the Western Front.

SHEET MUSIC FOR A MARCHING SONG

AMERICAN TROOPS SEE ACTION
Following the victory of **British and Commonwealth** troops at Amiens, in August **≪ 304–05** the Germans knew they could no longer take the offensive. Instead, they sought to **delay the Allied advance** with a stubborn defence.

Throughout the summer of 1918, ever-increasing numbers of US troops in France **tipped the balance** of forces against Germany. Formally created in August, the American First Army entered combat at the **St Mihiel salient** on 12 September **≪ 306–07**. After swiftly capturing the salient, the army moved northwards in preparation for the Meuse-Argonne Offensive.

The Meuse-Argonne Offensive was a daunting task for which General John Pershing's First Army was inadequately prepared. The Americans were to advance up the west bank of the Meuse river, supported by the French Fourth Army on their left. The forested, hilly terrain was described by US General Hunter Liggett as a "natural fortress". The Germans had improved on nature, creating a formidable defensive network in depth. This was manned by the battle-hardened soldiers of the German Fifth Army under General Max von Gallwitz.

Short on resources
Although 600,000 US soldiers were available for the offensive, most of them had not previously experienced combat and many were poorly trained. The Americans were strong on infantry numbers but remained heavily dependent on the British and French for tanks, artillery, and aircraft. Since the Meuse-Argonne attack was timed to coincide with British and French offensives elsewhere on the front, the Allies had withdrawn equipment and personnel to meet their own needs, leaving Pershing with far fewer tanks and aircraft than for the smaller battle of St Mihiel two weeks earlier.

Battle scarred
US infantry advance through the village of Varennes, taken by 28th "Keystone" Division on the first day of the offensive. The ruins are evidence of the hard fighting that was needed to seize the village.

Launched on 26 September, the Meuse-Argonne Offensive soon ran into trouble. German forward positions were overrun by weight of numbers but US losses were heavy. Inexperienced American officers flung men forwards in frontal attacks only for them to be mown down by machine-gun fire. Pershing was concerned by the poor coordination between artillery and infantry, with some units forced to carry out assaults without any artillery support.

In contrast, German artillery fire, both with explosive and gas shells, was terrifyingly effective, the gunners benefiting from intelligence provided by German observation aircraft, which dominated the sky. US logistical problems meant that, as advances were made, food and ammunition supplies often failed to reach troops engaged in combat on the front. Even the weather was hostile, with persistent rain adversely affecting the US soldiers' morale.

By 28 September, the offensive had bogged down and the Germans were mounting counterattacks. One of these severely mauled the US 35th Division (National Guardsmen from Missouri and Kansas) and forced its withdrawal from battle. Then, poorly-trained African-American troops of the 92nd Division, under the command of indifferent white officers, broke and fled under German fire at Binarville, in the Argonne Forest. This episode later became a point of reference for those who wanted to denigrate the fighting spirit of African-Americans, which was, in fact, amply demonstrated elsewhere in the war.

Pershing regroups
After the battle, Allied Supreme Commander Marshal Ferdinand Foch believed US generals had proved incapable of handling a large-scale offensive and made a move to bring US troops under French command. Pershing, however, clung to his independence. After a pause for reorganization, on 4 October he relaunched the offensive with more experienced troops in the lead.

US SOLDIER (1887–1964)

ALVIN C. YORK

American war hero Alvin C. York came from a poor background in rural Jamestown, Tennessee. In 1917, he requested exemption from the draft on religious grounds, but his application was denied. By the time of the Meuse-Argonne Offensive, York was a corporal in the 82nd Infantry Division. He killed 32 German soldiers with rifle fire, helped capture 132 others, and seized 35 machine-guns during action outside the French village of Châtel-Chéhéry on 8 October 1918.

York was awarded the Medal of Honor for his bravery and, after the war, was promoted as a celebrity. His life story formed the basis for the 1941 film *Sergeant York*, directed by Howard Hawks.

"We were stumbling over **dead horses** and **dead men...** shells were **bursting** all around.**"**
CORPORAL ALVIN C. YORK, DIARY ENTRY, 5 OCTOBER 1918

US troops mostly fought with outstanding courage and enthusiasm, but again the gains were hard-won and losses severe. In one notable episode, six companies of the 77th Division, led by Major Charles Whittlesey, were surrounded by German forces, their only method of keeping in touch with the rest of the army being by carrier pigeon. This "Lost Battalion" held out for six days before it was rescued from encirclement. Only 194 of its original force of 554 men were still fit for action.

Gradually and painfully, progress was made. By 12 October, the Germans had been cleared from the Argonne Forest and US troops were facing the Kriemhilde Stellung, the southernmost part of the Hindenburg Line.

Heroic pigeon
The homing pigeon Cher Ami lost a leg while carrying a message from the "Lost Battalion" through German fire. The pigeon was honoured for its bravery with the Croix de Guerre medal. Its stuffed body is preserved in the Smithsonian Institution in Washington, D.C.

Momentum had again been exhausted, however, and Pershing decided to reorganize his forces. To accommodate increasing numbers of troops – about 1 million by mid-October – he created a new Second Army under General Robert Bullard. At the same time, he transferred command of the First Army to General Liggett, allotting himself a supervisory role.

Liggett was an excellent fighting general. While the desperate attritional struggle continued through the second half of October, he strove to imbue his army with the tactical sophistication it had lacked under Pershing. Infantry were to advance in small units, some firing to cover the movement of others; artillery was to coordinate closely with infantry, providing a creeping barrage behind which they could advance. Tanks and aircraft were to support the infantry.

Hard-won victory

On 1 November, it all came together when an assault by the US V Corps broke the Kriemhilde Stellung. Exploiting their training and experience, the US soldiers crossed the Meuse river and advanced along opposite banks, driving back the German forces. By 9 November, the Americans had progressed 40 km (25 miles) to reach the hills overlooking the city of Sedan. When the Armistice stopped the fighting two days later, Pershing claimed the Meuse-Argonne Offensive as a victory, even if it was achieved at great cost.

The Americans suffered 122,000 casualties in the Meuse-Argonne Offensive, including 26,277 dead. German losses were on a similar scale.

GERMANY SUCCUMBS

The relentless pressure kept up by the US and supporting French troops in the Meuse-Argonne sector prevented the Germans from reinforcing the **Hindenburg Line** further north. This was **taken by the British and French** in late September and early October **312–13 »**.

Along with the defeat of Germany's allies on other fronts – Turkey in Palestine, Bulgaria in Macedonia, and Austria-Hungary in Italy – these German setbacks on the Western Front led Germany to **seek an armistice 322–23 »** on 11 November. By that time, the American Expeditionary Force (AEF), like other armies on the Western Front, was in the grip of an **influenza epidemic** that would kill 25,000 Americans, compared with a total of 53,000 killed in combat.

Montfaucon in ruins
The village of Montfaucon d'Argonne was held by the Germans from September 1914 until its capture by US forces in September 1918. The remains of a German observation post is on the left of the ruined church.

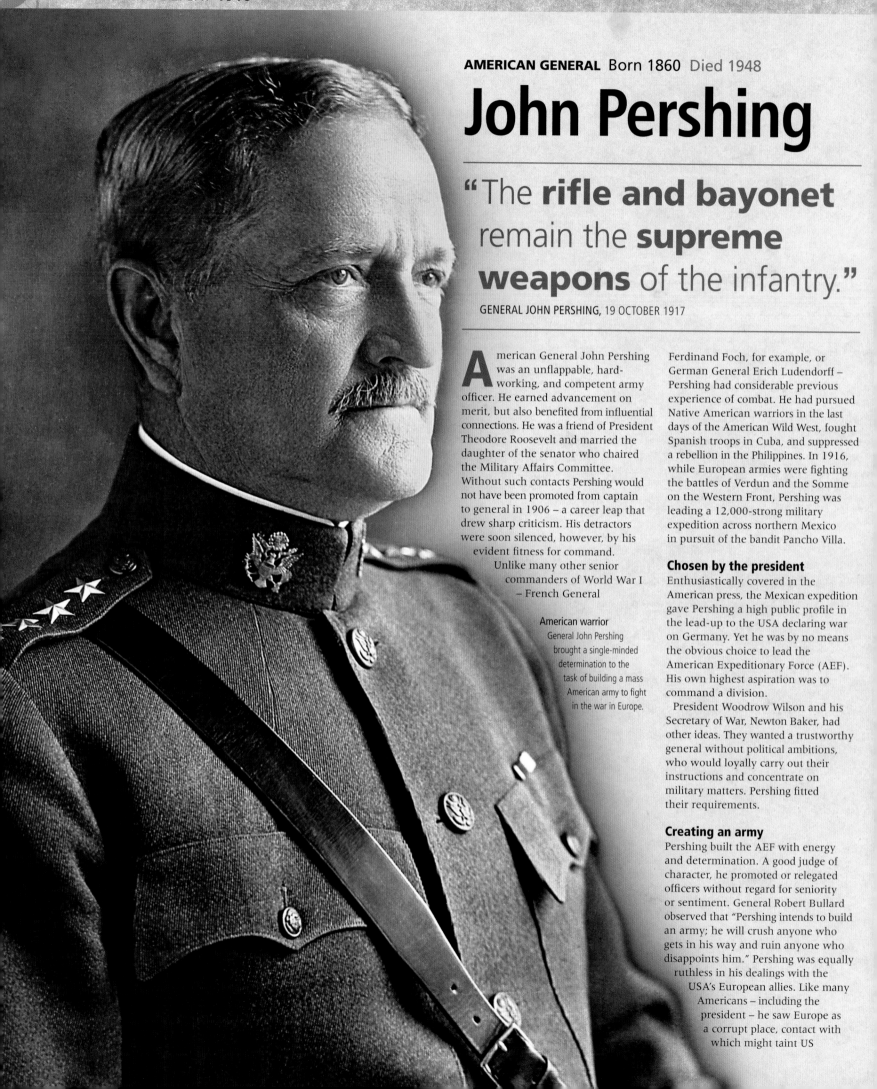

AMERICAN GENERAL Born 1860   Died 1948

John Pershing

> "The **rifle and bayonet** remain the **supreme weapons** of the infantry."

GENERAL JOHN PERSHING, 19 OCTOBER 1917

A merican General John Pershing was an unflappable, hard-working, and competent army officer. He earned advancement on merit, but also benefited from influential connections. He was a friend of President Theodore Roosevelt and married the daughter of the senator who chaired the Military Affairs Committee. Without such contacts Pershing would not have been promoted from captain to general in 1906 – a career leap that drew sharp criticism. His detractors were soon silenced, however, by his evident fitness for command.

Unlike many other senior commanders of World War I – French General

American warrior
General John Pershing brought a single-minded determination to the task of building a mass American army to fight in the war in Europe.

Ferdinand Foch, for example, or German General Erich Ludendorff – Pershing had considerable previous experience of combat. He had pursued Native American warriors in the last days of the American Wild West, fought Spanish troops in Cuba, and suppressed a rebellion in the Philippines. In 1916, while European armies were fighting the battles of Verdun and the Somme on the Western Front, Pershing was leading a 12,000-strong military expedition across northern Mexico in pursuit of the bandit Pancho Villa.

Chosen by the president

Enthusiastically covered in the American press, the Mexican expedition gave Pershing a high public profile in the lead-up to the USA declaring war on Germany. Yet he was by no means the obvious choice to lead the American Expeditionary Force (AEF). His own highest aspiration was to command a division.

President Woodrow Wilson and his Secretary of War, Newton Baker, had other ideas. They wanted a trustworthy general without political ambitions, who would loyally carry out their instructions and concentrate on military matters. Pershing fitted their requirements.

Creating an army

Pershing built the AEF with energy and determination. A good judge of character, he promoted or relegated officers without regard for seniority or sentiment. General Robert Bullard observed that "Pershing intends to build an army; he will crush anyone who gets in his way and ruin anyone who disappoints him." Pershing was equally ruthless in his dealings with the USA's European allies. Like many Americans – including the president – he saw Europe as a corrupt place, contact with which might taint US

Cheering for victory
Soldiers of the Irish Guards raise their helmets aloft to cheer the announcement of the Armistice at Maubeuge in northern France.

agreement were discussed, but there were no real negotiations. Erzberger read out a statement of protest, concluding: "A people of 70 million are suffering, but they are not dead."

At 5:10am the Armistice was signed by Foch and British First Sea Lord Admiral Rosslyn Wemyss for the Allies, and by Erzberger and three of his colleagues for Germany. It was agreed that, since it was the eleventh day of the eleventh month, hostilities would cease at 11am, to complete the coincidence.

The last shots

The war continued until the last moment. Everywhere Allied troops were advancing. The Belgians had just retaken Ghent, the Canadians Mons,

Celebratory feast
The annual Thanksgiving Day celebrations had special significance for Americans in November 1918. As this menu shows, the traditional turkey dinner was served in London to US soldiers who had survived the war.

and the Americans Mézières. There were 11,000 Allied casualties on the morning of 11 November, as officers ordered attacks to seize key points ahead of the ceasefire. Outside Mons, three British soldiers who had survived four years of combat were killed by a burst of machine-gun fire.

Canadian Private George Price is recognized as the last British and Commonwealth fatality of the war, shot dead by a sniper at 10:58.

"No more **slaughter,** no more **maiming,** no more **mud** and **blood,** and no more **killing.**"

BRITISH LIEUTENANT R. G. DIXON, ROYAL ARTILLERY, ON THE ARMISTICE

As the watches of the officers ticked to 11 o'clock, the order was given to cease firing. An uncanny silence fell along the front. Soldiers realized, with amazement, that the war really had stopped. As the guns fell silent, reactions were mixed. At the front there was no fraternization between opposing troops. Allied soldiers still manned their positions, while to the rear reactions ranged from decorous thanksgiving ceremonies to riotous celebrations with the local population.

Public reactions

The most joyous scenes took place in Allied cities. In London's Trafalgar Square, on Broadway in New York, and along the Seine in Paris, crowds danced and sang. Political leaders – Georges Clemenceau in France, David Lloyd George in Britain – made speeches. In some places, such as Chicago in the USA and Melbourne in Australia, celebrations degenerated into disorder. More frequently well-behaved street parties took place, as families waited to be reunited with loved ones.

For many people, in mourning for relatives killed in the fighting or struck down by the deadly influenza epidemic then sweeping the world, the rejoicing seemed inappropriate. The family of the English poet Wilfred Owen

Anglo-American celebrations

In Paris, on 11 November 1918, two British soldiers, an American sailor, and an American nurse celebrate the Armistice together. An apparently interminable conflict had come to a surprisingly sudden end.

received the telegram announcing his death in combat as the bells were ringing for the Armistice. In Belgium, celebration of the German defeat was accompanied by retribution against collaborators and profiteers. Belgian women alleged to have had relationships with German soldiers were forced to walk naked through the streets with their heads shaved, and traders believed to have exploited food shortages for profit had their shops looted and burned.

There was no rejoicing in the defeated countries. In Germany, shock and bitterness were widespread among civilians who had thought their country would win the war and soldiers who could not believe the

The Armistice was followed by a peace conference in Paris in 1919, at which the victors discussed the terms to be imposed on the defeated.

THE FALLOUT
The delay in finalizing peace terms slowed the **demobilization of Allied armies**, and soldiers demanded the right to go home. Many civilians in Germany and former Austria-Hungary suffered hardship through the continuing Allied blockade and economic and political dislocation. All countries experienced high death rates from an **influenza pandemic** that in total probably killed more people than the war. The **Treaty of Versailles 338–39 »**, signed by the Germans under protest in June 1919, formally ended the war. Matthias Erzberger was assassinated by German nationalist extremists in 1921 for his "crime" in signing the Armistice.

SPANISH FLU OVERTAKES THE ANGEL OF PEACE

German army had been beaten. One corporal, Adolf Hitler, heard the news of the Armistice while in hospital recovering from a gas attack. In his memoirs, *Mein Kampf*, he described his anguish at the realization that four years of fighting had "all been in vain". The reactions of men such as Hitler to the experience of defeat were to become a dangerous factor in postwar German political life.

Victory parade
French civilians and US soldiers celebrate the conclusion of the war. The collapse of the German army led the country's leaders to sign an armistice with the Allies on 11 November 1918.

German hardship

Women stoop to salvage food from a rubbish dump in Berlin in the aftermath of the war. Malnutrition was rife and the death toll high.

Adolf Hitler, were drawn into nationalist extremist groups that blamed socialists and Jews for the debacle. Unable to reintegrate in civilian life, many ex-soldiers joined paramilitary organizations called Freikorps. The German government, led by moderate Social Democrats intent on founding a parliamentary democracy, used the Freikorps to crush an attempted communist uprising in Berlin in January 1919. A socialist republic proclaimed in Bavaria, southern Germany, in May 1919 was also brutally suppressed.

Pitiful living conditions

Life remained a miserable struggle for most Germans, who faced poverty, cold, and hunger, induced by political chaos and the effects of the Allied naval blockade, which under the terms of the Armistice was maintained until a final peace agreement was signed.

It was a similar picture in other countries shattered by the war. In the Turkish capital Constantinople (Istanbul), typhus was rampant, food scarce, fuel unobtainable, and transport at a standstill. In the former Austro-Hungarian and Russian empires, the condition of many people was pitiful.

New conflicts

There were outbreaks of fighting as new states sought to establish their borders – for example, between Poland and Czechoslovakia. In Hungary, a communist revolutionary, Bela Kun, seized power in March 1919 and proclaimed a Soviet Republic. He was overthrown by an invasion of Romanian and Czechoslovak forces, which allowed Hungarian Admiral Miklos Horthy to take power.

The victor countries were not immune to conflict and disorder. Italy was swept by riots and strikes. In the USA, the authorities made widespread arrests of anarchists and socialists in the "Red Scare" from April 1919. The British Empire was challenged by revolts in Ireland, Egypt, and India. Meanwhile, Belgium and France faced the daunting challenge of reconstruction in the war-devastated zone of the Western Front, with its ruined or obliterated towns and villages, wrecked factories and mines, gas-poisoned soil, and dangerous litter of unexploded munitions. Even neutral countries such as Norway and the Netherlands were stalked by hunger.

The establishment of the American Relief Administration in February 1919, to provide food aid to Europe, was an attempt at a civilized international response to the catastrophe. But mostly individuals and states had to seek their own way back to normality.

Clearing the ruins

German prisoners of war are set to work clearing debris in the ruined French town of Béthune in 1919. It took about seven years to return the devastated areas of northeastern France to normality.

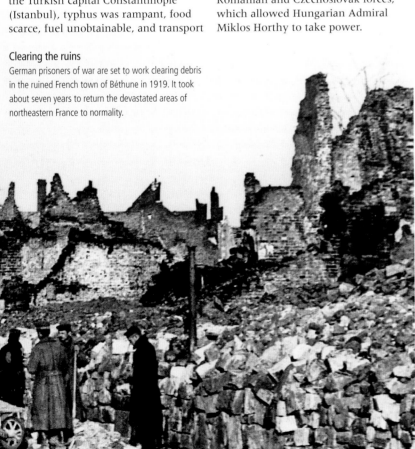

Leaders of the victorious powers gathered for a conference in Paris in January 1919, leading to the agreement of a series of treaties to formally end the war.

SEEDS OF FUTURE CONFLICT
The crucial peace agreement with Germany, the **Versailles Treaty 338–39 >>**, was signed in June 1919. Accepted by the Germans under duress, it included provision for **substantial reparations payments.** The German Weimar Republic was formally created in August 1919, but Germany continued to be racked by **civil conflict and hyperinflation** until 1924. In Italy, discontent with the outcome of the war was a major factor in the rise to power of **Benito Mussolini's Fascist Party** in 1922. In places, warfare continued into the 1920s, notably in the **Russian Civil War** and the **Greco-Turkish War 342–43 >>**.

> "We have won the war. Now we will **have to win the peace.** That may **prove harder.**"
>
> FRENCH PREMIER GEORGES CLEMENCEAU, 11 NOVEMBER 1918

GERMAN DICTATOR (1889–1945)

ADOLF HITLER

The future German dictator Adolf Hitler was Austrian. He moved to Munich in Germany as a young man, joining the German army as a volunteer in August 1914. After the war, he drifted into nationalist politics, and in 1921 became leader of the small Nazi Party.

In 1923, his attempt to seize power in the Munich Putsch failed. After a spell in prison, he built up mass support by arguing that all Germany's ills were due to the Treaty of Versailles. Taking power in 1933, he sought to reverse the result of World War I, eventually leading Germany to catastrophic defeat in World War II.

The Paris Peace Conference

In January 1919, world leaders met for a peace conference in Paris. Hopes were high for the creation of a new and better world that would justify the sacrifice of the war. The conference ended in disillusion, however, as the participants haggled over conflicting interests.

BEFORE

Wartime agreements between Allied countries and public statements by political leaders set the complex agenda for the peace conference.

QUEST FOR NATIONHOOD

US President Woodrow Wilson had declared that the war would **"make the world safe for democracy" ‹‹ 212–13**. Britain and France had agreed with the Americans to allow national groups such as the Poles to form **independent states ‹‹ 168–69**. But Italy expected to gain territory in Dalmatia, which had a mainly Slav population. The **Arabs** had been promised **independence ‹‹ 196–97**, contradicting an Anglo-French agreement to share former Turkish land and British **promises to Jewish Zionists**.

ITALIAN POLITICIAN (1860–1952)

VITTORIO ORLANDO

A law professor and politician from Sicily, Vittorio Orlando was Italy's minister of the interior before being appointed prime minister in the wake of the Caporetto disaster in 1917. His firm leadership secured a degree of national unity in support of the war effort. At the peace conference, he staged a walkout in protest at the treatment of Italy, but Italian nationalists still condemned him for failing to secure territorial expansion. They forced his resignation in June 1919.

The Paris Peace Conference was a vast, unwieldy event. Thirty-two states were represented, each with its entourage of diplomats, advisers, and secretaries. The most significant absentees were the defeated powers, who were not invited, and Bolshevik Russia. The leaders of all the major Allied states attended in person – David Lloyd George for Britain, Georges Clemenceau for France, Italian premier Vittorio Orlando, and US president Woodrow Wilson. The first US president to travel abroad on official business, Wilson was greeted in Europe by adoring crowds.

Initially, the most important issues at the conference were discussed by a Council of Ten, consisting of two representatives from each of the five major powers – the USA, Britain, France, Italy, and Japan. By March, this had been ditched in favour of a Council of Four – Wilson, Lloyd George, Clemenceau, and Orlando.

The League of Nations

The European Allies had broadly accepted the principle of a "just peace" based on democracy and national self-determination, as proposed by President Wilson. Lloyd George and Clemenceau both supported Wilson's idea for an international organization, the League of Nations, to preserve future peace. But each representative was there to promote his country's interests and ambitions. Victors expected to be rewarded for their war effort and compensated for their losses. Many were soon disappointed.

Japan proposed that the League support racial equality between members, but this was rejected.

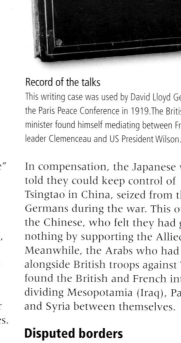

Record of the talks
This writing case was used by David Lloyd George at the Paris Peace Conference in 1919. The British prime minister found himself mediating between French leader Clemenceau and US President Wilson.

In compensation, the Japanese were told they could keep control of Tsingtao in China, seized from the Germans during the war. This outraged the Chinese, who felt they had gained nothing by supporting the Allied cause. Meanwhile, the Arabs who had fought alongside British troops against Turkey found the British and French intent on dividing Mesopotamia (Iraq), Palestine, and Syria between themselves.

Disputed borders

The peacemakers are sometimes said to have redrawn the borders of Europe, but except for the crucial case of Germany, most changes were decided elsewhere. Poland, Czechoslovakia, and the Kingdom of Serbs, Croats and Slovenes (Yugoslavia) had already declared

Arab representatives
Prince Feisal and his delegation, including British officer T.E. Lawrence (to the right of Feisal), at the conference. Having supported the Allies against Turkey, the Arabs expected to be rewarded with independence.

independence. The peacemakers could only intervene over the detail of borders, and sometimes, as in the case of Poland's eastern frontier, their decisions were later ignored.

Much time was spent discussing the fate of Fiume (Rijeka), which Italy and Yugoslavia both claimed. In April, Orlando walked out of the conference after his allies refused to back Italy. The frustration of its territorial ambitions fuelled discontent in the country in the postwar period. Overall, attempts to

NATIONAL SELF-DETERMINATION
The right of ethnic groups to form independent nation-states instead of living under foreign rule.

match borders to ethnicity revealed how impossible it was to apply self-determination to Europe's complex web of people.

A series of peace treaties were signed with the defeated powers: the Treaty of Versailles with Germany in June 1918, the Treaty of St Germain with Austria in September, the Treaty of Neuilly with Bulgaria in November, the Treaty of Sèvres with Turkey in April 1920, and the Treaty of Trianon with Hungary the following June. The treaties were complex, detailed, and partially ineffectual. The compromises between justice and revenge, and idealism and self-interest, left grounds for resentment, fuelling hostility and conflict for decades to come.

AFTER

In the 1920s and 30s, two of the peace treaties were nullified. Some of the disputes were settled by force.

BROKEN PROMISES

The **Treaty of Versailles 338–39 ››** with Germany included provision for reparations that the Germans had difficulty in paying. The treaty was overturned by the Nazi regime from 1933. The **Treaty of Sèvres**, signed with Ottoman Turkey, was invalidated by the overthrow of the Sultan and success of Turkish Republican forces in a war with Greece. The **Treaty of Lausanne**, far more favourable to Turkey, replaced it in July 1923.

SHIFTING TERRITORIES

After a war between Poland and Bolshevik Russia, in March 1921 the **Peace of Riga** pushed the Polish border further east. Yugoslavia accepted Italian rule of disputed Fiume by the **Treaty of Rome** in 1924.

Peace conference delegates
Irish artist William Orpen was commissioned to paint this group portrait of the conference. Entitled *A Peace Conference at the Quai d'Orsay*, it shows Orlando, Wilson, Clemenceau and Lloyd George seated around the table.

FRENCH PRIME MINISTER Born 1841 Died 1929

Georges Clemenceau

"You ask what are **my war aims.** Gentlemen, **they are very simple: Victory.**"

GEORGES CLEMENCEAU, SPEECH, 20 NOVEMBER, 1917

In 1914, Georges Clemenceau was a 72-year-old maverick politician and journalist approaching the end of a long and chequered career. As a young man he had made his reputation as a radical critic of government, whose speeches in the Chamber of Deputies denounced colonialism, militarism, and the power of the Catholic Church.

When French life was torn apart in the 1890s by the Dreyfus affair – a scandal involving the mistaken condemnation of a Jewish army officer for treason – Clemenceau was among those who upheld Dreyfus's innocence. He became a hate figure for right-wing militarists, nationalists, anti-Semites, and Catholics. Around the same time, he was accused of taking bribes to cover up the bankruptcy of the Panama Canal Company.

In 1906, a time of political unrest in France, he accepted the post of minister of the interior. Socialists and anarchists were added to his list of enemies when he employed the army and police to suppress strikes and disturbances. In a subsequent three-year spell as prime minister, he earned respect for his tough handling of domestic issues and strengthened the Entente Cordiale (informal alliance) between France and Britain.

Outspoken critic
In the run-up to World War I Clemenceau founded a newspaper, *L'Homme libre* (The Free Man), to warn against the German threat to France and campaign for military preparedness. He described France as "neither defended nor governed" and fulminated against socialists who preached anti-militarism. When the war broke out in 1914, he turned down the offer of a government post as minister of justice. Instead, he stayed on the sidelines, using his newspaper to criticize the government and to demand a more competent execution of the war. After an issue of *L'Homme libre* was suppressed by military censors in September 1914, Clemenceau renamed it *L'Homme enchaîné* (The Shackled Man).

Clemenceau was no champion of the freedom of others, however. He denounced

Ferocious reputation
French wartime prime minister Georges Clemenceau was known as "the Tiger" because of his fierce temperament. He was 77 years old at the time of the Paris Peace Conference in 1919.

The doctor of France
This cartoon alludes to Clemenceau's qualification as a doctor, depicting him as a crude surgeon who has operated on France's sick body. He was renowned for his ruthlessness towards his numerous enemies.

Interior Minister Louis-Jean Malvy as a defeatist and traitor for allowing the publication of the left-wing journal *Le Bonnet Rouge* and for failing to arrest left-wing "subversives and saboteurs".

As well as running his newspaper, Clemenceau was a member of the Senate, the upper house of the French parliament. As head of its army and foreign affairs committee from 1915, he met the military and political leaders of the Allied war effort and gained an insider's understanding of the conflict.

Becoming prime minister

By autumn 1917, the government was in disarray and public morale was low. Political unity had disintegrated. The fall of Paul Painlevé's government, defeated in parliament, left President Raymond Poincaré with two credible candidates for the job of prime minister: Joseph Caillaux, the leading advocate of a negotiated peace, and Clemenceau, the best known proponent of a fight to the death. He chose Clemenceau.

Clemenceau visits the troops
In 1918, the French prime minister made weekly visits to the front, both to talk with his generals and to meet ordinary soldiers in the trenches. His public appearances strengthened morale.

More like a dictator than a prime minister, Clemenceau filled his cabinet with nonentities and kept the key post of minister for war for himself. In an impassioned speech, he declared victory his sole aim and committed France to war "to the end". Alleged traitors and defeatists were arrested, including Caillaux and Malvy. Strikes in factories were resolved by addressing grievances while cracking down on anti-war activists.

Clemenceau's passionate commitment to the war tightened bonds with France's Allies during the fluctuating battles of 1918. He could claim a large part of the credit for installing Ferdinand Foch as Supreme Commander of the Allied Armies in spring 1918 and for the aggressive pursuit of the war on the Western Front from July 1918. His eloquent speeches raised French morale on the home front and in the army.

Tough stance

Celebrated at the Armistice as the architect of victory, he entered the Paris Peace Conference determined to ensure the security of France against a future resurgence of German militarism. Surviving an assassination attempt by anarchist Emile Cottin – which left a bullet lodged in his chest for the rest of his life – Clemenceau argued tirelessly against what he saw as the naive idealism of US President Woodrow Wilson. Faced with the refusal of Britain and the USA to support his aims, however, he was forced to accept compromises. As a result, the Treaty of Versailles was denounced by French nationalists as too lenient on Germany.

Exploiting Clemenceau's prestige, a "bloc national" of right-wing politicians campaigned under his banner at elections in November 1919 but then deserted him. Failing in a bid for the presidency, Clemenceau retired in 1920. He died nine years later at the age of 89.

Prime ministerial seal
Used by Georges Clemenceau during his tenure as prime minister of France, this seal was fashioned out of red gold and silver. It had a carved monogram – "GC".

> "With **snarls and growls,** the ferocious, aged, dauntless beast of prey **went into action.**"
>
> WINSTON CHURCHILL, DESCRIBING CLEMENCEAU AS WAR LEADER

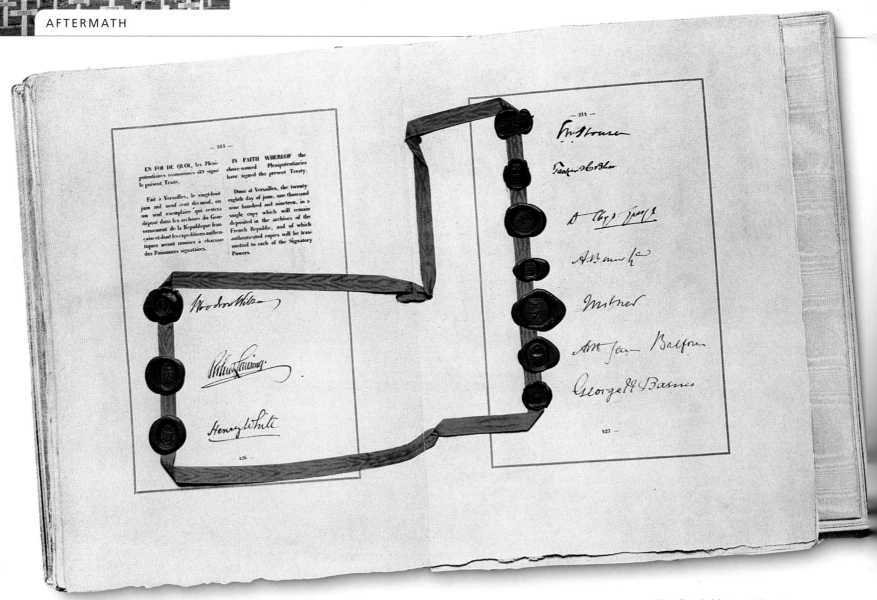

Signed, sealed, but not delivered
This page of the treaty was signed by all the main delegates at the conference. At the top is the signature of Woodrow Wilson, who later failed to get the treaty ratified by the US Congress.

The **Versailles Treaty**

The peace treaty signed by the Allies and Germany has remained controversial. The product of acrimonious debate between the leaders of the victorious powers, the terms it imposed on Germany were regarded by almost all Germans as excessively harsh and unjust.

BEFORE

The Armistice, signed on 11 November 1918, paved the way for a permanent peace settlement.

VICTORY AND DEFEAT
In Germany, a **revolution ‹‹ 320–321** overthrew the Kaiser and established a republic. The country was in political turmoil and its people suffered severe hardship, worsened by the continuation of the Allied blockade. In fulfilment of the Armistice terms, **German troops withdrew from foreign soil** and Allied forces occupied German territory west of the Rhine. Allied leaders assembled for the **Paris Peace Conference ‹‹ 334–35** in January 1919.

Discussion of the peace terms was primarily in the hands of three men: US President Woodrow Wilson, French Prime Minister Georges Clemenceau, and British Prime Minister David Lloyd George. Wilson and Clemenceau were very different characters. Wilson rejected the cynicism and self-interest of the European states; Clemenceau believed the American president was naive in his dealings with Germany.

Wilson believed in a settlement based on just principles. Future peace would be guaranteed through a League of Nations committed to oppose any act

Germany faces the guillotine
Commenting on the Paris Peace Conference, the German satirical magazine *Simplicissimus* shows a captive Germany facing execution at the hands of President Wilson, Lloyd George, and Clemenceau.

of aggression. Clemenceau, steeped in European history, did not believe in a future ruled by principle rather than force. He told Wilson: "Do not believe the Germans will ever forgive us. They will seek only the chance of revenge." For Clemenceau, Germany had to be

permanently incapacitated. Lloyd George, for his part, won an election in December 1918 with promises to "hang the Kaiser" and make Germany pay for the war. But Britain was satisfied with seizing the German fleet and German colonies. Lloyd George had no interest in backing French aims in Europe.

Key points
The easiest ground for Allied agreement was the founding of a League of Nations. Interpreted by Wilson as initiating a new era in international relations and by Clemenceau as a permanent military alliance against Germany, it was enshrined in Part I of the treaty.

There was also agreement on limiting Germany's armed forces. The German army was to be restricted to 100,000 men without tanks or aircraft, and the navy to a few small surface warships.

Territorial arrangements posed intractable problems. The Allies were committed in principle to "national self-determination", but they also

White forces and could claim victory in the Civil War, but the Bolsheviks reigned over depopulated cities and a devastated countryside that was ravaged by famine.

Meanwhile, Bolshevik Russia was defeated in a crucial conflict with Poland. War broke out when the newly established Polish Republic, keen to advance its borders as far eastward as

15 MILLION The number of people estimated to have died in the Volga famine in Russia in 1921–22, a direct result of the Russian Civil War.

possible, sent troops into Belarus and Ukraine. A counter-offensive by the Red Army launched in June 1920 drove the Poles back and by August the advancing Bolsheviks were threatening Warsaw.

As Soviet forces pushed on towards Germany and Hungary, Polish leader Marshal Josef Pilsudski regained the initiative, executing a series of bold manoeuvres that inflicted a crushing defeat on the Red Army. Bolshevik leader Vladimir Ilyich Lenin was forced

to agree a peace that left the Poles in control of large areas of Belarus and Ukraine.

Greece versus Turkey
In 1919, Greece exploited the weakness of defeated Ottoman Turkey to launch a military occupation of parts of western Anatolia that had a substantial ethnic Greek population. Turkish nationalists led by General Mustafa Kemal defeated the Greek army in large-scale fighting through 1921 and 1922. Mustafa Kemal, later known as Ataturk, proclaimed Turkey a republic and deposed the Ottoman sultan.

Rejecting the option of reopening war with the Turks, the Allied powers accepted the need

OTTOBRE 1922

ADVNATA CAMICIE NERE A ROMA

ED. DALL'UFFICIO STAMPA

Fascist propaganda postcard
A fanciful postcard celebrates the "march on Rome" by Italian fascist blackshirts in October 1922. A carefully stage-managed demonstration, the march led to Benito Mussolini becoming head of the Italian government.

AFTER

By the mid-1920s, some of the consequences of the chaotic aftermath of World War I were being addressed, although the return to normality proved shortlived.

RIGHTING WRONGS
In 1924, a US-brokered agreement, the **Dawes Plan**, created a basis for German payment of reparations and led to the **withdrawal of French and Belgian troops** from the Ruhr. In 1925, the **Locarno Treaty** settled outstanding issues with Germany, which was admitted to the **League of Nations** the following year. In the Middle East, Egyptian independence was granted in 1922 and Prince Feisal was made king of Iraq.

ECONOMIC CRASH
Normalization was ended by worldwide **economic depression** from 1929. Mass unemployment undermined democracy in Germany and brought Adolf Hitler's **Nazi Party** to power in 1933. Hitler tore up the Versailles Treaty and Germany rearmed.

Fleeing the flames
Greeks leave Smyrna (now Izmir, Turkey), as its Greek quarter burns to the ground at the end of the Greco-Turkish War. Around 1.5 million Greeks left Turkey.

to renegotiate the peace treaty that had been imposed in 1920. The Treaty of Lausanne, signed in 1923, set Turkey's new borders, which it still holds today. The ethnic Greek population was expelled, leaving many towns and villages emptied of their inhabitants.

The rise of fascism
In Western Europe, the economic and social disruption caused by World War I led to chronic political instability. In Italy, nationalist extremist Benito Mussolini, who had served as a soldier in the war, led black-shirted Fascist paramilitaries in a violent campaign against socialists and trade unionists. In 1922, when Mussolini threatened to lead his followers in a "march on Rome", King Victor Emmanuel III allowed him to form a government, setting Italy on the road towards an eventual fascist dictatorship.

In Germany, postwar chaos peaked in 1923. In response to German failure to make reparations payments, France and Belgium sent troops to occupy the Ruhr region. The German government responded with a campaign of passive resistance. Hyperinflation led to the collapse of the German currency, wiping out savings.

When Nazi Party leader Adolf Hitler attempted a coup modelled on Mussolini's "march on Rome", however, his "Munich putsch" was suppressed by the army. The postwar world was still seeking stability.

The occupation of the Ruhr
An illustration from a French newspaper shows French soldiers confronting German workers in the Ruhr in 1923. The French and Belgians occupied the Ruhr in an effort to force Germany to make reparations payments.

> "I don't know if **war** is an **interlude in peace,** or **peace** an **interlude in war.**"
> FRENCH PRIME MINISTER GEORGES CLEMENCEAU

Bringing home the Unknown Soldier
In 1920, the body of a British soldier, selected at random, was brought back from France to be buried in the Tomb of the Unknown Warrior in Westminster Abbey.

≪ BEFORE

Never Again

The experience of World War I cast a long shadow over the postwar period. Nations sought appropriate forms of public mourning and commemoration to grieve and honour the dead. There was an overwhelming desire that such a war should never be repeated.

During the war, Allied political leaders promised that a better, more peaceful world would result from victory over German militarism. These promises proved hard to keep.

THE WAR TO END ALL WARS
Declaring war on Germany in April 1917, US President Woodrow Wilson said his object was to **"bring peace and safety to all nations".** Celebrating the Armistice on 11 November 1918, British Prime Minister David Lloyd George said: "I hope we may all say that thus, this fateful morning, came to an end all wars."

The aspiration to a permanent peace was embodied in the founding of the **League of Nations** at the **Paris Peace Conference ≪ 334–35** in 1919. Member-states of the League committed themselves to progressive disarmament and the peaceful resolution of disputes.

The emotional impact of World War I and its place in collective memory varied between countries. In Russia, for example, the war was almost forgotten, quickly eclipsed by the shattering upheaval of the Bolshevik Revolution.

In Britain and France, the war was commemorated intensively, with an annual Remembrance Day on 11 November established from 1919. By common accord they honoured the sacrifice of the dead rather than celebrated a victory. A two-minute silence was observed throughout Britain and its empire at 11am, a practice so rigorously followed in the early years that all traffic stopped,

factories turned off machinery, and pedestrians stood still in the street. Memorials to the war dead were erected in most towns and villages.

Unknown warriors
On Remembrance Day 1920, the British held a state funeral in Westminster Abbey for an Unknown Warrior, burying a soldier chosen at random from among the wartime dead. The French held a similar ceremony at the Arc de Triomphe in Paris, and the USA followed suit in 1921, burying an Unknown Warrior at Arlington National Cemetery in Virginia. The Unknown Warrior represented all those who had lost their lives, without

distinction of rank. This democratic spirit infused all commemoration of the war. Tens of thousands of plaques and monuments were erected in cities, towns, and villages, typically listing the fallen in alphabetical order, the officers intermingled with ordinary soldiers regardless of rank.

Britain decided against repatriating the dead. Instead, the Imperial (now Commonwealth) War Graves Commission created vast war cemeteries in France. Unidentifiable remains were marked: "A Soldier of the Great War Known unto God." The French placed the bones of their unidentified dead in ossuaries, such as the one at Douaumont near Verdun.

"Anything rather than war! Anything!… **No trial, no servitude** can be **compared to war.**"

FRENCH NOVELIST AND PACIFIST ROGER MARTIN DU GARD, PRIVATE LETTER, SEPTEMBER 1936

For Germany, remembrance was complicated by deeply divided attitudes towards the war. Local memorials were erected to the dead, but the Weimar Republic failed to agree on a national remembrance day, and commemorative events were often the occasion for political protests. Germany did not bury an Unknown Warrior until 1931.

Ireland was another place in which the memory of the war was politically contentious. For Irish Catholics, war service in the British Army became an embarrassment and commemorative ceremonies drew hostility from many republicans. For Protestants in Northern Ireland, war service was a badge of loyalty to the British Crown and Remembrance Day became a demonstration of Protestant superiority to the allegedly disloyal Catholics.

When the French erected a monument to mark the site of the signing of the armistice, they inscribed it with the words: "Here on the 11 November 1918 succumbed the criminal pride of the German Reich… vanquished by the free peoples which it tried to enslave." Such ringing endorsement of the purpose of the war was not often heard during the postwar decades. Disillusion was partly fuelled by the fate of ex-servicemen, who received far less attention from governments than the dead. Many

ended up unemployed, although veterans' organizations provided a source of support and companionship. The peace treaties were seen as unworthy of the soldiers' sacrifice.

A flood of memoirs and novels published during the late 1920s and 1930s – Erich Remarque's *All Quiet on the Western Front* the most prominent among them – fed the popular imagination with images of the horrors of the war. Americans in particular viewed the war as a mistake into which they had been lured by British propaganda.

US isolationism

Throughout the 1920s and 1930s, in reaction against the war, an isolationist mentality predominated in the USA. In Britain, pacifism grew into a mass movement, led by organizations such as the Peace Pledge Union. In 1933, students debating at the Oxford Union at Oxford

Pacifist protest
The youth section of the British Peace Movement at a demonstration in 1924. The movement was part of War Resisters International, founded in 1921.

University famously voted that "this House will in no circumstances fight for its King and Country".

Public promises

Governments were also inspired by the desire to fulfil the promise that World War I would prove "a war to end war". In the 1920s, there were international arms limitation agreements, while the League of Nations sought to substitute "collective security" and negotiation for armed confrontation. In 1928–29, all major countries signed the Kellogg-Briand Pact – named for US Secretary of State Frank Kellogg and French foreign minister Aristide Briand – publicly renouncing the use of war as an "instrument of national policy".

Nationalists and militarists in countries defeated in the war or disappointed by the peace drew a different lesson from the conflict. In the 1920s, the German Stahlhelm veterans' organization and the Italian Fascist movement harked back to the wartime experience of national unity. Fascist leader Benito Mussolini stated that war "put the stamp of nobility on those nations that had the courage to face it". Another ex-soldier who longed to reverse the defeat of 1914–18 was German Nazi Party leader Adolf Hitler. His accession to power in Germany in 1933 set the world on course for an even more destructive war.

World War I shows no signs of being forgotten a century after it was fought.

GONE BUT NOT FORGOTTEN
Despite the **deaths of the last surviving soldiers** from World War I, including Harry Patch in Britain in 2009 and Frank Buckles in the USA in 2011, the war continues to stir powerful emotions in the nations that were involved. Annual **commemorative ceremonies** – for example, Remembrance

36,000 The number of communes in France that erected monuments to those who died in World War I.

Day in Britain, Veterans Day in the USA, and Anzac Day in Australia and New Zealand – continue to be well attended, with the fallen in subsequent wars also remembered.

THREE OF THE WAR'S LAST VETERANS IN 2008

Ombler / By kind permission of The Trustees of the Imperial War Museum, London (cl). **50-51 Dorling Kindersley:** Gary Ombler / Courtesy of the Royal Museum of the Armed Forces and of Military History, Brussels, Belgium (b). **51 Dorling Kindersley:** Gary Ombler / Courtesy of the Royal Artillery Historical Trust (tl, cl); Gary Ombler / Courtesy of the Royal Museum of the Armed Forces and of Military History, Brussels, Belgium (tr, cr, br). **52 akg-images:** IAM (c). **Getty Images:** Popperfoto (b). **53 Corbis:** Bettmann (bc). **54 akg-images:** ullstein bild (t). **Lebrecht Music and Arts:** RA (bc). **55 Dorling Kindersley:** Imperial War Museum, London (tr). **56 Mary Evans Picture Library:** Rue des Archives / Tallandier (l). **57 Getty Images:** Popperfoto (tc). **Lebrecht Music and Arts:** leemage (br). **RMN:** Paris - Musée de l'Armée, Dist. RMN-GP / Emilie Cambier (bc). **58 Getty Images:** Hulton Archive (b); Topical Press Agency (tr). **59 The Bridgeman Art Library:** Musée de l'Armée, Paris, France (br). **60 akg-images:** Interfoto (bc). **Lebrecht Music and Arts:** Interfoto (cl). **60-61 Australian War Memorial:** Order 6167241 (c). **61 Alamy Images:** Arterra Picture Library (br). **Getty Images:** Hulton Archive (tr). **62-63 The Art Archive:** Imperial War Museum. **64 akg-images:** Interfoto (tr). **Getty Images:** Hulton Archive (b). **66 The Bridgeman Art Library:** Heeresgeschichtliches Museum, Vienna, Austria (bl). **66-67 akg-images:** Interfoto / Hermann Historica. **67 Alamy Images:** Pictorial Press Ltd (br). **Corbis:** Hulton-Deutsch Collection (tc). **68 akg-images:** Imagno (bc). **68-69 Nationaal Archief / Spaarnestad Photo:** Het Leven / Fotograaf onbekend (t). **69 Corbis:** (bl). **Dorling Kindersley:** Gary Ombler / Collection of Jean-Pierre Verney (cr). **70 akg-images:** Interfoto (b). **Alamy Images:** The Print Collector (c). **Getty Images:** Hulton Archive (tl). **71 Dorling Kindersley:** Gary Ombler / Collection of Jean-Pierre Verney (cr). **Mary Evans Picture Library:** AISA Media (b). **72-73 akg-images:** Interfoto (t). **Corbis:** Hulton-Deutsch Collection (b). **73 akg-images:** Interfoto (tr). **Australian War Memorial:** Order 6167241 (bc). **74 The Bridgeman Art Library:** Private Collection (ca). **75 akg-images:** ullstein bild (tr). **74-75 Lebrecht Music and Arts:** RA (b). **76 Dorling Kindersley:** Gary Ombler / Collection of Jean-Pierre Verney (cla). **Getty Images:** Images of Empire / Universal Images Group (b). **77 Alamy Images:** Interfoto (tl). **Getty Images:** Hulton Archive (tr). **78 Corbis:** Bettmann (b). **79 Corbis:** Swim Ink 2, LLC (cr). **Dorling Kindersley:** Gary Ombler / By kind permission of The Trustees of the Imperial War Museum, London (b). **Getty Images:** SSPL (tl). **80 Australian War Memorial:** Order 6183492 (r). **80-81 The Art Archive:** Imperial War Museum. **82 Australian War Memorial:** Order 6180421 (cl). **83 Alamy Images:** The Print Collector (bl). **Dorling Kindersley:** Harry Taylor / Trustees of the National Museums Of Scotland (br). **Lebrecht Music and Arts:** Sueddeutsche Zeitung Photo (tr). **84-85 Lebrecht Music and Arts:** Pictures from History / CPAMedia. **85 Australian War Memorial:** Order 6173929 (tc). **Dorling Kindersley:** Imperial War Museum, London (cr). **86-87 Dorling Kindersley:** Gary Ombler / Courtesy of the Royal Museum of the Armed Forces and Military History, Brussels, Belgium. **88 Alamy Images:** Photos 12 (bc). **The Art Archive:** Imperial War Museum (tc); Marc Charmet (bl). **Getty Images:** Hulton Archive (tl). **Mary Evans Picture Library:** Interfoto / Pulfer (tr). **89 Corbis:** Bettmann (tr). **Corbis:** Lebrecht Authors / Lebrecht Music & Arts (tl). **Lebrecht Music and Arts:** Pictures from History / CPAMedia (bc). **90 Corbis:** Derek Bayes Aspect / Lebrecht Music & Arts (tr); Hulton-Deutsch Collection (cl). **Dorling Kindersley:** Gary Ombler / By kind permission of The Trustees of the Imperial War Museum, London (cr). **Getty Images:** Leemage (br). **Museum Victoria, Melbourne:** Order 18373 (ca). **91 akg-images:** (clb); Interfoto (tr). **The Art Archive:** Imperial War Museum (c). **Dorling Kindersley:** Gary Ombler / Collection of Jean-Pierre Verney (cl); Gary Ombler / By kind permission of The Trustees of the Imperial War Museum, London (br). **TopFoto.co.uk:** Roger Viollet (bl). **92 The Art Archive:** Imperial War Museum. **93 The Art Archive:** Musée des 2 Guerres Mondiales Paris / Gianni Dagli Orti (tr). **Lebrecht Music and Arts:** Sueddeutsche Zeitung Photo (bl). **94 Alamy Images:** Trinity Mirror / Mirrorpix (bl). **Australian War Memorial:** Order 6173929 (c). **94-95 akg-images. 95 Toucan Books Ltd:** Imperial War Museum / Norman Brand (c). **96-97 Corbis. 98 Getty Images:** Popperfoto (cla). **99 The Art Archive:** Imperial War Museum / Eileen Tweedy (t). **Dorling Kindersley:** Imperial War Museum, London (bl). **100 Dorling Kindersley:** Gary Ombler / John Pearce (cl); Imperial War Museum, London (br). **100-101 Dorling Kindersley:** Gary Ombler / Collection of Jean-Pierre Verney. **101 Dorling Kindersley:** Gary Ombler (r, bc); Imperial War Museum, London (tc); Gary Ombler / © The Board of Trustees of the Armouries (cr). **102 Corbis:** Lebrecht Authors / Lebrecht Music & Arts (clb). **102-103 Canadian War Museum (CWM):** Detail of The Second Battle of Ypres, 22 April to 25 May CWM 19710261-0161 Beaverbrook Collection of War Art / www.warmuseum.ca (t). **103 akg-images:** (bl). **Lebrecht Music and Arts:** RA (tr). **104 Dorling Kindersley:** Gary Ombler / By kind permission of The Trustees of the Imperial War Museum, London (tr). **Getty Images:** Hulton Archive (b). **105 Australian War Memorial:** Order 6180421 (c). **Corbis:** Hulton-Deutsch Collection (cra); (tc). **106 Getty Images:** Leemage (tr). **106-107 Corbis:** Hulton-Deutsch Collection (b). **107 akg-images:** Electa (br). **Dorling Kindersley:** Gary Ombler / Collection of Jean-Pierre Verney (tc). **108 Corbis:** Bettmann (bl). **108-109 Australian War Memorial:** Order 6173929 (c). **109 Alamy Images:** Global Travel Writers (r). **Australian War Memorial:** Order 6173929 (cb). **Museum Victoria, Melbourne:** Order 18373 (tc). **110 Corbis:** Bettmann (cra, clb). **Dorling Kindersley:** Gary Ombler / By kind permission of The Trustees of the Imperial War Museum, London (cb). **111 Getty Images:** Philip Schuller / The AGE / Fairfax Media (tr). **112 Getty Images:** Keystone-France / Gamma-Keystone (tc). **112-113 The Art Archive:** Imperial War Museum (b). **Dorling Kindersley:** Gary Ombler / Courtesy of the Royal Artillery Historical Trust (t). **113 Dorling Kindersley:** Gary Ombler / Collection of Jean-Pierre Verney (br). **Getty Images:** Keystone (tr). **114-115 Corbis. 116 Alamy Images:** Photos 12 (b). **117 akg-images:** ullstein bild (tr). **Corbis:** Atlantide Phototravel (br). **Dorling Kindersley:** Gary Ombler / Collection of Jean-Pierre Verney (bl). **118 akg-images:** (tr). **Alamy Images:** Photos 12 (b). **119 Dorling Kindersley:** Gary Ombler / © The Board of Trustees of the Armouries (cr). **Lebrecht Music and Arts:** Pictures from History / CPAMedia (bc). **Mary Evans Picture Library:** Imperial War Museum / Robert Hunt Library (tc). **120-121 Mary Evans Picture Library:** Rue des Archives / Tallandier. **122 Lebrecht Music and Arts:** Sueddeutsche Zeitung Photo (t). **Mary Evans Picture Library:** Imperial War Museum / Robert Hunt Library (tr). **123 Dorling Kindersley:** Gary Ombler / Courtesy of the Royal Artillery Historical Trust (c). **Toucan Books Ltd:** Imperial War Museum / Norman Brand (crb). **124 Mary Evans Picture Library:** Robert Hunt Library (c). **124-125 The Art Archive:** Imperial War Museum (b). **125 Mary Evans Picture Library:** Imperial War Museum / Robert Hunt Library (tl). **Toucan Books Ltd:** Imperial War Museum / Norman Brand (cra). **126 Corbis:** Bettmann (b). **Dorling Kindersley:** Gary Ombler (cl). **127 Corbis:** Hulton-Deutsch Collection (cr). **Dorling Kindersley:** Gary Ombler / By kind permission of The Trustees of the Imperial War Museum, London (tl). **National Maritime Museum, Greenwich, London:** (br). **128 The Art Archive:** Eileen Tweedy (tr); Imperial War Museum / Eileen Tweedy (clb). **Getty Images:** Buyenlarge (bl); DEA / G. Dagli Orti (tc); Universal History Archive (br). **Mary Evans Picture Library:** Interfoto / Pulfer (cr, bc). **129 akg-images:** (tr). **Corbis:** (cl); Heritage Images (bl); K.J. Historical (fbl). **Getty Images:** Archive Photos (br); DEA / G. Dagli Orti (tl); The Bridgeman Art Library (tc). **Smithsonian Institution, Washington, DC, USA:** Armed Forces Division, National Museum of American History, Kenneth E. Behring Center (bc). **130 Getty Images:** Boyer / Roger Viollet (br). **Library Of Congress, Washington, D.C.:** Harris & Ewing Collection (t). **131 Alamy Images:** The Protected Art Archive (cr). **TopFoto.co.uk:** Roger Viollet (tc). **U.S. Air Force:** (bc). **132 Dorling Kindersley:** Imperial War Museum, London (tl). **Getty Images:** Hulton Archive (cra, bl). **133 Corbis:** Derek Bayes Aspect / Lebrecht Music & Arts. **135 akg-images:** (bl). **Alamy Images:** The Print Collector (br). **Dorling Kindersley:** Gary Ombler / Collection of Jean-Pierre Verney (t). **136-137 Corbis:** Underwood & Underwood. **138 Dorling Kindersley:** Matthew Ward (c); Gary Ombler / © The Board of Trustees of the Armouries (cr). **138-139 Canadian War Museum (CWM):** CWM 19390002-268 (t). **139 Australian War Memorial:** Order 6175160 (tl). **Dorling Kindersley:** Gary Ombler / © The Board of Trustees of the Armouries (br, cr, cl, tr); Gary Ombler / Collection of Jean-Pierre Verney (cla, bl). **140 The Art Archive:** Marc Charmet (b). **Getty Images:** Universal History Archive (tr). **141 Getty Images:** Hulton Archive (br). **Toucan Books Ltd:** Imperial War Museum / Norman Brand (c). **142 Alamy Images:** Military Images (ca). **142-143 Photo Scala, Florence. 143 The Stapleton Collection:** (cra). **144 akg-images:** ullstein bild (b). **145 Alamy Images:** Interfoto (bl). **Dorling Kindersley:** Clive Streeter / Science Museum, London (tl). **Getty Images:** SSPL (cra). **Lebrecht Music and Arts:** Sueddeutsche Zeitung Photo (tc). **146-147 Dorling Kindersley:** Gary Ombler. **148 The Art Archive:** Imperial War Museum (bl). **Corbis:** dpa (bc). **148-149 The Bridgeman Art Library:** Private Collection (t). **Dorling Kindersley:** Anthony Haughey (tl). **Lebrecht Music and Arts:** Sueddeutsche Zeitung Photo (tc). **TopFoto.co.uk:** (br). **149 Getty Images:** MPI (bc). **Lebrecht Music and Arts:** Imagno (tl). **150 Corbis:** (c). **Dorling Kindersley:** Andy Crawford / By kind permission of The Trustees of the Imperial War Museum, London (br); Gary Ombler / Courtesy of the Royal Museum of the Armed Forces and Military History, Brussels, Belgium (cr); Gary Ombler / Collection of Jean-Pierre Verney (cl/a, tr). **Getty Images:** Universal History Archive (bl). **151 Alamy Images:** Pictorial Press Ltd (tl). **The Bridgeman Art Library:** Dublin City Gallery, The Hugh Lane, Ireland (br). **Dorling Kindersley:** Gary Ombler (cr). **Getty Images:** Galerie Bilderwelt (bc); Mansell / Time & Life Pictures (cl). **152 Australian War Memorial:** Order 6185010 (cl). **Dorling Kindersley:** Gary Ombler / Collection of Jean-Pierre Verney (tr). **Getty Images:** Hulton Archive (bl). **152-153 Alamy Images:** Trinity Mirror / Mirrorpix (b). **153 Getty Images:** Hulton Archive (tc). **154 Alamy Images:** Interfoto (t). **Lebrecht Music and Arts:** Sueddeutsche Zeitung Photo (bc). **155 Alamy Images:** Interfoto (cl). **Lebrecht Music and Arts:** RA (tr). **156-157 Lebrecht Music and Arts:** RA. **158 Getty Images:** Universal History Archive (l). **159 akg-images:** (c). **Getty Images:** Apic (bl); Galerie Bilderwelt (crb). **160 Corbis:** adoc-photos (c). **Dorling Kindersley:** Gary Ombler / Courtesy of the Royal Museum of the Armed Forces and Military History, Brussels, Belgium (bl). **161 Alamy Images:** Hemis (bl). **Getty Images:** Galerie Bilderwelt (tl). **162-163 Mary Evans Picture Library:** westernfrontphotography.com. **164 The Bridgeman Art Library:** Private Collection (cl). **Dorling Kindersley:** Anthony Haughey (cla, t). **165 Alamy Images:** Trinity Mirror / Mirrorpix (t). **166 Getty Images:** Hulton Archive (b). **167 Getty Images:** Leemage (cra). **Lebrecht Music and Arts:** RA (bc). **168 Alamy Images:** Interfoto (bc). **169 akg-images:** Rainer Hackenberg (tr). **Getty Images:** Hulton Archive (br). **170 Alamy Images:** Interfoto (br). **The Bridgeman Art Library:** Private Collection (b). **171 Alamy Images:** Mary Evans Picture Library (tr). **Dorling Kindersley:** Andy Crawford / By kind permission of The Trustees of the Imperial War Museum, London (bc); Gary Ombler (t). **172-173 akg-images:** Erich Lessing. **174 akg-images:** RIA Novosti (cl). **Lebrecht Music and Arts:** Imagno (tr). **175 Alamy Images:** Interfoto (c). **Dorling Kindersley:** Gary Ombler / Collection of Jean-Pierre Verney (tr). **176 Corbis:** Daniel Deme / epa (cl). **Getty Images:** Central Press (b). **177 The Art Archive:** Imperial War Museum (br); Musée des 2 Guerres Mondiales Paris / Gianni Dagli Orti (cl). **Getty Images:** Hulton Archive (tr). **178 Getty Images:** Topical Press Agency (r). **hemis.fr:** Francis Cormon (l). **179 Alamy Images:** David Osborn (crb). **Bonhams Auctioneers, London:** (t). **Getty Images:** Topical Press Agency (bc). **180 The Bridgeman Art Library:** National Museum Wales (b). **181 The Art Archive:** Imperial War Museum (cr). **Corbis:** Michael St. Maur Sheil (tr). **Dorling Kindersley:** Gary Ombler / Courtesy of Birmingham Pals (bc). **182-183 Alamy Images:** Pictorial Press Ltd. **184 Cody Images:** (bl). **184-185 Lebrecht Music and Arts:** Sueddeutsche Zeitung Photo (b). **185 Getty Images:** Scott Barbour (cr). **186 Corbis:** (b). **187 Corbis:** (c). **Dorling Kindersley:** Jerry Young (b); Gary Ombler / Collection of Jean-Pierre Verney (crb). **Toucan Books Ltd:** Imperial War Museum / Norman Brand (t). **188 Getty Images:** Fotosearch (bl). **189 Alamy Images:** Classic Image (tr). **Lebrecht Music and Arts:** Sueddeutsche Zeitung Photo (br). **190-191 Ministry of Defence Picture Library:** UK MoD / Crown Copyright 2012. **192 Dorling Kindersley:** Gary Ombler / Courtesy of the Royal Museum of the Armed Forces and of Courtesy of the Royal Museum of the Armed Forces and of Military History, Brussels, Belgium (crb, cl). **192-193 Dorling Kindersley:** Martin Cameron / Courtesy of the Shuttleworth Collection, Bedfordshire (b). **193 Dorling Kindersley:** Gary Ombler (crb, cr); Gary Ombler / Courtesy of the Royal Museum of the Armed Forces and Military History, Brussels, Belgium (cl). **194 Mary Evans Picture Library:** Illustrated London News Ltd (r); Sueddeutsche Zeitung Photo (bl). **195 Lebrecht Music and Arts:** Sueddeutsche Zeitung Photo (bc). **Roland Smithies:** Luped.com (crb). **196 The Art Archive:** Liddell Hart Centre (tr). **Dorling Kindersley:** Gary Ombler / © The Board of Trustees of the Armouries (c). **TopFoto.co.uk:** (b). **197 Alamy Images:** Interfoto (tc). **The Bridgeman Art Library:** The Illustrated London News Picture Library, London, UK (br). **198 Corbis:** dpa (tr); Hulton-Deutsch Collection (bl). **Dorling Kindersley:** Gary Ombler / Collection of Jean-Pierre Verney (tl). **199 The Art Archive:** (b). **200 Getty Images:** Mansell / Time & Life Pictures (l). **201 Corbis:** Hulton-Deutsch Collection (br); Underwood & Underwood (tl). **Mary Evans Picture Library:** (bl). **202 Corbis:** Bettman (tr). **Dorling Kindersley:** Karl Shone (bl).

Pictures (br); Popperfoto (cl). **203 akg-images:** (l). **Dorling Kindersley:** Gary Ombler / © The Board of Trustees of the Armouries (cra). **204-205 Dorling Kindersley:** Andy Crawford / By kind permission of The Trustees of the Imperial War Museum, London. **206 akg-images:** (br, c). **The Art Archive:** Imperial War Museum (bl). **Corbis:** (tr). **Getty Images:** Bentley Archive / Popperfoto (tl). **207 Corbis: (tr);** Bettmann (tc). **Getty Images:** DEA / G. Dagli Orti (tl). **Mary Evans Picture Library:** Imperial War Museum / Robert Hunt Library (cb). **208 akg-images:** Interfoto (tl); ullstein bild (b). **Alamy Images:** akg-images (clb). **Dorling Kindersley:** Gary Ombler / Collection of Jean-Pierre Verney (tr, crb). **TopFoto.co.uk:** RIA Novosti (c). **209 Corbis:** (bl). **Getty Images:** Universal History Archive (crb). **Lebrecht Music and Arts:** RA (cra). **Smithsonian Institution, Washington, D.C., USA:** Armed Forces Division, National Museum of American History, Kenneth E. Behring Center (cr). **TopFoto.co.uk:** Imagno (cl). **210 Dorling Kindersley:** Sergio (cl). **210-211 Getty Images:** Popperfoto (b). **211 Dorling Kindersley:** H. Keith Melton, spymuseum.org (br). **Getty Images:** Popperfoto (tl). **TopFoto.co.uk:** RIA Novosti (tr). **212 Corbis**. **213 Corbis:** Bettmann (cl). **Dorling Kindersley:** Gary Ombler / Collection of Jean-Pierre Verney (br). **214 Corbis:** Bettmann (clb, r). **215 Corbis:** Smithsonian Institution (br). **Getty Images:** Fotosearch (bl); SuperStock (tl). **216 akg-images:** (cra). **217 Corbis:** (t). **Smithsonian Institution, Washington, D.C., USA:** Armed Forces Division, National Museum of American History, Kenneth E. Behring Center (bl). **218 Corbis:** Bettmann (tr). **Getty Images:** Bentley Archive / Popperfoto (bl). **219 Alamy Images:** akg-images. **220 Getty Images:** Time Life Pictures / Mansell / Time Life Pictures (cl). **220-221 Getty Images:** MPI (b). **221 akg-images:** (cla). **Dorling Kindersley:** Gary Ombler / By kind permission of The Trustees of the Imperial War Museum, London (tr). **222 Alamy Images:** akg-images (bl). **Getty Images:** Imagno (r). **223 akg-images:** (tc). **Corbis:** Hulton-Deutsch Collection (b). **Mary Evans Picture Library:** SZ Photo / Scher (crb). **224 akg-images:** ullstein bild (b). **225 Alamy Images:** World History Archive (tl). **Dorling Kindersley:** Gary Ombler / Collection of Jean-Pierre Verney (cl). **226 Dorling Kindersley:** Gary Ombler / Collection of Jean-Pierre Verney (cr). **226-227 akg-images:** ullstein bild (t). **227 Dorling Kindersley:** Gary Ombler / Collection of Jean-Pierre Verney (c). **Lebrecht Music and Arts:** RA (bc); Sueddeutsche Zeitung Photo (bl). **228-229 Corbis**. **230 Corbis:** Bettmann (b). **Dorling Kindersley:** Gary Ombler / Collection of Jean-Pierre Verney (tr). **231 The Art Archive:** Culver Pictures (bc). **Corbis:** Reuters / Chris Wattie (br). **Getty Images:** Buyenlarge (tl). **232 akg-images:** ullstein bild (tr). **Dorling Kindersley:** Gary Ombler / Courtesy of Royal Airforce Museum, Hendon (cl); Gary Ombler / Courtesy of the Royal Museum of the Armed Forces and Military History, Brussels, Belgium (bl). **233 akg-images:** ullstein bild. **234 Alamy Images:** RIA Novosti (bl). **The Art Archive:** Musée des 2 Guerres Mondiales Paris / Gianni Dagli Orti (tr). **234-235 Corbis:** Bettman (b). **235 Corbis:** Hulton-Deutsch Collection (tc). **Dorling Kindersley:** Imperial War Museum, London (cra). **236-237 Alamy Images:** The Print Collector. **238 Alamy Images:** The Print Collector (tr). **The Bridgeman Art Library:** Moore-Gwyn Fine Art (bl). **239 Dorling Kindersley:** Gary Ombler / Collection of Jean-Pierre Verney. **Getty Images:** Travel Ink (tr). **240 Dorling Kindersley:** Karl Shone (cla). **241 The Art Archive:** Imperial War Museum (t). **Dorling Kindersley:** Gary Ombler / Collection of Jean-Pierre Verney (b). **242 Canadian War Museum (CWM):**

19390001-759 (tl). **242-243 The Art Archive:** (b). **243 Australian War Memorial:** Order 6189723 (tl). **Dorling Kindersley:** Gary Ombler / Collection of Jean-Pierre Verney (cr). **244-245 The Bridgeman Art Library:** The Fine Art Society, London (b). **246 Corbis:** Hulton-Deutsch Collection (b). **247 Dorling Kindersley:** Gary Ombler / Collection of Jean-Pierre Verney (c). **Getty Images:** Universal History Archive (bl). **248 Mary Evans Picture Library:** Robert Hunt Collection (tr). **248-249 Dorling Kindersley:** Gary Ombler / By kind permission of The Trustees of the Imperial War Museum, London (b). **249 The Art Archive:** (tr). **Dorling Kindersley:** Imperial War Museum, London (br). **250 Alamy Images:** Martin Bennett (c). **Dorling Kindersley:** Gary Ombler / Courtesy of the Royal Artillery Historical Trust (bl). **250-251 Corbis:** Underwood & Underwood (b). **251 Bovington Tank Museum:** (cra). **Dorling Kindersley:** Andy Crawford / By kind permission of The Trustees of the Imperial War Museum, London (tc); Kim Sayer (br). **252 Alamy Images:** ITAR-TASS Photo Agency (ca). **The Art Archive:** Private Collection / CCI (ca). **252-253 Dorling Kindersley:** Imperial War Museum, London (b). **253 akg-images:** Erich Lessing (tc). **The Art Archive:** (tc). **254 akg-images:** Interfoto (bl). **Lebrecht Music and Arts:** Sueddeutsche Zeitung Photo (r). **255 akg-images:** (tl); ullstein bild (crb). **Alamy Images:** Interfoto (bl). **256 Alamy Images:** Interfoto (cla). **Mary Evans Picture Library:** Robert Hunt Library (c). **256-257 Getty Images:** Hulton Archive (b). **257 Dorling Kindersley:** Karl Shone (cra). **Mary Evans Picture Library:** Robert Hunt Library (tl). **258 akg-images:** (cla). **Alamy Images:** Prisma Bildagentur AG (cra); Yagil Henkin (b). **259 Corbis:** (br). **Dorling Kindersley:** Gary Ombler (tc). **260-261 Dorling Kindersley:** (b). **261 The Art Archive:** Imperial War Museum (cb). **Dorling Kindersley:** Gary Ombler / Collection of Jean-Pierre Verney (cr). **Toucan Books Ltd:** Imperial War Museum / Norman Brand (tl). **262-263 Dorling Kindersley:** Gary Ombler. **264 Corbis:** Bettmann (br). **Getty Images:** Galerie Bilderwelt (tc). **TopFoto.co.uk:** (tr); ullstein bild (bl). **265 Corbis:** (tr); K.J. Historical (c). **TopFoto.co.uk:** Fine Art Images / Heritage-Images (tl). **266 akg-images:** ullstein bild (cr). **Australian War Memorial:** Order 6191798 (c). **Mary Evans Picture Library:** (cla, cra). **TopFoto.co.uk:** (br); ullstein bild (bl). **267 akg-images:** Interfoto / Hermann Historica (bc). **Corbis:** Reuters / Chris Wattie (cb). **Dorling Kindersley:** Gary Ombler / Courtesy of the Royal Museum of the Armed Forces and Military History, Brussels, Belgium (clb). **Lebrecht Music and Arts:** Interfoto (cr). **Library Of Congress, Washington, D.C.:** (tc). **Canadian War Museum (CWM):** The Signing of the Armistice / CMW 19830483-001 Beaverbrook Collection of War Art © Canadian War Museum / www.warmuseum.ca (cr). **268 Getty Images:** A. R. Coster / Topical Press Agency (b); Popperfoto (cla). **269 Corbis:** Bettmann (br). **Dorling Kindersley:** Gary Ombler / By kind permission of The Trustees of the Imperial War Museum, London (bl). **Lebrecht Music and Arts:** Interfoto (tr). **270-271 The Bridgeman Art Library:** SZ Photo / Scherl. **272 The Art Archive:** Imperial War Museum (b). **Australian War Memorial:** Order 6191798 (tr). **273 The Art Archive:** John Meek (cr). **Australian War Memorial:** Order 6203877 (tl). **Dorling Kindersley:** Imperial War Museum, London (bc). **274 Dorling Kindersley:** Gary Ombler (clb, br, tr, b); Gary Ombler / © The Board of Trustees of the Armouries (c). **275 akg-images:** Interfoto / Hermann Historica (tl). **Dorling Kindersley:** John Pearce (cra); Gary Ombler / Collection of Jean-Pierre Verney (tc); Gary Ombler / John Pearce (r, c, bc); Gary Ombler / Courtesy of the 5te. Kompagnie Infanterie Regiment

nr.28 'Von Goeben' (bl). **276 Corbis:** Hulton-Deutsch Collection (bl). **276-277 akg-images:** ullstein bild (b). **Mary Evans Picture Library:** (cla). **277 akg-images:** ullstein bild (tl). **278 akg-images:** Interfoto (t). **Australian War Memorial:** Order 6191798 (br). **Dorling Kindersley:** Geoff Dann / Courtesy of David Edge (bl). **279 akg-images:** ullstein bild (bl). **Lebrecht Music and Arts:** Sueddeutsche Zeitung Photo (cra). **280-281 Corbis:** Bettmann. **282 Dorling Kindersley:** Andy Crawford / By kind permission of The Trustees of the Imperial War Museum, London (cb); Gary Ombler / Collection of Jean-Pierre Verney (tr). **283 Mary Evans Picture Library:** (tc); Sueddeutsche Zeitung Photo (br). **284 TopFoto.co.uk:** Buyenlarge (cl); Pictorial Parade (bc). **286 Dorling Kindersley:** Gary Ombler (bl). **Getty Images:** Universal History Archive (cl). **286-287 Dorling Kindersley:** Gary Ombler / Courtesy of the Royal Museum of the Armed Forces and Military History, Brussels, Belgium. **287 The Art Archive:** Culver Pictures (bc). **Corbis:** Bettman (tr). **288-289 The Art Archive:** Imperial War Museum. **290 Getty Images:** Leemage (cl); Universal History Archive (r). **291 age fotostock:** Dennis Gilbert (br). **Getty Images:** Hulton Archive (tl); Three Lions (bc). **292 akg-images:** Interfoto (bl). **TopFoto.co.uk:** (tr). **293 Australian War Memorial:** Order 6206941 (tc). **Getty Images:** A. R. Coster / Topical Press Agency (br); FPG / Archive Photos (cl). **294 Dorling Kindersley:** Gary Ombler (tl). **294-295 Dorling Kindersley:** Martin Cameron / Courtesy of the Shuttleworth Collection, Bedfordshire (t). **295 Dorling Kindersley:** Imperial War Museum, London (crb). **TopFoto.co.uk:** (bl). **296-297 akg-images:** ullstein bild. **298 Dorling Kindersley:** Imperial War Museum, London (clb). **TopFoto.co.uk:** ullstein bild (r). **299 akg-images:** (bc). **Alamy Images:** National Geographic Image Collection (br). **Corbis:** Bettmann (tc). **300 Alamy Images:** Interfoto (br). **The Art Archive:** Musée des 2 Guerres Mondiales Paris / Gianni Dagli Orti (c). **Corbis:** Underwood & Underwood (clb). **301 TopFoto.co.uk:** Fine Art Images / Heritage-Images (tc, b). **302 Getty Images:** Universal History Archive (b). **303 Corbis:** (tl). **The Kobal Collection:** Universal (cra). **Lebrecht Music and Arts:** Ben Uri Art Gallery (c). **TopFoto.co.uk:** (bc). **304 Australian War Memorial:** Order 6206941 (tr). **305 Corbis:** Bettmann (t). **TopFoto.co.uk:** (br). **306 Dorling Kindersley:** Gary Ombler / Collection of Jean-Pierre Verney (bc, bl). **TopFoto.co.uk:** The Granger Collection (tr). **307 Corbis:** (b). **TopFoto.co.uk:** The Granger Collection (tc). **308 Dorling Kindersley:** Gary Ombler / Collection of Jean-Pierre Verney (tl). **Lebrecht Music and Arts:** RA (cr). **TopFoto.co.uk:** The Granger Collection (bc). **309 Smithsonian Institution, Washington, D.C., USA:** Armed Forces Division, National Museum of American History, Kenneth E. Behring Center (tl, b). **310 Library Of Congress, Washington, D.C.:** (l). **311 Corbis:** David Pollack (c). **Getty Images:** Hulton Archive (bl); MPI (tl); Paul J. Richards / AFP (br). **312 Dorling Kindersley:** Gary Ombler / © The Board of Trustees of the Armouries (cl). **TopFoto.co.uk:** (bl). **313 TopFoto.co.uk:** (tc) Fine Art Images / Heritage-Images (t). **314-315 Getty Images:** Three Lions. **316 TopFoto.co.uk:** (bc, cr). **Toucan Books Ltd:** Imperial War Museum / Norman Brand (cl). **317 Corbis:** Bettmann (b). **Dorling Kindersley:** Gary Ombler / Collection of Jean-Pierre Verney (tl). **Mary Evans Picture Library:** Grenville Collins Postcard Collection (r). **318 TopFoto.co.uk:** Imagno (tr). **319 Alamy Images:** Interfoto (c). **Dorling Kindersley:** Andrzej Chec / National Museum, Cracow (bl). **TopFoto.co.uk:** Imagno (tr). **320 Dorling Kindersley:** Gary Ombler / Collection of Jean-Pierre Verney (cl). **Getty Images:** Galerie Bilderwelt (tr). **TopFoto.co.uk:**

ullstein bild (bc). **321 TopFoto.co.uk:** ullstein bild (t, bc). **322 Canadian War Museum (CWM):** The Signing of the Armistice / CMW 19830483-001 Beaverbrook Collection of War Art © Canadian War Museum / www.warmuseum.ca (t). **323 Dorling Kindersley:** Gary Ombler / Collection of Jean-Pierre Verney (cl). **Getty Images:** Hulton Archive (t). **Mary Evans Picture Library:** (cr). **TopFoto.co.uk:** (br). **324-325 TopFoto.co.uk:** The Granger Collection. **326-327 Alamy Images:** Glen Harper. **328 akg-images:** Rainer Hackenberg (bc). **Alamy Images:** Global Travel Writers (tr). **Corbis:** Bettmann (tc, br); Hulton-Deutsch Collection (tl). **Getty Images:** Time Life Pictures (bl). **329 Corbis:** Bettmann (tc). **Mary Evans Picture Library:** (cb). **330 Alamy Images:** DBI Studio (br). **The Bridgeman Art Library:** Imperial War Museum, London (tl). **Corbis:** DaZo Vintage Stock Photos / Images.com (bl); Hulton-Deutsch Collection (cr). **Lebrecht Music and Arts:** Interfoto (tr). **Toucan Books Ltd:** Imperial War Museum / Norman Brand (bc). **331 age fotostock:** Jose Antonio Moreno c (bl). **akg-images:** Andrea Jemolo (cl); ullstein bild (br). **Alamy Images:** The Print Collector (tr). **Corbis:** Hulton-Deutsch Collection (c). **332 Corbis:** DaZo Vintage Stock Photos / Images.com (c). **Lebrecht Music and Arts:** RA (tl). **332-333 Getty Images:** Hulton Archive (t). **333 akg-images:** ullstein bild (br). **Corbis:** Bettmann (tc). **334 Corbis:** Bettmann (bc). **Lebrecht Music and Arts:** Interfoto (c); RA (clb). **335 The Bridgeman Art Library:** Imperial War Museum, London. **336 Mary Evans Picture Library:** (bl). **336-337 Alamy Images:** Photos 12. **337 The Art Archive:** (tr). **Lebrecht Music and Arts:** Interfoto (bc). **TopFoto.co.uk:** Roger Viollet (tc). **338 The Bridgeman Art Library:** Roger Viollet (t). **Mary Evans Picture Library:** (bc). **339 Alamy Images:** DBI Studio (cr). **Getty Images:** Hulton Archive; Popperfoto (br). **340-341 Getty Images:** Time Life Pictures. **342 Corbis:** Hulton-Deutsch Collection (tl). **342-343 Corbis:** Hulton-Deutsch Collection (b). **343 akg-images:** Andrea Jemolo (cr). **Alamy Images:** The Print Collector (crb). **344 Corbis:** Hulton-Deutsch Collection (t). **345 Corbis:** (tl); Hulton-Deutsch Collection (br). **Getty Images:** Peter Macdiarmid (cr). **346-347 age fotostock:** Jose Antonio Moreno c. **138. 8 Dorling Kindersley:** Gary Ombler (b)

Endpaper image: Jean-Pierre Verney

All other images © Dorling Kindersley

For further information see:
www.dkimages.com